Contract Management

Contract Management

Core business competence

Peter Sammons

KoganPage

Publisher's note
Every possible effort has been made to ensure that the information contained in this book is accurate at the time of going to press, and the publishers and authors cannot accept responsibility for any errors or omissions, however caused. No responsibility for loss or damage occasioned to any person acting, or refraining from action, as a result of the material in this publication can be accepted by the editor, the publisher or the author.

First published in Great Britain and the United States in 2017 by Kogan Page Limited

Apart from any fair dealing for the purposes of research or private study, or criticism or review, as permitted under the Copyright, Designs and Patents Act 1988, this publication may only be reproduced, stored or transmitted, in any form or by any means, with the prior permission in writing of the publishers, or in the case of reprographic reproduction in accordance with the terms and licences issued by the CLA. Enquiries concerning reproduction outside these terms should be sent to the publishers at the undermentioned addresses:

2nd Floor, 45 Gee Street	c/o Martin P Hill Consulting	4737/23 Ansari Road
London	122 W 27th St, 10th Floor	Daryaganj
EC1V 3RS	New York, NY 10001	New Delhi 110002
United Kingdom	USA	India

www.koganpage.com

© Peter Sammons, 2017

The right of Peter Sammons to be identified as the author of this work has been asserted by him in accordance with the Copyright, Designs and Patents Act 1988.

ISBN   978 0 7494 8064 6
E-ISBN 978 0 7494 8065 3

British Library Cataloguing-in-Publication Data

A CIP record for this book is available from the British Library.

Library of Congress Cataloging-in-Publication Data

Names: Sammons, Peter A., author.
Title: Contract management : core business competence / Peter Sammons.
Description: 1st Edition. | New York, NY : Kogan Page Ltd, [2017] | Includes
   bibliographical references and index.
Identifiers: LCCN 2017001794 (print) | LCCN 2017004775 (ebook) |
   ISBN 9780749480646 (pbk.) | ISBN 9780749480653 (ebook)
Subjects: LCSH: Management. | Management contracts. | Performance.
Classification: LCC HD31.2 .S26 2017 (print) | LCC HD31.2 (ebook) | DDC
   658.4/058–dc23
LC record available at https://lccn.loc.gov/2017001794

Typeset by Integra Software Services, Pondicherry
Print production managed by Jellyfish
Printed and bound by CPI Group (UK) Ltd, Croydon CR0 4YY

CONTENTS

Foreword ix

Introduction 1

01 Contract management as a value driver 6
Setting the scene 6
Understanding value in the commercial context 8
What are the benefits of good contract management? 10
Endnote 11

02 What is the task? 12
What do we (universally) want from our contracts? 12
The contract management team 15
Understanding contract materiality 17
Completion of the BCMR form 19
Materiality 25
Endnotes 26

03 Role and importance of effective contract management 27
Effective counterparty performance management 27
Upside opportunities versus downside risks 30
Six foundation stones 32
Market making 33
Stakeholder management 34

04 Contract administration 37
An eye for detail 37
What has to be administered? 40
Contract management plan – yes or no? 42
When should the contract management
  plan be developed? 43

What should be included in the contract management plan? 44
Who develops the contract management plan? 45
Contract administration tasks 46
Managing the money 49

05   Commercial strategy 51
Back to basics 51
Project strategy 54
Laying foundations 56
Gestation and birth 59

06   Contract design 61
Back to basics 61
NEC3 contract system 63
Old-fashioned lawyers 66
Endnote 67

07   Mobilization 68
Getting started 68
Mr or Ms 2 per cent 70
We're underway! 71
Monitoring performance – what do we monitor? 74
Contract correspondence 79
Notices of poor performance and variations 80
Endnotes 82

08   When things go wrong 84
Why contracts need to be managed 84
Sammons' Five Forces! 87
Remedies 90
When delinquency becomes a claim 93
Pulling the levers! 97
Up the escalator! 99
Endnotes 101

09 Managing for success 103
Core style versus adaptive style 103
Details, details, details! 108
All good things come to an... 114
Endnote 116

Practical tools and checklists 117

1. Preparing specification documents: an approach to support client–supplier contract negotiations 119
2. Supply contract risks: an approach to support client–supplier contract negotiations 127
3. Contract management plan 144
4. Project Memo format 150
5. Project Memo system – guidance notes 151
6. Basic Contract Materiality Review 153
7. Vendor Relationship and Contracts Manager – job description 158
8. Vendor Manager – job description 162
9. Outsourced services: exit management – planning guidelines 165
10. Contract variation – letter 186
11. Formal written notification of unsatisfactory contract performance 188
12. Formal written notification of improved contract performance 190
13. Formal written notification – repeat of poor contract performance 191
14. Notices 193
15. A dozen things I wish they'd told me when I started 197
16. Conditions of contract for purchase 198
17. Master Services Agreement: Buy Research 2016 207
18. Miscellaneous terms 235
19. Model form of Statement of Work 248
20. Letter of comfort 252

21 Letter of intent (limited liability commence) 253
22 Inspection arrangements – clause 255
23 Availability of information – clause 257
24 Supply chain transparency – clause 259

Index 261

FOREWORD

Commercial history is littered with contracts that have gone wrong, resulting in millions wiped off a company's profitability, not to mention reputational and market share damage, costly litigation and protracted dispute settlements. Most business people in their day-to-day activity are directly or indirectly involved in contracts – whether sales or purchase – yet few have any practical training in what to do or how to read the signs of impending danger. Contract management remains a neglected business discipline.

This book is a valuable resource. Business people – and those in the public sector – need to get to grips with the issue of *ensuring* commercial success with their contracting counterparties. Too many organizations enter into contracts with only a superficial consideration of how things will actually be managed once the ink has dried on the contract signature! This needs to change!

Commercial pressures and the demands to deliver on contractual promises will only increase in the future. One aspect of preparing for that future is to tighten up and systemize the management of contracts. No business, whether private or public sector, can afford to be seen as incapable of basic contract management. This book sets out the essential building blocks to ensure contract success.

Steve Wills, MBA, FCIPS
Managing Director, Procurement Central

Introduction

The business of making money – through contracts

Businesses exist to make money. They must deliver what their customer wants. They must deliver what they are contracted to deliver. Public-sector organizations are mission-driven (at least in principle). Both public and private organizations use *third-party* providers, acting under contract, to assist in achieving mission targets.

Along the value chain, whether buying or selling – and often both – organizations have a practical and legal interest in the successful conclusion of contracts. This book is prepared from a private sector (industrial–commercial) perspective, but its lessons are equally applicable across the public sector and the so-called third sector.

This book is aimed at three readerships:

1 general managers carrying responsibility for budgets and personnel, and who, sooner or later, will find themselves dependent upon external third parties to deliver on contractual promises;
2 senior managers, who ultimately carry executive responsibility for effective use of shareholder funds or taxpayer money;
3 legal advisers, who are sometimes tasked to assist organizations to ensure contractual performance

This is not a legal book. It does not seek to tell you what conditions of contract will make life easy, or transfer risks onto someone else. Indeed, it is a foundational principle of this book that *we recognize that what is written on bits of paper will not ensure satisfactory outcomes.*

This is a real-world book for real-world professionals. Let us go back to basics for a moment; Tim Boyce, in his book *Successful Contract Administration*,[1] makes the valid point that:

> A business or a company is a money machine. If it does not make money it will not survive. It makes money by winning and performing on contracts. With no contracts, there is no business.

He goes on:

> Without contracts, there is no business. Without profitable contracts, there is no business. It must therefore be a truism that the work of the contract administrator lies at the very heart of the success of the business.

It is unlikely that anyone has ever put this more succinctly. Let us for a moment critique what Boyce said: the task of the contract administrator is key to the success of any business. Since we all depend upon contracts, it is remarkable that so little effort is directed towards understanding the essential organizational conditions required to guarantee success. How many managers reading this book have had any training in how to manage a contract? Most will not. Boyce's book uses the term 'administration' to describe the task to be undertaken. There is a sense in *which administering tasks and activities* is in reality what is required of a *Contract Manager* – but we suggest that the task of contract management is broader than 'just' contract administration. This book sets out a range of issues of which a top-flight Contract Manager must be aware and be able to manage. Contract management is a key management skill, yet it is underplayed in most organizations, which usually default to *project management* skills as a proxy for contract management skills. Whilst project management skills are equally essential, they are not the same thing.

In this book, we make a clear distinction between contract management and contract administration. The second is a sub-set of the first. The definitions we use are as follows.

Definitions

Contract management

A strategic management task to achieve…

Planning, stakeholder engagement (and ongoing management), commercial and contract strategy development, alignment with business strategy and objectives, risk appreciation, negotiation and execution. In addition, contract administration including through-life monitoring and exception reporting with remedial actions, controlling, problem resolution, and ultimate closure of liabilities between the contracting parties, as well as ensuring that all commercial objectives and planned business benefits are achieved and all expenditure is justified on commercial grounds.

Contract administration

A tactical administrative task to achieve…

The tasks required (and performed) to ensure that all elements of a commercial contract are performed by both (all) counterparties in accordance with the terms of the contract, in particular that:

1 payments are made;
2 deliveries are received;
3 communications are tracked/monitored and acted upon;
4 intellectual property rights (IPRs) are respected;
5 good 'title' from seller to buyer is achieved;
6 business reviews are carried out and associated MI (management information) is received and acted upon.

This is a non-exhaustive description of the tasks and associated disciplines and actions required to ensure that *a contract delivers on its promises*. There is some overlap between contract management and contract administration – and contract administration is a sub-set of contract management.

An administrator will be frustrated in delivering their professional service if the strategic foundations underpinning a particular contract are inadequate. Contract management is a broad discipline, then, and requires a degree of gravitas and experience within any organization. This is not to suggest that relatively junior managers cannot manage contracts but there must be a degree of 'clout' that the manager can apply, even if only indirectly via their own senior managers. This underlines the second point about contract management: it is a team-based activity. The members of the team need to know:

a) a team exists and they are a part of it;

b) what their role is and deliverables are within that team;

c) what the other team members are expected to deliver.

A Contract Manager can sometimes find themselves 'out on a limb' and deemed to be solely responsible/accountable for successful outcomes. In practice, however, this is rarely the case – and delegation (or even abdication) to a junior manager acting as the Contract Manager may be a sign of organizational weakness or, bluntly, of senior manager incompetence.

This book accordingly looks at the wider contract management picture, and helps to set out typical structures and processes that assist the contract management task. There are two other points to make about this book before we launch into the first chapter:

1 A picture is worth a thousand words! We use diagram representations wherever possible to depict complex ideas. This book is not a literary exercise; it is a handbook designed for the busy practical business manager.

2 'Learning points' are highlighted in boxes. Where we think a 'lesson' can be learned, or where individual thought/reflection or review will be beneficial, we 'flag' it using a stand-alone box. This can be a catalyst for discussion within any organization, to encourage us to consider – just how do we handle this problem? And is there anything for our organization to learn, or are there procedure changes required to enhance our commercial performance?

What this book delivers – payback

Allowing that in most organizations there is room to improve contract management disciplines, this book should prove to deliver two key benefits:

1 A catalyst for discussion on best practice – and how our organization might better move towards best practice.

2 A handbook for individual managers to review their own skills and practices.

This book has emerged from practical experience across a number of industries. I have been fortunate to work with many excellent people in the commercial sphere, from whom I have learned a great deal. It is expected that this book will remain current and up to date for the next 15 years. Whilst commercial law develops progressively, there are no significant legal developments presently on the horizon that might fundamentally alter the way contracts are entered into, or the way they are properly managed. It is expected, then, that managers can 'personalize' this book and make it their first reference point.

I wish to thank my colleagues at Procurement Central for providing the bandwidth for me to undertake the writing of this book. Also Neil Robertson at Compleat Software Ltd, who provided some valuable insights into the question of IT-based contract management systems. His thoughts found their way into Chapter 9. Finally, sincere thanks to my long-suffering wife, Joyce, who graciously tolerated me disappearing into 'the den' for long periods of writing – no doubt neglecting other important tasks!

It is hoped that this proves to be an intensely practical book. For a slightly ironic view of what we can learn from each other, readers might want first to cast a weather eye over Appendix 15 – 'A dozen things I wish they'd told me when I started'. We are all learning all the time, and we need to keep our feet firmly on the ground as we enter into, and subsequently manage, our contracts. Have a quick look at Appendix 15 and keep those ideas at the back of your mind as you work through, and hopefully enjoy, this book.

Endnote

1 Tim Boyce (1992) *Successful Contract Administration*, Hawksmere, ISBN 1-85418-0980-8.

Contract management as a value driver 01

Setting the scene

First things first: what do we mean by *value driver*? The term has several definitions that rather depend on who uses it. Let us think about value for just a moment, and its meaning to differing audiences:

- *Accountants* – monetary worth of assets, businesses, services rendered.
- *Economists/lawyers* – monetary worth of all the benefits and rights arising from ownership.
- *Marketing* – the extent to which a good or a service is perceived by customers to meet needs/wants, measured by their willingness to pay for it.
- *Maths* – a magnitude or quantity represented by numbers.

From the perspective of contract management, value is about the accurate translation of benefits from one contracting party to another, measured in terms of goods/services received, or profit earned. The term *value driver* is generally considered as anything added to a product or service that increases its value to customers. These 'additions' differentiate a product or service from those of competitors and make them more appealing to consumers. A true value driver provides a competitive advantage to a business and may come in many forms, such as superior brand awareness or leading-edge technology. So how can contract management be a value driver? Look for a moment at typical value drivers associated with competitive businesses (Figure 1.1)

Contract Management as a Value Driver

Figure 1.1 Value drivers and value creation

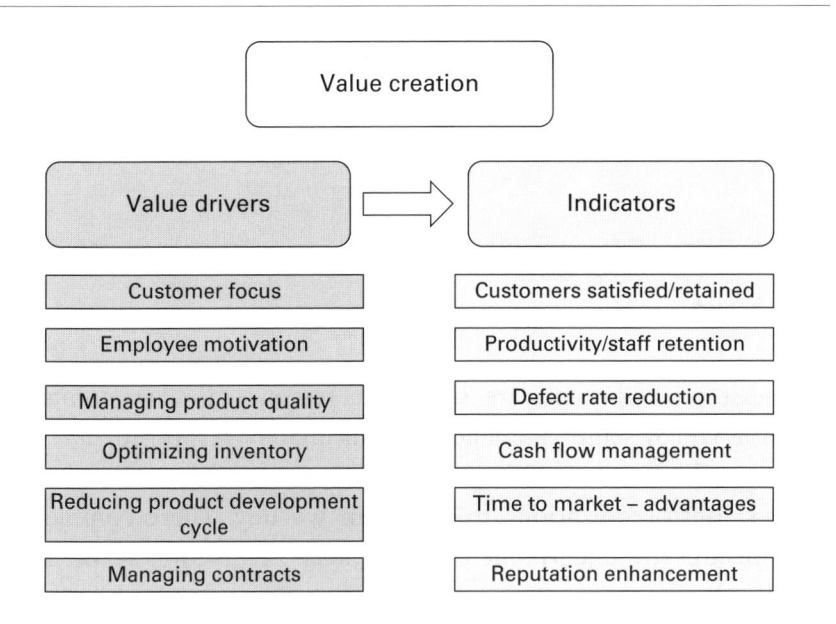

```
                    ┌─────────────────┐
                    │ Value creation  │
                    └─────────────────┘

    ┌───────────────┐            ┌───────────────┐
    │ Value drivers │    ⇨       │   Indicators  │
    └───────────────┘            └───────────────┘

    Customer focus                Customers satisfied/retained
    Employee motivation           Productivity/staff retention
    Managing product quality      Defect rate reduction
    Optimizing inventory          Cash flow management
    Reducing product development  Time to market – advantages
    cycle
    Managing contracts            Reputation enhancement
```

In the figure above, contract management is one typical value driver, alongside several others. Good and effective contract management achieves these business benefits:

- **More business certainty** = promises will be kept = stronger business case for investment (investor confidence).
- **Operational risk reduction** = lower insurance premiums.
- **Product quality enhancement** = fewer complaints = fewer 'latent defects' = satisfied customers.
- **Counterparty dependability** = reduced management time in exception management and problem resolution = more certainty.

Viewed in these terms, contract management, whether sales contracts or purchase contracts, will be seen to drive business performance by providing greater certainty. And certainty is valuable in business! Good contract management enhances reputation amongst customers and suppliers. Customers see your business as competent and capable – and hopefully trading on terms that are reasonable to both parties. Suppliers, similarly, see your business as competent and capable. In dealing with your firm, they know they will be held to account, but are more likely to be seen as a business partner, and one that will be used repeatedly if they perform well under contract. Similarly, they expect your business to also behave competently and do what you are expected to do under the contract. Performance becomes a two-way street!

Understanding value in the commercial context

Businesses, whether private or public sector, will have a mission task for which senior managers are ultimately responsible. Within the value chain there will be persons/organizations to whom we sell, and persons/organizations from whom we buy. These commercial relationships are underpinned by contracts. Let us look at one more definition – the term *value chain*.

The value chain can be thought of as interlinked value-adding activities that convert 'inputs' into 'outputs'. These activities impact the bottom line in terms of costs or profits. Typically, a value chain consists of suppliers and customers, and it is always instructive for a business to understand clearly where it 'sits' within the overall value chain, and which external organizations are typical contracting counterparties. The value chain will consist of internal and external activities such as:

- contract negotiations and agreements;
- optimized contract prices;
- inbound distribution or logistics;
- manufacturing operations;
- outbound distribution or logistics;
- marketing and selling;
- after-sales service.

The value chain is impacted within organizations through their business infrastructure, ie:

- Sales and Marketing;
- Purchasing or Procurement;

- Research and Development;
- Human Resource Development.

It is of note that most of these are generally supported by, or involved in, contract relationships with third-party organizations. Figures 1.2a and 1.2b summarize this.

The relationships within the value chain clearly have to be managed on an ongoing basis, which raises questions as to who is responsible for this at an organizational level and what specific qualities (and qualifications?) do they need? If you are a senior manager, just pause for a moment and reflect: you have legal obligations along the value chain. You are RESPONSIBLE for the correct management of contracts along the value chain to:

- customers/suppliers;
- investors/shareholders;
- creditors;

Figure 1.2a Generic value chain

Suppliers — The Business (You!) — Customers

The Value Chain

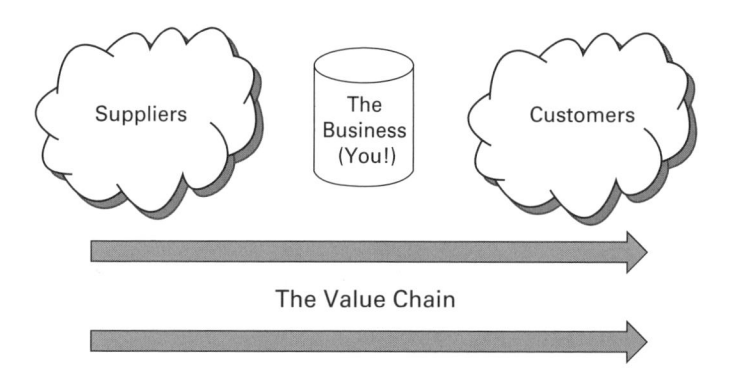

Figure 1.2b Contractual relationships

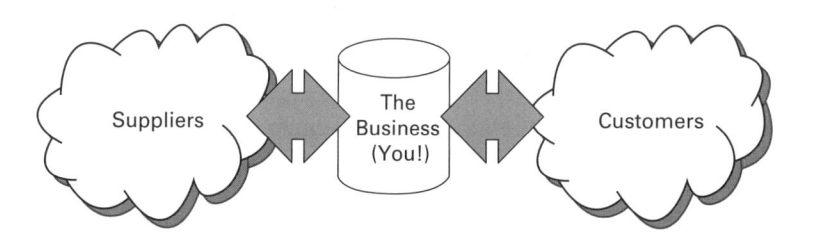

Suppliers ⇔ The Business (You!) ⇔ Customers

Contractual relationships = Contractual obligations

- directors;
- stakeholders.

You are *responsible* for ensuring that obligations/risks are adequately recorded so that your organization can ascertain a reasonably accurate understanding, at any given point in time, of your current financial and contractual liabilities. Contracts can be inter-linked, so problems under one contract could potentially impact other contracts – possibly unrelated ones. A reasonably effective contract repository is therefore a normative prudent management objective. If directors cannot lay their hands on their company's legal obligations, then they are failing adequately to discharge their director duties with appropriate due diligence, and may therefore be failing in a core director duty. This has become more important with the greater general penetration of outsourcing and third-party management.

> **LEARNING POINT**
>
> Part of 'Value' in the commercial contracting sphere is the management of contractual obligations. How comfortable are you that you have the relevant bases covered in the terms of this book? Do you know what your key contractual obligations are?
> Can you lay your hands on your contracts right now?

What are the benefits of good contract management?

Good contract management will reduce risk and increase certainty. There are a range of techniques, at strategic and at tactical levels, that enhance the contract management activity. And these are the issues we review and explore in the remainder of this book! How can we summarize these key benefits, so as to focus minds? Contracts need active management for four principal reasons:

- Rapidity of business change.
- Things go wrong!

Figure 1.3 Why contracts need managing

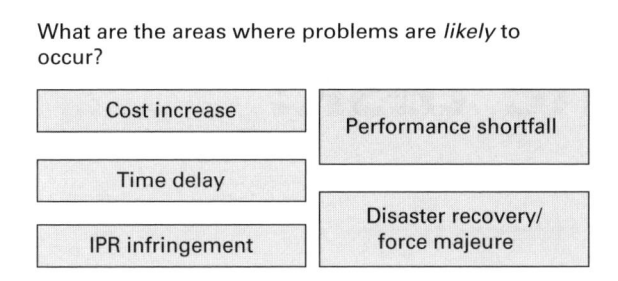

What are the areas where problems are *likely* to occur?

- Cost increase
- Time delay
- IPR infringement
- Performance shortfall
- Disaster recovery/force majeure

- People lose interest/focus.
- They create (archive) an audit trail.

Part of this is controlled and influenced by plain, good old-fashioned management. But if we focus on areas prone to 'go wrong' then we can maximize our influence on outcomes. Figure 1.3 suggests the likely problem areas.

Each of these areas can be analysed, understood and managed.[1] Cost and performance shortfall are closely associated with value. Time delay can lead to delays further down the value chain, and can cause on-costs in subsidiary contracts (such as supplier sub-contracts) or up the value chain, such as contracts with our key clients. Disasters happen from time to time, and we need to plan for them. Finally, intellectual property rights are increasingly important in this information age. It is quite possible to inadvertently (and innocently) infringe someone else's rights – and good management practices can be a powerful defence against this risk.

Enough said! Some organizations might consider contract management to be a cost centre – it is seen as an administrative burden on the organization that many would like to avoid if it were possible. Perhaps, however, we should think of contract management skills as a value driver – an opportunity to enhance the value of our projects and take risk (and cost) out of our business. That is the approach we adopt in this book.

Endnote

1 See Chapter 8 under heading 'Sammons' Five Forces!'

What is the task?   02

What do we (universally) want from our contracts?

We have already seen the areas prone to go wrong in any contract relationship – areas that need to be managed by contracting counter-parties (Figure 1.3). At one level, we can say simply, if we have these areas sewn up, then hopefully we will avoid the 'routine' problems that sap management time, attack business reputation and undermine value.

A contract is a set of promises – we sometimes forget this. A contract, strictly speaking and measured from an English Law viewpoint, is a legally enforceable agreement by which one party agrees to do something (usually supply a good or service) in exchange for the other party doing something (normally paying a price of money, or of money's worth). The key point about a contract is that the promise is to be specified in terms that both parties can understand and against which performance can be measured. In most contract documents there will be a sub-section that sets out, in technical or commercial terms, what has to be done – and by whom.

Please refer to Appendix 1 for some background on writing effective, watertight specifications. Once again we find that there are several terms commonly used to describe the specification, so let us review them briefly; you need to know which type of specification you intend to use – and then whether it is fit for purpose:

- **Specification** – this defines in detail what is required and who will do what. The term is often associated with technical products (physical things). Appendix 1 focuses on this type of document.
- **Terms of Reference** or **Statement of Work** – this is a specification of tasks required under a services contract.

- **Service Level Agreement** – this sets out service levels which, when measured over time, provide evidence that a contractor is satisfactorily and professionally meeting the requirements set out in a Statement of Work (SoW). Note that SLAs are often associated with outsourced tasks such as cleaning services, catering, or security. But SLAs might be applied to any service-based task where performance will fluctuate over time – it is only when measured in aggregate, over time, that a client is able to determine whether a contracting counterparty is meeting the required service levels. Note that a Statement of Work or a Specification might incorporate an SLA – possibly as an Appendix document.

For what it is worth, your author prefers to use the term 'Specification' wherever possible. Most organizations, whether buying or selling, should *specify* in precise terms what will be done – and by whom. Statements of Work and SLAs are by their nature less precise and perhaps are written with the understanding that there will be variables in performance and that it is not possible or realistic to expect 100 per cent performance 100 per cent of the time. Accordingly, service levels that fluctuate may be quite acceptable to a client, providing they remain within pre-set parameters.

Note that there are commercial specification-writing training courses available, and personnel regularly involved in writing specifications should probably attend such a course.

What is important in preparing specifications?

- **Terminology** – using terms that are recognized and understood.
- **Clarity** – people need to be clear about what is required.
- **Roles and responsibilities** – people need to know who will do what.

One US study on litigation, arbitration and contractual disputes noted that the most common specification problem areas include:

- 'or equal' references: counterparties can debate endlessly just what is 'equal' to something else;
- lack of alignment between specification documents and associated technical drawings (clerks may be issued with incorrect or out-of-date drawings);

- defective specifications: something incorporated into the specification was incorrect and caused confusion or delay;
- inaccurate technical data, or lack of technical information such as 'interfacing data';
- performance deficiencies post-delivery, where performance parameters are either not adequately specified or the goods/services simply fail to meet expectations.

Eight key questions before signing off a specification

We should ask ourselves some routine questions before signing off on a specification. These will include:

1. Do we truly know what we are buying (or selling)?
2. Is the specification clear to me? (If not, it will not be clear to others.)
3. What MI (management information) will be required during contract performance so that both parties can readily identify that progress is on track?
4. What, Why, Who, Where and When? Are these set out clearly?
5. Delivery – precisely how will this be effected?[1]
6. What information does the counterparty need from me – have I provided it? Do I actually have it? When will I need to get it?
7. What happens if things go wrong? How will we know? Who will put them right?
8. What is the remuneration (payment) strategy chosen for the proposed contract? Does it support the process of transfer of legal title from party A to party B?

We universally require certainty from our contracts. Of course, contract management skills help to provide that certainty. Some organizations (or possibly their legal advisers) think that it is possible, or desirable, to offload contractual risk – as far as possible – onto the other party. The point needs to be made quite clearly that this is not risk management, and in practice it is rarely good business either! It can build resentment if terms that might be considered as 'unfair' are being dictated and inflicted by a party operating in a dominant negotiating or market position. Prudent organizations have a basic business dictum when handling business and technical risk via contracts. It is a dictum that all business people should know and take to heart:

> Risk should lie where risk is best managed.

What this means is that the party best able to control a risk at a practical level should be the party that shoulders that risk (carries that risk) under the contract. We will not pursue this thought any further here, but Appendix 2 sets out a rationale via a formalized CREF (Contract Risk Evaluation Framework). Most organizations do not sit down and formally articulate their attitude to risk – sometimes called risk appetite. But most organizations probably should!

There is another business dictum we should take to heart:

> Profit is the reward for risk.

Some business people think that they can earn high profits and accept no risk. This is quite unrealistic. Generally speaking, those businesses which are prepared to accept greater risk can demand greater profit. The 'trick' in all this is to be aware of typical risks and to mitigate and manage them. We return to this in Chapter 5.

The contract management team

We make a very simple case in this book that there is, in reality, more than one person who is responsible for delivering a contract. This might be stating the obvious, but most organizations seem to devolve day-to-day management down to one person – the titular Contract Manager – who is seen to be the organization's eyes, ears, muscles, conscience and all-round superhero as regards contract delivery. Whilst that role holder is certainly accountable, we can challenge the idea that they are solely responsible. We strongly argue in this book that there should be a single point of contact for all management issues and in Appendix 7 we offer a typical job description for a Contract Manager role in a modern, well-managed organization.

But let us just pause for one moment to consider what is really going on! In any organization there will be certain stakeholders who have a practical interest in the outcome of any contract. In the next chapter, we review stakeholder management – as this is a semi-professionalized technical task in its own right! In addition to the stakeholders, however, there is inevitably a chain of command at managerial level, and technical expertise at operational level. Both groups have tasks to perform and have a practical interest in outcomes. In that sense there is some mutual accountability, illustrated in Figure 2.1.

We will not express in detail what the various organizational and operational stakeholder roles are – in fact it would be difficult to do so, as all organizations differ in terms of their 'chain of command'. But we can make this generalization: *at organizational level there should be clarity about which grade of manager holds responsibility for successful contract delivery – certainly for any contract of any 'materiality'*. For a major strategic investment, or a high-risk sale, it may well be that the board holds collective responsibility, or else a senior operational director, acting within their delegated financial authority. For a large project, perhaps the project manager might be responsible, with a Contract Manager reporting direct to them. For smaller contracts,

Figure 2.1 Who is responsible for delivering the contract?

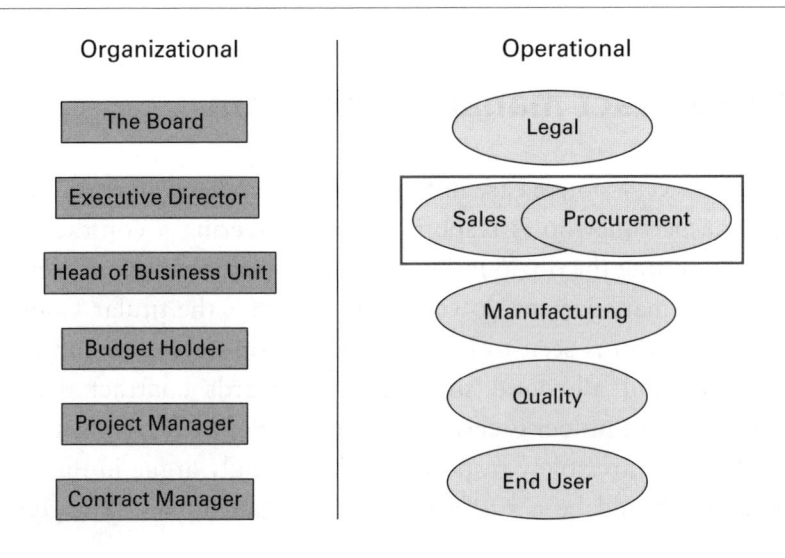

Organizational	Operational
The Board	Legal
Executive Director	Sales, Procurement
Head of Business Unit	Manufacturing
Budget Holder	Quality
Project Manager	End User
Contract Manager	

perhaps, the Contract Manager might hold accountability, working within their personal delegated financial authority, and within their managerial *span of control*. Operationally, the legal adviser may have an ongoing responsibility, or at least an oversight role. Depending on whether the transaction is a sale or a purchase, the relevant accountable department may carry primary responsibility and so provide the resource known as the Contract Manager. And in some organizations the quality department or the end user/budget holder might be considered both accountable and sufficiently knowledgeable to provide contract management capabilities.

It is important that the contract management team (a) knows that it is a team and (b) knows what role each team player has in the successful delivery of a contract. As we will see in Chapter 9, when we consider contract documentation and document repositories, being able to account to shareholders and other key stakeholders as to the location and status of live contracts is ultimately a senior manager responsibility – they carry this due diligence-type responsibility as senior directors. They cannot delegate that responsibility for any transaction that is in any way 'material' to their organization.

Understanding contract materiality

All contracts need to be managed, but the amount of effort that we assign to the management/administration task will be determined by the materiality of the transaction to our own organization. We have already referred to the idea of *materiality*, so now we will define it.

Any contracting organization, whether buying or selling, needs to understand the importance of a proposed contract and how, potentially, it might impact the organization – especially if it goes wrong! The idea of materiality helps us to recognize the importance of the contract measured with direct reference to the issues that are important to our organization, using a 'language' that is meaningful to our organization, and readily recognized and understood by our people. This can be systemized by undertaking a standardized *materiality assessment* (we call it a BCMR – a Basic Contract Materiality Review).

What is the point of this? Surely people know what is important – almost intuitively? Or surely the contract value (sales value or purchase value) is a good enough proxy for a proposed contract's importance to our organization? In reply, we argue that value alone does not tell you anything about market conditions, the state of the marketplace and the difficulties of changing (or escaping from) a contract if things go badly wrong. A BCMR helps to remedy these shortcomings and gives us a consistent view that is meaningful in our terms. It enables management to better understand risk exposure.

By materiality we mean *how significant the arrangement is to our organization and what direct impact non-performance or legal dispute might have on our organization.*

Materiality is not just a question of the financial size of the arrangement. Smaller third-party arrangements may have the capacity to adversely impact our organization in its marketplace, especially in terms of reputational damage and loss of confidence. These are both of concern to our own directors, but also potentially of concern to local regulatory agencies. For example, in the UK, the Financial Conduct Authority (FCA) shows considerable interest in its regulated sector (banks, insurance firms and other financial services companies) having a good appreciation of contracts with third parties (selling or buying), especially where such contracts might seriously impact or inconvenience the general public.

Some firms use Excel to create a simple tool such as the BCMR as a mechanism to assess any third -party contractual relationship against dimensions of risk assessed as important to their business. There are typically five dimensions:

- contract value;
- legal risk;
- reputation risk;
- market concentration risk;
- business risk of change.

Figure 2.2 reflects this idea. The use of the BCMR enables *our organization* to characterize any existing, or proposed, third-party contractual arrangement in terms of its potential risk, and so to adopt

Figure 2.2 Five commercial dimensions through which contract 'materiality' can be accessed

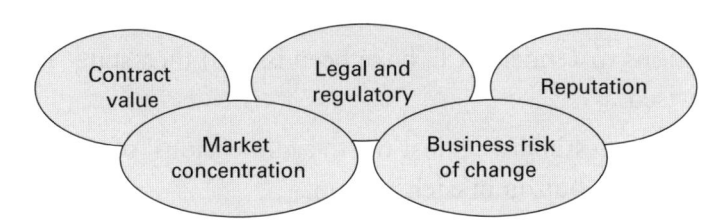

- Contract value
- Legal and regulatory
- Reputation
- Market concentration
- Business risk of change

the appropriate strategies to proactively engage company managers and select the right commercial tools to set up the arrangement. A BCMR helps risks to be recognized, visualized, measured and registered, and then managed and reviewed on an ongoing basis, as well as mitigated in practice.

A BCMR is quite simply a consistent and systematic review of the likely impact *to our organization* of any proposed new contract, using pre-defined simple questions. The model recommended in this book consists of a simple spreadsheet survey form, identifying risk using algorithms that are meaningful in our business context. It is best practice for completed 'materiality assessments' to be approved by the relevant business unit director. This means the director signs and dates a *hard copy* of the completed document, which is retained on file. If our company has a Risk Department, then this department will periodically audit BCMRs. Any assessment that registers as 'high' or 'exceptional' risk should typically be flagged to the Risk Department (or the relevant executive director) at project initiation.

Completion of the BCMR form

Please refer to Appendix 6 (a template BCMR form). Each section of the form should be completed. The project manager or business process owner responsible for the third-party contractual relationship would typically be responsible for initiating the BCMR unless this role is specifically delegated to a competent alternative – eg to a procurement director. Such delegation should be evidenced in writing. There are three things to note in terms of the use of a systematic BCMR:

- At project inception, if it is too early to know who the likely contracting partner will be (eg this is at outset of project, before Requests for Information (RFI), Requests for Porposals (RFP) or Invitations to Tender (ITT) have been issued) then state 'TBA = to be advised'.
- Make a best estimate against the five 'dimensions' of risk by clicking one radio button in each section.
- Use the comments box to fill in as much background (and references to other controlled documentation) as is necessary to get a good overall appreciation of what the project is about and how the BCMR assessment has been carried out.

Complete separate *Assessment Notes* (in our template BCMR spreadsheet this is located at Tab 2) with your rationale for making your earlier assessments in Tab 1. Note that some form of internal audit will be applied to these BCMRs for correctness and consistency. Reviewers/auditors would typically pay as much attention to the supporting notes as to the overall score registered by the BCMR tool. Project managers or contract managers are expected to use their common sense and good business judgement in completing a BCMR. Managers should be diligent in making it as accurate as possible. Where they make assumptions or estimates then they should be open about this, and explain their rationale.

Once the BCMR form is completed by its 'owner', it should then be discussed with their line manager and/or the project owner/budget holder. The BCMR form should be reviewed at an appropriate level of seniority given its overall ranking. For example, if a proposed contract is deemed to be of 'high' or 'exceptional' materiality, then it should typically be referred directly to a board-level director.

Once appropriate internal stakeholders are satisfied, then the final BCMR form should be presented to the relevant business unit director who should typically be briefed and then physically sign off the form. It is best practice for a copy to be retained on the director's risk file and the original BCMR filed along with other project information either as hard copy or scanned image/pdf.

We consider here, for a few moments, the types of contract relationship that might be encountered by typical businesses and subjected to the BCMR process. The headings on the 'template' BCMR set out in Appendix 6 can be characterized as follows, *but note that any business implementing a BCMR approach would need to devise headings specific for their business requirements.*

BCMR: Seven headings for review

In this section we consider how a BCMR might be completed for a financial services firm. Readers should consider, as they review this, what equivalent questions and financial parameters will be meaningful in their own business context. Where, immediately below, we refer to a '3P', this means 'third party', which might be the counterparty in either a sales contract or a purchase contract. The BCMR is applicable to both types of relationship. 3P really means 'contracting counterparty', but some organizations feel comfortable with the simple adjective 3P to describe these relationships. The examples below are for an insurance firm but are applicable to a wide range of relationships.

Heading 1: Contract value (type of relationship – examples for an insurance firm)

Typical third-party contracting scenarios for this type of business:

1 *Claims handling arrangements* – including third-party claims administrators and suppliers of goods where such suppliers have claims-handling authority.

– *Contract value*: annual value of claims payments.

2 *Intermediary or underwriting contracts* – includes delegated underwriting authorities, policy administration, introducer arrangements, corporate partners, reinsurance, and the provision of underwriting expertise and capacity for risks that the *insurer* does not want to write.

– *Contract value*: annual gross written premium.

3 *Policy administration services* – third parties under contract administering insurer policies.

– *Contract value*: the value of the fee charged by the third-party service provider.

4 *General expenses, goods and services* – goods and services such as professional advice, major IT systems, FM services. Exclude purchases (one-off purchases < £5K or any purchase against an existing call-off/framework arrangement).

- *Contract value*: total expected spend over the lifetime of the contract.

Heading 2: Market concentration risk (type of relationship – examples for an insurance firm)

How difficult would it be to find an alternative business partner or supplier if the insurer needed to switch? In assessing this risk consider the following:

- How many other 3Ps can perform the function?
- Can they provide the same service standard (eg regional or national coverage)?
- Can the insurer handle the activity in-house?
- Does the insurer have a documented exit strategy for the *existing* 3P (where there is an existing 3P)?
- What proportion of the insurer's activities of this type will be handled via this particular 3P?
- What proportion of the total market for this activity does this arrangement (or proposed arrangement) represent?

Brief comments on how you have arrived at your view should be in the Assessment Notes section of the BCMR.

Heading 3: Business risk of counterparty change (type of relationship – examples for an insurance firm)

How difficult would it be for the insurer to move to a different 3P? In assessing this risk consider the following:

- How dependent will the insurer be on the service or the product? (eg is it part of a core process?)

- Does the 3P have a unique level of influence over the sector concerned? (eg through holding a major market share)
- Can an alternative supplier adequately replace the current 3P? Does the insurer have the expertise, staff or other facilities to take on the work in-house?
- How complex and expensive would it be to change? (eg where the insurer has an existing third-party administrator handling claims for several different insurer business groups)

Brief comments on how you have arrived at your view should be in the Assessment Notes section of the BCMR.

Heading 4: Legal risk (type of relationship – examples for an insurance firm)

This section deals with the insurer's potential loss of funds through:

a) loss of funds through insolvency of third party;

b) impact of any legal action or sanctions by FCA/PRA or other Regulators;[2]

c) other losses arising from terms and conditions of the proposed contract. In assessing this third area, BCMR users would consider, for example, the following issues and discuss them as appropriate with their legal adviser(s), sales department, purchasing department or anyone else best placed to understand potential losses. These sorts of questions would need to be answered:

- Does the insurer have investment in the 3P that it might lose (eg a loan)?
- Does the 3P hold large financial balances on the insurer's behalf (eg premiums or claims floats)?
- How long is the credit period given to the 3P?
- How might the financial health of the 3P affect our ability to recover damages?
- Does the 3P act as an appointed representative of the insurer?

- Has the 3P in the past had any legal or regulatory problems that remain unresolved?
- Would it be an inconvenience or might they be unable to carry on their normal business activities – perhaps because they don't have current insurance certificates?
- In event of 3P service failure to the insurer, might the insurer be liable to other third parties, especially clients?
- Are there any unusual terms and conditions in the proposed contract?

A major loss of funds for an insurer of any size would typically run into > £200K (or equivalent non-Sterling). A minor loss (middle category) would be < £100K. In the low category, an insurer's losses would be primarily internal losses/expenses such as an internal audit investigation.

Brief comments on how you have arrived at your view should be in the Assessment Notes section of the BCMR.

Heading 5: Reputation risk (type of relationship – examples for an insurance firm)

This covers the impact on the insurer's ability to positively influence the customer to perceive the insurer as an insurer of choice and/or to trade with the insurer. If the insurer is subject to a high volume of customer complaints that are reported in the media etc, this may cause potential customers to avoid the insurer, impacting their ability to conduct business successfully. In assessing this risk, consider the following:

- Is there potential for issues to be reported in the national press for extended periods (eg dealing with vulnerable customers)?
- Could the insurer incur significant penalty from courts/regulators which might later be reported (or re-run) alongside unrelated cases?
- Are large numbers of customers, or premium customers, likely to be impacted by any disruption to service – or will impact on them be particularly severe?

- Do any of the insurer's clients that might be directly impacted have a particularly high media profile, eg charities?

Brief comments on how you have arrived at your view should be in the Assessment Notes section of the BCMR.

Heading 6: Summary comment

This field of the BCMR describes the nature of the 3P relationship, references any specific controlled documents for review, and outlines the overall rationale of the assessment. The business case (or provisional business case) will probably be referenced.

Heading 7: Assessment notes

In the model BCMR referenced in Appendix 6, Tab 2 of the spreadsheet requires more narrative detail on the reasoning adopted by the manager who completes the form. Really it is asking, why did you make the choices you made on Tab 1? BCMR assessors will pay great attention to this narrative, so the form needs to be completed professionally. It is part of the project's overall 'audit trail'.

Materiality

Once the preceding risk dimensions have been considered and 'entered' by selecting the appropriate radio button, and the associated assessment notes have been completed, a materiality status (exceptional, high, medium, low) is automatically generated by the Excel-based BCMR tool. In most cases, completion of the template will produce an appropriate and usable assessment. There may be circumstances where the assessment simply does not 'feel right'. In these cases, re-work the overall assessment, taking soundings from relevant parts of the business (eg Finance or Legal) and see if this produces a more accurate picture. If, at the conclusion of the BCMR exercise, there remains unease that the overall assessment may not be right, then propose a higher or lower 'level' of materiality, explaining your reasons in a covering e-mail to your line manager.

Endnotes

1 Your author remembers a case where a very large and expensive machine was purchased for delivery within a commercial building. When the machine arrived it was too big to squeeze through any door! Cue – knock a wall down!

2 These are UK regulators. BCMR users would necessarily consider whether a regulator specific to their industry should be specifically inserted to the BCMR form at this point.

Role and importance of effective contract management 03

Effective counterparty performance management

We do not need to labour this point, but it is worth emphasizing: a *counterparty* is the person or group with whom we enter a contract. Whilst, in the normal course of events, we might expect both parties to pay appropriate attention to their obligations under the contract, this does not always happen. Accordingly, well-managed organizations typically devote some effort to 'managing' their counterparty – as well as their own contractual activities – to assure that both parties do what is required. Seller and buyer typically have an analogous mechanism to evaluate each other. Again, we will not labour the point, but *supplier positioning* is a well-known management approach first described by Peter Kraljic (see Chapter 7).

Through understanding the different types of supplier available to them, buying organizations do not allocate time and resources uniformly across all their suppliers – they focus where there is most payback. Figure 3.1 helps to express this. Where, naturally, will we focus most effort?

Similar reasoning is applied by sellers. They also will focus effort where the payback is greatest, as Figure 3.2 suggests.

These frameworks of reference are fairly intuitive. Some organizations do in practice seek to formally 'position' their clients and suppliers using this type of thinking. It is surprising, however, that

Contract Management

Figure 3.1 Kraljic supplier positioning – managing suppliers from a buyer's perspective

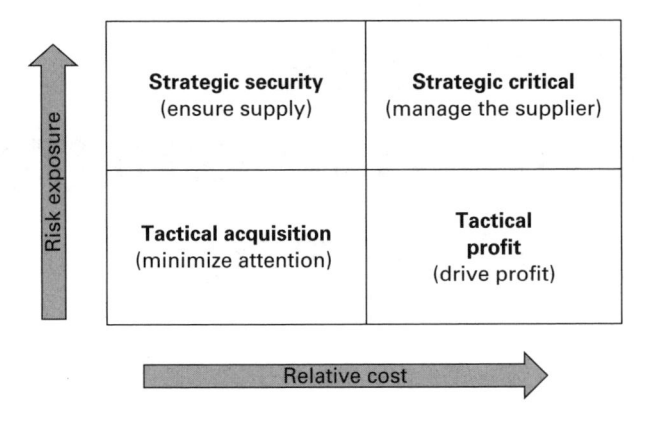

	Strategic security (ensure supply)	Strategic critical (manage the supplier)
	Tactical acquisition (minimize attention)	Tactical profit (drive profit)

Risk exposure ↑ / Relative cost →

Figure 3.2 Client positioning – managing customers from a seller's perspective

Development	Core
• nurture client • expand business • seek opportunities	• cosset client • defend vigorously • expand if possible
Nuisance	**Exploitable**
• give low attention • lose without pain • no proactivity	• drive premium price • short-term advantage • risk losing the client

Account attractiveness ↑ / Relative value of business →

many buyers and sellers can be almost oblivious as to where they 'fit' in this type of supplier (or client) positioning matrix. Most organizations, not unreasonably, will devote their contract management investment towards the top right-hand quadrant of each matrix. This does not mean the other three quadrants are ignored, but the approach adopted may be subtly different for these less *material* relationships.

LEARNING POINT

Do you typically understand your clients/suppliers in this systematic way? If not, are you misdirecting contract management resources?

Role and Importance of Effective Contract Management

What, then, are we 'driving at' in terms of counterparty performance management? All business effort should be devoted towards doing things effectively. So what does this mean in terms of contract management? We define four key terms in Figure 3.3.

In order to determine what is important to our organization, there are several inter-related aspects that have to be kept in mind as we determine our contract strategy and the associated management techniques we will apply to individual contracts. A contract is not created in a commercial vacuum (or it should not be!). A contract will arise from a business need and this in turn will be 'informed' by matters such as:

- our organization's overall corporate strategy and objectives;
- the associated commercial strategy that supports that corporate strategy;
- the individual contract strategy that best reflects these needs;
- the terms and conditions of the proposed contract.

In addition, do we need to apply some form of systematic supplier relationship management (SRM) or its equivalent customer relationship management (CRM)? Next, precisely what contract administration protocols will be applied and finally, exactly how do we propose to manage the payment process? What is important to us,

Figure 3.3 Defining four terms...

Effective	The process and activities WILL deliver the planned/required results.
Counterparty	Typically this will be a customer (selling) or a supplier (buying). Emphasis, of course, is on those that are strategically important.
Performance	Deliverables/outputs should be specified accurately, measured, tracked against a 'standard' and improved over time.
Management	This is about directing and prioritizing effort systematically to achieve organizational goals.

Figure 3.4 Corporate strategy to payment management – making connections

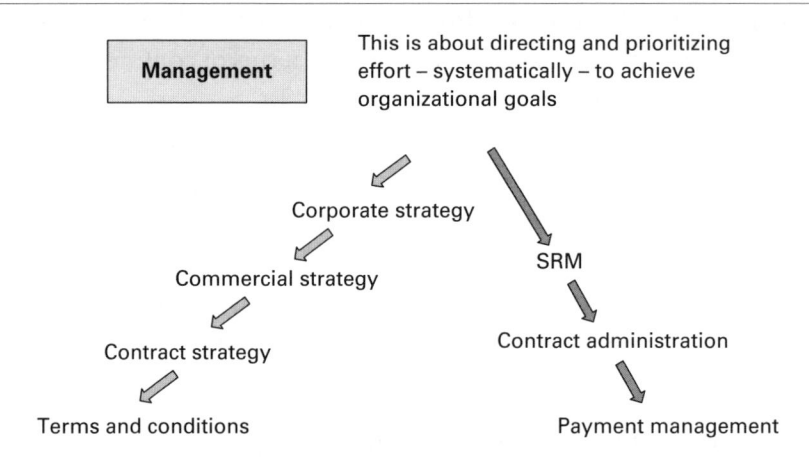

```
                    This is about directing and prioritizing
   [ Management ]   effort – systematically – to achieve
                    organizational goals

                    ↙       ↘
           Corporate strategy
              ↙                SRM
     Commercial strategy        ↘
         ↙                  Contract administration
  Contract strategy              ↘
     ↙                       Payment management
Terms and conditions
```

especially in terms of progressive transfer of legal ownership (or title, to use the correct legal term)? Will progressive payments reflect our ambition in terms of transfer of title and transfer of contract deliverables from Party A to Counterparty B? These ideas are expressed in Figure 3.4. Who in your organization carries responsibility for ensuring these various issues are kept in view as we determine our overall contract strategy for individual commercial transactions?

Upside opportunities versus downside risks

A second aspect needs to be kept in mind as we consider our commercial approach to potential future contracts. What is our organization's overall risk appetite? Are we risk-averse, or do we have a more nuanced approach to running and managing risks? This book does not aim to provide a definitive rationale for risk. This is very much down to the management board of each individual organization, whether private or public sector. But today in this 21st century, we can say that for all organizations there are typical *upside opportunities* to be weighed against typical *downside risks*. These opportunities and risks dovetail around social change, legal change and technological change. As pundits say – change is the only constant! Upside opportunities and downside risks represent a continuously changing series of commercial opportunities and risks that need to be kept in balance.

Typical upside opportunities in today's commercial world:

- convergent technologies/'plug and play';
- better commercial legal regime;
- more available sources of finance;
- more transparent trading;
- supplier diversity;
- supply chain intelligence;
- globalization;
- global suppliers/global markets;
- common standards (eg ISO);
- sophisticated financial instruments, including security for advance or progress payments;
- through-life costing;
- sophisticated economic awareness;
- better risk tools;
- the internet of everything (more informed customers, and greater sales 'reach');
- disruptive technologies create new possibilities for supply and marketing.

Typical downside risks in today's commercial world:

- regulatory compliance/corporate governance restrictions;
- consolidation – fewer suppliers;
- quality;
- supply chain disruption;
- wrong terms and conditions;
- BCM – business continuity management;
- time delay;

- consumer rights;
- product liability;
- health and safety;
- uncompetitive price;
- intrusive NGO accountability/adverse PR;
- cartels;
- rapid moving technology and obsolescence.

As commercial managers we need to hold in tension these basic business opportunities with the 'downside' that lurks just around the corner! Our contracts, then, need to be created and managed with both these ideas, upside and downside, in mind. Whilst the world is a risky place, most risks can be managed and/or mitigated.

Six foundation stones

Six elements comprise the concept of end-to-end contract management. Figure 3.5 identifies these. It is unnecessary for us to discuss them in detail, as much of that discussion would belong to the discipline of *strategy development* and that, in turn, many business people will typically encounter (in an academic sense) in a business studies course such as an MBA degree. For our purposes, however, we make a simple connection: a contract is not created in splendid isolation; it should reflect overall business objectives, which in turn will suggest the strategies and tactics to be used with our markets and with our contracting counterparties. We will assume, therefore, that foundations 1 to 4 are properly articulated and managed. If they are properly managed, then we can assume that some high-level appreciation of supply and sales markets has been undertaken and we currently know which suppliers and clients are important to us now – and into the foreseeable future. We focus our thoughts, then, on foundations 5 and 6.

Figure 3.5 Foundations of contract management

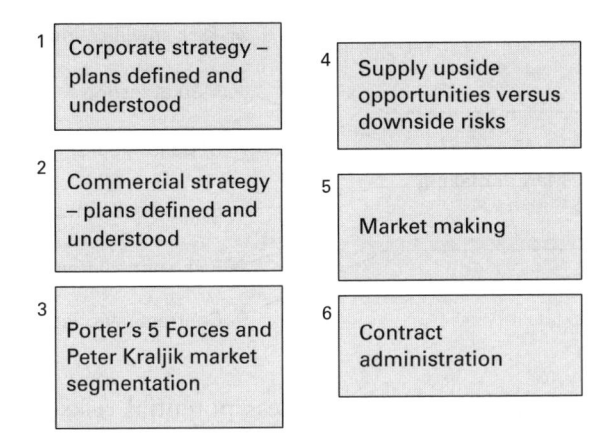

#		#	
1	Corporate strategy – plans defined and understood	4	Supply upside opportunities versus downside risks
2	Commercial strategy – plans defined and understood	5	Market making
3	Porter's 5 Forces and Peter Kraljik market segmentation	6	Contract administration

Market making

Market making is the activity of engaging with external markets, whether supply or sales, in such a way that we influence to our advantage the way those markets respond to us. This may sound a very ambitious objective, especially if our organization is a small one and therefore relatively insignificant. It can be said, however, that markets do respond to clear signals given out by trading counterparties, and to this extent we can 'make' a market, whether it is a sales market or a supply market. Figure 3.6 suggests the various elements of market making.

Whether buying or selling, the task or the product needs to be specified in a way that contractual promises can safely be made (and accepted) by each counterparty. In specifying what we want (or what we have to sell) we are already influencing the market and it will begin to adjust to meet needs and aspirations. For the buyer, some formal or informal market testing will begin to 'shape' the way the sales market will respond. Alongside this is supplier goal setting, where suppliers begin to appreciate in detail what is expected of them, and they consider how (in turn) they will meet those requirements. For both sides, there is a need for a good grounding in supply economics – just how remunerative will this project prove to be?

Figure 3.6 Market making

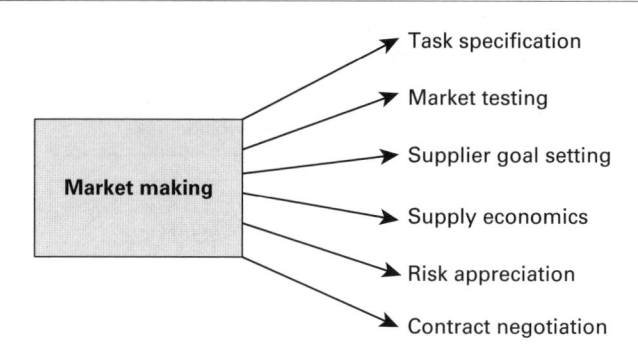

```
Market making ──→ Task specification
              ──→ Market testing
              ──→ Supplier goal setting
              ──→ Supply economics
              ──→ Risk appreciation
              ──→ Contract negotiation
```

Both parties should be trying to assess potential risks, and in some cases should establish a formal risk register to track and manage risks during the future contract period. Lastly, the contract needs to be negotiated with a view to settling all issues (specification, service levels, prices and transfer of title) prior to signature. In all these ways, both sides are setting expectations within the broader market, and in this sense they are market making.

Contract administration is a sufficiently large subject to require a separate chapter. We consider this in Chapter 4.

Stakeholder management

In Chapter 2, we commented that there are generally a number of 'stakeholders' who have a practical interest in the outcome of any contract. It is important for the success of any business to identify, influence and manage a (sometimes) diverse group of stakeholders. Some business commentators argue that stakeholder management is a key sub-element of people management generally. For the purposes of this book we make the simple point that we need to be able to recognize and understand that there is usually a range of people or groups that have a 'stake' in the success of a contract. Accordingly, we need to know who they are, what is the precise nature (and importance) of their 'stake' and whether they will positively or negatively impact the outcome of the contract in question. Bluntly, there are some stakeholders that have a legitimate 'stake'; there are others that believe they have or ought to have a 'stake', but who in reality are very much on the fringes of the project. Of these, we might go so far as to say they are non-legitimate stakeholders – or even busy-bodies who need to be excluded from the process!

Let us be precise: in contract management, a stakeholder is some person or group that has a genuine vested interest in the successful delivery of the objectives of the contract, typically:

- sales and marketing department (or procurement);
- manufacturing department;
- key external clients (users).

Others who may have a passing interest include Design, Operations, Legal, Compliance, Safety, and the board. There is a considerable body of literature available that illustrates the 'science' of stakeholder management, so we will merely summarize here.

Often it will be fairly obvious and intuitive as to who is likely to have a legitimate interest in a proposed contract. In complex organizations, however, some type of formal mapping process is useful, so as to ensure we identify the right targets – and possibly exclude those whose interest is only tenuous. A quick 'brainstorm' exercise within the commercial department should highlight who are the most likely external 'stakeholders'. A list (possibly in Excel format) of these persons or groups will focus minds. Then it is useful to contact each of them formally to ask the simple question: do you agree that you should be involved in the planning cycle of this proposed contract? Following informal confirmation of involvement – which may be as simple as an e-mail affirmative statement – we might consider holding a formal stakeholder meeting and discussion. At this meeting roles, responsibilities and timescales will be formally recorded and thereafter, in principle, these 'stakeholders' know what is expected of them. What we are really seeking is stakeholder buy-in and alignment with the project objectives, and this will include contract objectives. Stakeholders will go on being represented at project development and project execution phases – and possibly have some sort of oversight role in external contracts. The overall stakeholder management task typically involves these sub-steps:

- 'mapping';
- initial engagement;
- confirmation of involvement;

- roles and responsibilities assigned (audit trail);
- project governance agreed (audit trail);
- project objectives agreed (audit trail);
- outline business case prepared;
- market making (sourcing or sales activities as appropriate);
- negotiation phase completed;
- final business case agreed (audit trail);
- contract entered into (audit trail);
- contract performed.

One key element of stakeholder mapping is to establish, early on, to what extent a stakeholder is a supporter, or an enemy, of the project. If this is new to readers, then we would recommend that you take a look at a stakeholder management training course or business book on this subject. Suffice to say, if we have happy stakeholders then a contract will probably be performed well. If we have unhappy stakeholders there is much more risk of behind the scenes lobbying against the project, lack of buy-in and lack of support. Each of these can undermine a contract from an early stage. As process steps, stakeholder mapping, engagement and ongoing management are relatively straightforward. This is a time 'investment' that should prove to be well worthwhile. A final benefit, as suggested above, is that we can establish an audit trail for future reference – we then know who agreed to what (and when!) so it is difficult for critics, at a later stage, to argue that they were not sufficiently consulted.

> **LEARNING POINT**
>
> Does your company adequately manage stakeholders? Do you have a formalized process to do so?

Contract administration   04

An eye for detail

Chapter 3 explored the six key foundation stones upon which contract management success will be built. In this chapter, we consider the contract administration task. Let us go back to our original definitions:

1 **Contract management.** A strategic management task to achieve:

 The planning, stakeholder engagement (and ongoing management), commercial and contract strategy development, alignment with business strategy and objectives, risk appreciation, negotiation and execution. Also contract administration including through-life monitoring and exception reporting with remedial actions, controlling, problem resolution, and ultimate closure of liabilities between the contracting parties. Ensuring that all commercial objectives and planned business benefits are achieved and all expenditure is justified on commercial grounds.

2 **Contract administration.** A tactical administrative task to achieve:

 The tasks required (and performed) to ensure that all elements of a commercial contract are performed by both (all) counterparties in accordance with the terms of the contract. In particular that:

 a) payments are made;
 b) deliveries are received;
 c) communications are tracked/monitored and acted upon;
 d) IPRs are respected;

e) good 'title' from seller to buyer is achieved;

f) business reviews are carried out and associated MI (management information) is received and acted upon.

This is a non-exhaustive description of the tasks and associated disciplines and actions required to ensure that *a contract delivers on its promises*. There is some overlap between contract management and contract administration – and contract administration is a sub-set of contract management.

Clearly, without adequate administration of the day-to-day relationships and tasks, the strategic contract management objectives will almost certainly remain unrealized. Again, let us think in a 'systematic' way about all the things that are likely to happen whether or not they are done formally, or seen as being formal steps in a process. A contract is like a human; it goes through a life cycle. Let us explore the analogy!

A contract will traverse a life cycle with activities and tasks that begin when the possibility of a formal commercial contract is merely 'a twinkle in a commercial manager's eye'! So the *conception* stage is one where commercial objectives are matched to broader company strategies, to ensure that all work, all tasks and all activity reflect what our company is trying to achieve in its competitive and regulatory environment. Only then will there be a *gestation* period, where we are 'market making' (as we considered in Chapter 3) and both buyers and sellers (customers and contractors) will be developing the various commercial proposals that will deliver expected commercial benefits. Then comes the *birth*. The contract is 'birthed' when it is physically executed and both parties know that they are in agreement and in a contractual relationship. We might say, that is when the hard work really starts!

Life and death follow, as Figure 4.1 suggests. The contract administration task may have an indistinct beginning and end, but generally speaking, they tend to fall in the middle, as Figure 4.2 suggests.

If there is a separate *contract management plan*, it is likely this will be used as a governance protocol for the contract administration phase. We will consider this shortly. For now, we simply note that, if there has been a *project development team* responsible for all the pre-contractual activity (possibly acting under the direction of a

Contract Administration

Figure 4.1 Stages in the life of a contract

Conception	• Corporate strategy • commercial strategy • need identification • budget allocation • contract strategy
Gestation	• Market test (buyer) • negotiation • business case • bid (seller)
Birth	• Drafting • negotiation • 'execution' (signature) • copies to key stakeholders
Life	• Mobilization • contract management plan • progress monitoring • changes to scope or duration • dealing with problems • SRM • CRM • progress payments • transfer of legal title • progress meetings • project memo system for communications
Death	• Final delivery • final payment • final 'sign-off' (issue certificates) • expiry of warrantees/guarantees • latent defects period • IPR provisions expire • archival of documentation • document retention and destruction policy

project manager or a sales manager, purchasing manager etc), it may be that at *mobilization* stage, a Contract Manager will be formally appointed and will now become largely responsible for the day-to-day running (and success) of the contract. We will consider the role of the Contract Manager in Chapter 5.

Figure 4.2 Contract administration phase

Conception	• Corporate strategy • commercial strategy • need identification • budget allocation • contract strategy
Gestation	• Market test (buyer) • negotiation • business case • bid (seller)
Birth	• Drafting • negotiation • 'execution' (signature) • copies to key stakeholders
Life	• Mobilization • contract management plan • progress monitoring • changes to scope or duration • dealing with problems • SRM • CRM • progress payments • transfer of legal title • progress meetings • project memo system for communications
Death	• Final delivery • final payment • final 'sign-off' (issue certificates) • expiry of warrantees/guarantees • latent defects period • IPR provisions expire • archival of documentation • document retention and destruction policy

There is no doubt that, whoever manages the contract in practice, this person must be able to handle detail, and generally be comfortable with detail. A lot of this boils down to plain old-fashioned 'administration', although a *project management* mindset and associated project management skills will certainly be a real boon to anyone who is tasked with looking after a commercial contract on a day-to-day basis. Conversely, if someone has a 'butterfly' mind and is uncomfortable with detail and management, it may be unwise to place them in charge of a contract, no matter what other skill sets they may possess. An eye for detail really counts.

What has to be administered?

This book does not seek to be overly prescriptive, trying to develop *one-size-fits-all* materials for our readers. What we seek to highlight are common themes across the task of contract management. Any contract is likely to have a complete life cycle, from cradle to grave (as it were) and this is the basic mindset we encourage businesses to adopt. It is important that businesses have a clear sense of precisely what stage their contract (or proposed contract) has reached, and

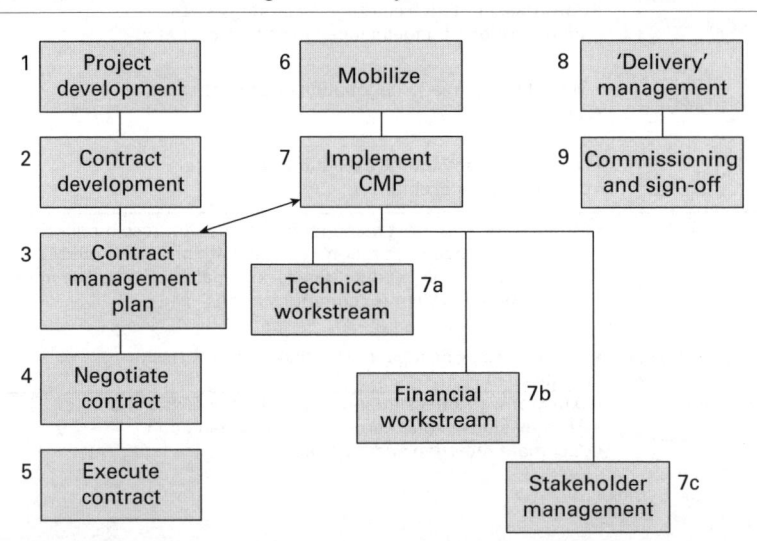

Figure 4.3 Contract management life cycle – workstreams

```
1  Project development          6  Mobilize                8  'Delivery' management
2  Contract development         7  Implement CMP           9  Commissioning and sign-off
3  Contract management plan        7a Technical workstream
4  Negotiate contract              7b Financial workstream
5  Execute contract                7c Stakeholder management
```

what are the next steps, or next tasks. Another way of considering the life cycle is suggested in Figure 4.3. We will return to this figure a number of times in this book, as it is a useful short-hand mechanism to understand contracts.

The task of the Contract Manager is to manage all these separate workstreams. We can of course acknowledge that workstreams #1–3 might actually be undertaken by a *commercial development manager* (such as a sales director or a procurement director – or even, in some cases, a lawyer). However, the practical day-to-day administration tasks will really commence at workstream #7, from which flow three sub-workstreams: all the *technical things* that need to be done under the contract, all the *financial things* and finally, keeping all the relevant *stakeholders engaged* and energized throughout the life cycle.

Dependent on the materiality of the contract to our organization (see Chapter 2), and the simplicity or complexity of the contract tasks, we might decide that it is prudent to develop a separate contract management plan (CMP).

> **LEARNING POINT**
>
> It is important to understand that the CMP is not an adjunct to the contract. It is not part of the specification or terms of reference. It is not used to interpret the contract terms.

Rather, the CMP helps individuals to understand what is expected of them and provides a structure for the mobilization and subsequent administration of the contract. It is a highly practical document for what is, in reality, the contract management team, but it is not referred to constantly. If the CMP is well drafted, it alerts all those personnel, at contract commencement, who will have primary interaction with the contractual obligations and tasks, as to how the whole programme will be carried out. In the next section, we consider the CMP.

Contract management plan – yes or no?

Why then do contracts need administration (or management, depending on your preferred term)? This is because, bluntly, four things can (and the fourth definitely should!) occur during the life of any contract:

- **Rapidity of business change** – circumstances change. Change happens so quickly that objectives are blown off course and so any commercial contract needs to keep pace with the change. This, in turn, might suggest renegotiation of certain aspects of a contract (or, in extremis, its cancellation). The administrator facilitates this.
- **Things go wrong!** One or both parties fail to meet their contractual obligations and the contract is now in some way delinquent in terms of its objectives. These issues need to be controlled as both parties are exposed to commercial risk thereby.
- **People lose interest/focus.** We are all human! For a number of reasons, people's focus can shift. This, in turn, brings the risk that contractual demands are allowed to slide. Someone needs to be accountable and energized to bring objectives and tasks back along the overall contract trajectory – all those things set out in any task specification (or terms of reference).
- **Create (and archive) an audit trail.** Records have to be kept, retained and managed, so that in the unfortunate event of a contractual disagreement (or dispute) both sides are able to determine quickly what the contract document itself actually intends. It is surprising how many businesses routinely do not know what are, in fact, their contractual arrangements and obligations!

A well-drafted CMP contains all the key information about how a contract will be managed. It sets out clearly systems and processes to ensure that the counterparty complies with the terms and conditions during the performance of the contract. A contract management plan enables the Contract Manager to:

- develop a good understanding of the contract, and the responsibilities of the parties involved; and

- establish a system against which the performance of both parties can be monitored and problems can be identified early – either before or as they occur.

How then do we determine if we require a CMP, and what should that CMP cover?

When should the contract management plan be developed?

A formal contract management plan is not required for all contracts, but is strongly recommended where the contract involves large financial investment relative to our organization, and/or where it includes complex technical requirements, or when the Contract Manager is responsible for managing a large number of contracts simultaneously. We refer again to the concept of materiality (see Chapter 2).

The CMP is a living document. Its development should commence during the contract planning stage, and it should be reviewed and updated throughout the project development phase process and the life of the contract. At the planning stage, consideration needs to be given to:

- which individual person will manage the contract;
- how the contractor's performance will be monitored;
- what risks are associated with the contract, and how they will be managed during the course of the contract; and
- what reporting requirements will be required of the contractor.

During the finalization of the contract document, details need to be agreed in relation to:

- measures to be used;
- confidentiality provisions – you may need to check your organization's broader policies in relation to this;
- milestones;
- reporting requirements; and
- implementation/transitional issues.

At the beginning of the contract management phase, the Contract Manager should finalize the plan by identifying the critical clauses in the contract and other requirements that may influence the management of the contract. The plan should be updated throughout the course of the contract as circumstances require.

What should be included in the contract management plan?

The level of detail included in a CMP will vary, depending on the nature of the commercial obligations undertaken by (generally speaking) *both* parties to the contract. Generally, the CMP should not be shared between the parties because, if it were to be so shared, it would be difficult to avoid the implication that the CMP was itself a document devised to help *construe* the contract. ('Construe' in this sense is a legal technical word, meaning interpret.)

Whilst it is entirely possible that both parties might have their own internal CMP, it is very often a client organization ('buyer') that has the biggest interest in close control and administration. It is they, after all, who are parting with their money and sheer prudence suggests it is they who need to ensure they achieve value for money. Not for nothing do we have the ancient English law dictum of *caveat emptor* (let the buyer beware!).

It should be noted that most of the information needed to draft and complete the CMP will be located in the contract documentation (including, for example, the technical specifications – or terms of reference – and possibly the contractor's tender documentation or technical proposal, where such documentation has been a feature of the negotiation phase). See Appendix 3 for more detail on what might be included and how the plan could be structured. It is worth emphasizing once again that the CMP should be seen as firmly distinct from the contractual documentation itself. Remember, the contractual documentation covers *legal rights and obligations*; the CMP and other typical ancillary documentation is far more about administering and managing the overall 'project' of which the

Figure 4.4 Contract Documentation Suite

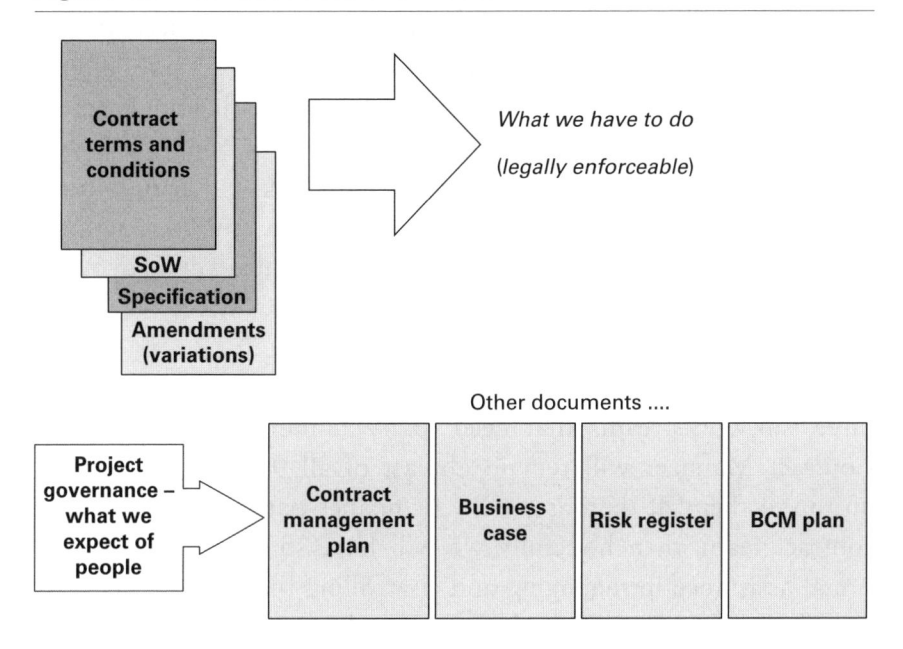

```
Contract terms and conditions
  SoW
  Specification
  Amendments (variations)
```
→ *What we have to do (legally enforceable)*

Other documents ....

Project governance – what we expect of people → Contract management plan | Business case | Risk register | BCM plan

contract is a part. This is illustrated in Figure 4.4, which suggests some of the ancillary documentation that will probably be devised for any sizeable ('material') contract.

Who develops the contract management plan?

Ideally the CMP should be developed by the Contract Manager, who preferably will have also been involved in the planning stages of the contract (boxes 1, 2 and 4 of Figure 4.3 above). This, of course, may not be possible if, for example, such a person has not yet been identified or nominated. But many organizations will have a clear view as to who that individual is likely to be, and so can include that person in developing the CMP. It is unlikely, however, that the CMP will be developed in isolation by any one individual and key stakeholders should probably review the draft CMP and actually approve the finalized document, again providing an audit trail and setting expectations very clearly.

As suggested in Figure 4.3, the CMP will prudently be developed during the project development phase, and we have placed this at box 3 in Figure 4.3. Assuming that a proposed contract does indeed go ahead, then at some point the CMP will be formally implemented, possibly in a contract mobilization ('kick-off') meeting. In Figure 4.3 we show this at box 7, and that kick-off task will also, in turn, initiate the typical workstreams associated with any contract: the technical (what actually happens), the financial (billing and payment) and stakeholder management (keeping everyone 'sweet' as far as possible!).

At this point, there is probably little for us to say about the three sub-workstreams that need to be administered. Ideally, the Contract Manager will remain abreast of all these tasks, keeping on top of them! If there is a CFO or finance partner as part of the contract team, then hopefully we will have some genuine professional assistance in managing and controlling the P2P activity. It is principally the technical workstream to which the organization will allocate primary resource – both sides have to perform their obligations under the contract effectively – otherwise we are heading for disputes! Stakeholder management is an art as much as a science, but the point is validly made that if stakeholders are unhappy, there are greater opportunities (and incentives) for negative behaviours that might adversely impact the project and/or any associated commercial contract.

Contract administration tasks

Once again we will avoid being overly prescriptive on this. What needs to be administered, and to what intensity, will vary from project to project and from contract to contract. Rather than become engaged in dense text, hopefully readers will appreciate the 'listing' of tasks under three main 'headings' that are required. We do this in Figures 4.5 a–j.

Contract Administration

Figure 4.5a The Contract Manager's main tasks

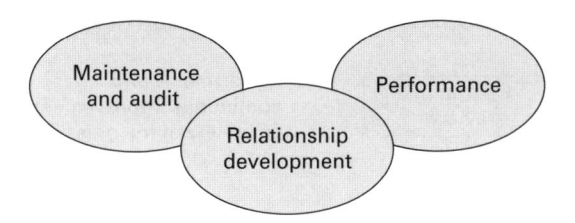

- Maintenance and audit
- Performance
- Relationship development

Figure 4.5b

Contract risk log maintenance
Change control maintenance
Financial strength review (?)
Trigger events – schedule
BCMR – annual update
BCM plans – annual review
IT security – review
Exit plan – review and maintenance
Quality audits (?)

Maintenance and audit

Figure 4.5c

Service levels
KPIs
Continuous improvement plan
Corrective action plans
MI and performance management dashboard
Validate performance information
Benchmark against competition (?)

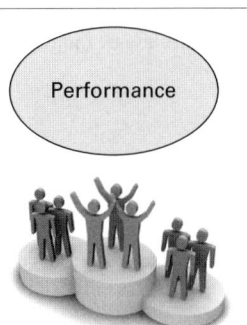

Performance

Figure 4.5d

Senior executive role
Joint working
Account plan
Relationship plan
Continuous improvement plan
Escalation

Relationship development

Figure 4.5e

RELATIONSHIP MANAGEMENT FRAMEWORK

Operational reviews — Performance and continuous improvement. Overview of major issues

Strategic reviews — Long-term relationship – improvement and development

Figure 4.5f

Operational reviews

CONTENT	ATTENDEES
Performance and continuous improvement	Contract Manager (chair)
	Key contact in counterparty
Overview of major issues	Specialist representative from business stakeholder/user
	Other key stakeholders

Figure 4.5g

Strategic reviews

CONTENT	ATTENDEES
Strategic agenda	Appropriate seniority group, reflective of size and scale of the contract relationship
Business development agenda	
Long-term strategic plans	+ Contract Manager
Long-term change programmes	

Contract Administration

Figure 4.5h

- Contracts should respond well to measurement (if contract is well drafted!).
- The Contract Manager's task is to facilitate measurement.

Figure 4.5i

What you cannot measure, you cannot manage

MEASURE YOUR SUCCESS

Figure 4.5j

- Measurements are key.
- If you cannot measure contract progress, you cannot control it.
- If you cannot control it, you cannot manage it.
- If you cannot manage it, you cannot improve it.

Managing the money

The 10 figures immediately above, 4.5a to 4.5j, are typical task requirements and reflect the sort of activities that a Contract Manager is expected to handle, certainly in larger organizations. Plainly, each organization needs to understand, and be clear about, the tasks to be handled by their Contract Managers which, in turn, will influence the sort of people selected for this task. What basic qualities will they need? We should not be too prescriptive about this, but Appendices 7 and 8 suggest two typical Contract Managers (in these cases 'Vendor' Managers, typically associated with major third-party outsourced arrangements, and therefore at the 'high end' of the relevant skill set) job role profiles. Readers may want to benchmark these against any job descriptions you currently use.

We stated in the introduction to this book that all contracts are about money – and that money needs to be managed. A Contract Manager, therefore, is responsible for ensuring that money is either received (if they are on the selling side) or paid (if they are on the client side) at the right time and in accordance with the detailed requirements of the contract. Let us just remind ourselves that payments are a contractual obligation! Where no time is specified, English courts take the view that payment will be made in a 'reasonable' time. Under most contracts there will be provisions covering legitimate delay to payment – and legitimate delay to further deliveries in the event of unjustified delayed payment. In the UK, businesses have the right to recover interest on delayed payment, assuming that payment has been unnecessarily delayed. We will leave this subject with the following thought.

> **LEARNING POINT**
> Poor payment practice prevents perfect project progression and presupposes probable pursuant penalty pain – penalizing profit.
> (= please pay promptly)

Commercial strategy   05

Back to basics

A contract is not created in isolation from the rest of the business – or it should not be! As explored in Chapter 1, any business is embedded somewhere within a broader value chain, and the very fact that *value* is delivered through a chain of different organizations gives rise to legally enforceable contractual relationships. In Chapter 3 and Figure 3.4, we began to flesh out the idea that businesses will inevitably have their own corporate strategy, which generally helps to answer the underlying question, *why are we in business and what do we want to achieve within this business?* From those decisions, we can then clarify the commercial strategies that will most assuredly help us to realize those corporate aims. From that, in turn, we can decide individual contract strategies that will best *deliver value* in practice. Whilst most businesses tend not to consider, in a systematic manner, individual contract strategies in context with broader corporate strategy, undoubtedly somewhere within the management hierarchy there is at least an intuitive understanding of these things, even if they are seldom articulated.

In this chapter, we want to go back to basics and ensure we have a common lexicon for considering these important issues. Really, this is all about giving everyone within our organization the same 'world view' of all these issues; as is often said, we should be 'singing from the same hymn sheet'! Through understanding these issues in the round, we can then decide, as Figure 3.4 suggests, our approach to supplier relationship management (SRM, if we are a buyer) or the equivalent customer relationship management (CRM, if we are a seller). And downstream from that clarification of relationship management will lie our approach to contract administration. In Chapter 4 and Figure 4.1

we began to explore the idea that there is in reality a *contract life cycle* which begins, as it were, at conception. It is at that very early stage, possibly long before individual contracts will be under active consideration, that an organization will consider how its commercial strategy (and tactics) supports its broader corporate strategy.

It was in Figure 4.3 that we first used the term 'Project Development' to describe how businesses will typically begin to think about upcoming contracts. Many organizations today utilize the skills and disciplines of project management to successfully plan, mobilize and deliver commercial tasks, considering many contracts to be discrete 'projects' in their own right. In this chapter, we flesh out this idea a little more, as we want readers to better understand how 'project strategy' helps us to determine an associated 'contract strategy'. Only once we have a good grasp of this are we really in the best position to determine what sort of commercial contract(s) will support these strategies. That, in turn, is called 'contract design', which we will explore in Chapter 6.

So, what do we mean by project strategy? A project strategy is the way in which a contracting organization intends to bring together all resources in order to deliver a project. So, a project will have technical objectives and a clear timeframe within which those objectives are to be delivered. The organization will then determine what combination of resources (finance, personnel, in-house manufacturing activity, materials, external suppliers and contractors, and interfacing with regulatory authorities (in some cases)) is required to achieve the desired end result. That is *The Project*. That is what must be delivered.

The sub-components will be:

- What is the *type of project* (technical components)? An example of this from the electricity-generating world would be:
  - Combined cycle gas turbine?
  - Coal-fired conventional plant?
  - Coal-fired with flue gas desulphurization?
  - Combined heat and power?
  - Major state-of-the-art retrofit?
  - Major refurbishment?

- What is the *client or funder structure* (purely in-house, or are we to combine with external third parties to realize the project objectives)?
- What sort of contract(s) will best 'fit' with these objectives? Examples might be:
  - turnkey;
  - management contracting;
  - multi-contract;
  - build-operate-transfer.

Having considered the *technical project strategy* and the *financial project strategy*, we can begin to address:

- operations input;
- HR input;
- manufacturing input;
- marketing (sales) input;
- purchasing input;
- stakeholder identification and management.

With internal and external resources martialled, we can turn to the associated commercial contracts that will best support these objectives. What sort of contract pricing strategy will support the commercial objectives? Examples might be:

- lump sum/fixed price;
- target cost;
- measure and value;
- cost reimbursable;
- estimated cost with financial ceiling (eg research and development projects).

Once our organization has clarity on the way the project is to be delivered, only then can it seriously begin to 'design' the terms of the contract. Yes, there will be *boilerplate* provisions incorporated, but bespoke terms around such variables as transfer of legal ownership

Figure 5.1 Back to basics

Conception	• Corporate strategy • commercial strategy • need identification • project strategy • budget allocation • contract strategy
Gestation	• Market test (buyer) • negotiation • business case • bid (seller)
Birth	• Drafting • negotiation • 'execution' (signature) • copies to key stakeholders
Life	• Mobilization • contract management plan • progress monitoring • changes to scope or duration • dealing with problems • SRM • CRM • progress payments • transfer of legal title • progress meetings • project memo system for communications
Death	• Final delivery • final payment • final 'sign-off' (issue certificates) • expiry of warrantees/guarantees • latent defects period • IPR provisions expire • archival of documentation • document retention and destruction policy

('title') will be devised to suit the particular circumstances. Referring to Figure 4.3 again, note that project strategy will generally be developed at Stages 1 and 2. The same message is indicated in Figure 5.1 above.

The earliest decisions that will impact a contract (and its subsequent management) are taken well 'up-stream' of the finalization of any contract document. Some connection between broader corporate strategy, and associated project strategies, is important.

> **LEARNING POINT**
>
> Who, in your organization, ensures that these necessary 'connections' are made?

Project strategy

Before we begin to design a contract, there will be a few large question marks that loom over the project. We can think of these as the key questions that a seller, or a buyer, will inevitably need to consider. For both parties, just how complex will this project prove to be? Is it in some way state of the art (technologically advanced, or in any way breaking new commercial, social or technical ground)?

If we are a client (buyer) then how attractive might be our 'account' to the potential supply market? A degree of realism is required here! Will the project be routine, or in any way 'special'? Will we need to deal directly with manufacturers or with other traders such as distributors? The equivalent questions for the seller will cover similar ground. Figure 5.2 summarizes this thought process. Both parties will have initial thoughts on the 'shape' of the potential contract that will best realize their commercial objectives.

Figure 5.2   Commercial project strategy – major considerations

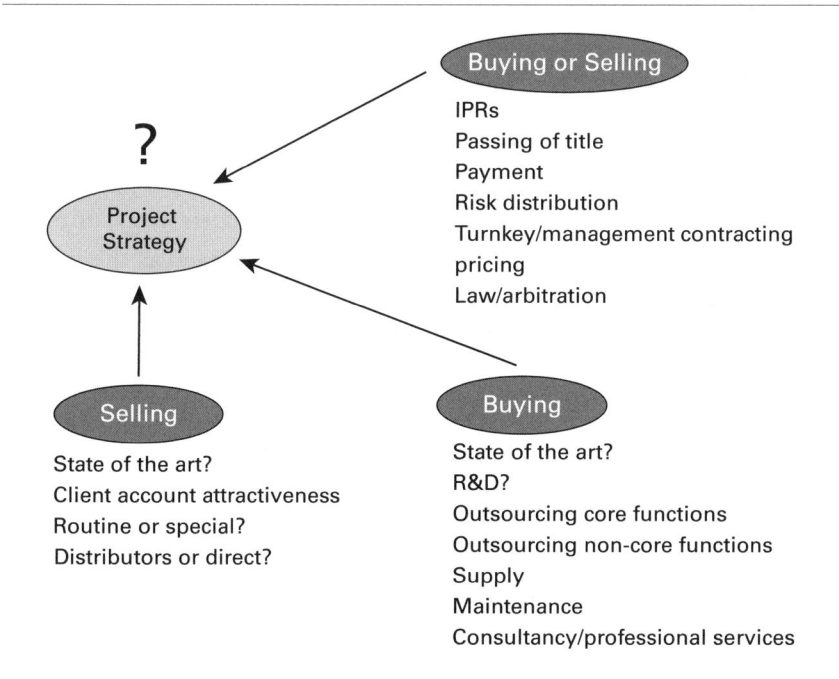

Buying or Selling
- IPRs
- Passing of title
- Payment
- Risk distribution
- Turnkey/management contracting
- pricing
- Law/arbitration

Project Strategy

Selling
- State of the art?
- Client account attractiveness
- Routine or special?
- Distributors or direct?

Buying
- State of the art?
- R&D?
- Outsourcing core functions
- Outsourcing non-core functions
- Supply
- Maintenance
- Consultancy/professional services

Let's 'cut to the chase' on this. The project strategy, once defined, helps us to think logically through the next steps, especially about the sort of contract that will best meet our needs. There are many factors that feed into our broad commercial strategy, not least of which is Professor Michael Porter's 'Five Forces' analysis technique. As this technique belongs in the area of corporate strategy we will say no more about it here, but there is plenty of material freely available on the internet for those seeking a quick overview. The chosen commercial strategy

Figure 5.3 Commercial strategy and contract strategy

- Fixed price
- Firm price
- Schedule of rates ('T&M')
- Cost plus percentage
- Cost plus fixed fee
- Maximum (estimated) price

Contract pricing method

Terms and conditions

Contract strategy

- Need for contract (broad)
- Make-or-buy?

Commercial strategy
'Project Strategy'?

- Market realities
- Company strategy
- Porter's 5 Forces
- Clients/partners/JVs etc
- Company values

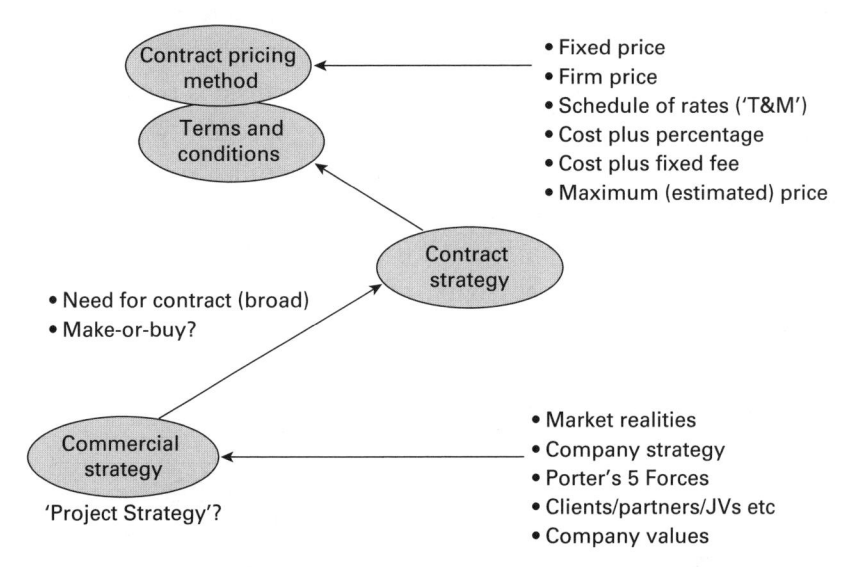

(or project strategy, depending on how your organization defines these things) will help us to define the optimum contract strategy, in terms of boilerplate and bespoke terms and conditions, as well as the pricing and payment mechanism to be used.

With these building blocks firmly in place, we can confidently design the contract.

Laying foundations

A few years ago, your author embarked on a small house extension and was surprised, if not a little shocked, at the seemingly vast hole that appeared beside the existing house as the new foundations were prepared. I had, a few years previously, been involved in a commercial dispute around inadequate legacy foundations dating from the 1950s, so perhaps should not have been so awed by the exacting building standards that are common in the UK in the early 21st century! A deep excavation, followed by successive layers of concrete and insulation, means that a modern dwelling sits upon a foundation 'raft' that should withstand all and any movement or disturbance that might reasonably be expected. Modern buildings tend to be very strong!

Figure 5.4 Foundations are vital

What is the position with modern contracts? How are their foundations laid, and who is responsible for this aspect of the commercial arrangements? Without labouring the point, which hopefully by now is becoming apparent, a contract is founded on a solid raft of commercial realities. This is explored in Figure 5.5. Our commercial (or project) strategy is the first layer to go down. Then the contract pricing strategy will begin to suggest the overall 'shape' and design of the contract itself. The contract management plan, explored in Chapter 4, will help us to understand on a day-to-day basis how we will control and administer events in such a way that the objectives are satisfactorily delivered. This tells us, prosaically, *who does what* – and how stakeholders are engaged and continue to contribute to the overall project objectives. Only then can we start to finesse the actual terms and conditions, our *contractual superstructure*, which we suggest comprises eight separate dimensions, outlined below.

The eight primary dimensions of any contract are:

1 **Privity and recitals.** This expresses, quite simply, who is party to the contract, and who, accordingly, can be held accountable and sue (or be sued) under the terms of the agreement.

Contract Management

Figure 5.5 Foundations and superstructure

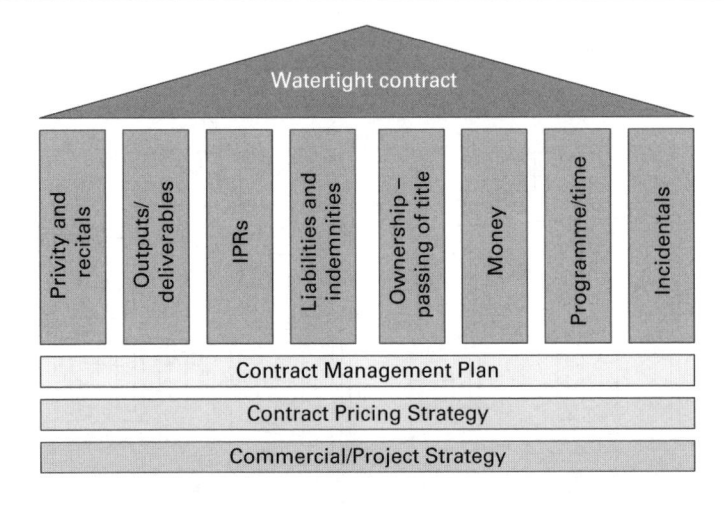

[Diagram: A temple-like structure with "Watertight contract" as the pediment, supported by eight columns labelled: Privity and recitals; Outputs/deliverables; IPRs; Liabilities and indemnities; Ownership – passing of title; Money; Programme/time; Incidentals. The foundation layers beneath are labelled: Contract Management Plan; Contract Pricing Strategy; Commercial/Project Strategy.]

2 **Outputs and deliverables.** Linked to the terms of reference (or specification) and any associated service level measures, this expresses at a technical level what actually must be achieved.

3 **Intellectual property rights (IPRs).** Increasingly important in today's knowledge-based economy, this underlines and makes a term the protection and non-disclosure of information that often has its own discrete commercial value and almost certainly an identifiable 'owner'.

4 **Liabilities and indemnities.** In the event of certain exigencies occurring, who is nominated to manage the situation and put things right? Insurance provisions will generally be incorporated under this heading.

5 **Ownership – passing of title.** At some point, what is owned by one party will become the property of another. The precise point at which this transfer takes place should be well expressed and well understood.

6 **Money.** Under English contract law (replicated in most places in the world), money is an essential element in any contract. It is generally referred to as consideration in the UK legal jurisdictions.

Money is ultimately what the contract is all about! Accordingly, when and how remittances become due, and payment is actually effected, needs to be expressed in a contract with great precision. Note that a failure to pay on time is technically a breach of contract and, in many jurisdictions, gives automatic rights to some element of financial compensation.

7   **Programme/time**. Again, time is an important element of any contract. Time delinquency on the part of one or other contracting party will often be a cause of friction, if not actual dispute. Time, again, should be clearly expressed in the contract documentation.

8   **Incidentals**. Many modern contract documents are nothing if not voluminous! They will often try cleverly to anticipate every conceivable situation and every conceivable exigency and provide specific contractual obligations to deal with such. Anything that is not an element of the preceding seven dimensions is, generally speaking, an incidental to the main purpose and the main metrics of any commercial contract. They can therefore be 'lumped together' under this dimension as an incidental.

Gestation and birth

Hopefully we can see the importance of commercial (or project) strategy to contract design. Everything we do has to ultimately match our corporate strategic objectives. This is not, of course, to suggest that all contracts must have the same management intensity applied to them. Our Basic Contract Materiality Review (BCMR), discussed in Chapter 2, will tend to focus management attention towards those that are most significant and represent greatest risk. Similarly, Figures 3.1 and 3.2 in Chapter 3 suggest, for both buyer and seller, where they must focus most attention.

A quick glance at Figure 5.1, above, reminds us that after conception there is a period when the putative contract is negotiated. In reality, what we have defined as gestation and birth are overlapping activities. Broadly, there will come a point at which one prospective party will make a formal offer to the other. Usually it is the buyer (or client) that prefers to manage and energize this activity – often through a formalized 'market test' activity. This activity is designed to gain business intelligence, set out the client's requirement(s) in such a way that the market can respond effectively, and in a structured manner, leading (ideally) to a prompt decision to award a contract.

During these phases, the contract document itself will be negotiated and prepared for signature ('drafting'). The extent to which the future Contract Manager will be involved in this activity is something for each organization to determine. A rudimentary understanding (at least!) of contract law, as well as a broad commercial awareness, will definitely assist the Contract Manager in discharging his or her duties. But in truth, in many situations, the skill sets required to administer and manage a contract on a day-to-day basis are rather different from the somewhat arcane and rarefied skill sets needed to dot every 'i' and cross every 't' of the commercial contract. Similarly, the skill sets and gravitas required to negotiate the terms and the economics of a given commercial deal are, again, subtly different from those of the person charged with day-to-day delivery. So we recommend no hard-and-fast rule on this. Suffice to say that at some point either a formal or an informal business case should be prepared so that the relevant manager with delegated authority is able to understand the contract, the risks, the rewards and the legal obligations to which they are being asked to assent and formally 'execute' (sign).

Contract design 06

Back to basics

Figure 4.3 in Chapter 4 outlines, in summary, the contract management life cycle. We have called Stage 2 in that life cycle *contract development* and, as suggested in Figure 4.2, there are various sub-tasks that must be undertaken before we are ready to physically sign-off ('execute') a contract and assume its legal obligations. In Chapter 5 we began to consider the main pillars of a typical commercial contract – refer again to Figure 5.5, 'Foundations and superstructure'. In this chapter, we consider contract design – the main elements that will typically be found in a commercial contract. In the sense of Figure 5.5, we might say that the superstructure of the contract is the terms and conditions document(s) and anything else that expresses the obligations of the contracting parties.

This chapter is necessarily short – no bad thing in a business book! As this is not a legal book per se, there is little benefit in trying to explore specific legal provisions or contractual clauses nor recommend any particular form of words as a sure-fire way to success. Instead we build upon Figure 5.5 and add some further thoughts around the structure or 'shape' of a typical contract. There are certain characteristics that must be found in any commercial contract. These are summarized as the *what*, the *where*, the *when*, the *how,* the *how much*, and the *what else* (see Figure 6.1). This is broadly analogous, incidentally, to our eight pillars in Figure 5.5.

The first five above reflect precisely what must be done under a contract, in which any *performance delinquency* will probably be a significant breach of the terms of the contract. All other contractual dependencies and minor provisions are encompassed in the *what else* provisions. We called those 'incidentals' in Figure 5.5. Without trying to make recommendations about particular wording or terms, then, we can make two simple observations (or 'truisms') about contract

Contract Management

Figure 6.1 Typical contract 'shape'

The WHAT	:	definition and specification
The WHERE	:	destination
The WHEN	:	timescales/timing of performance
The HOW	:	method of delivery
The HOW MUCH	:	price and payment
The WHAT ELSE	:	dependencies/incidentals

drafting. These are summarized in Figure 6.2 below. The point is that vagueness or a lack of detail may typically be of service to a seller, as they may then be best positioned to argue that vagueness in their favour. If a contract was vague then there might well be room to argue what was actually meant by its specific wording and so defend oneself against charges of performance delinquency or performance shortfall. Conversely, precision and clarity will always work to the benefit of the client (buying) organization, unless, exceptionally, excessive precision introduces a direct conflict between one part of the contract and another. (Indeed, this surely would be a case of imprecision, so perhaps we have sufficiently proved our point on this!)

But keep these two truisms in mind – especially if you are a client organization. As we say in the UK, this is a case of *caveat emptor*, which is Latin for 'let the buyer beware'!

Figure 6.2 Contract drafting – two 'truisms'

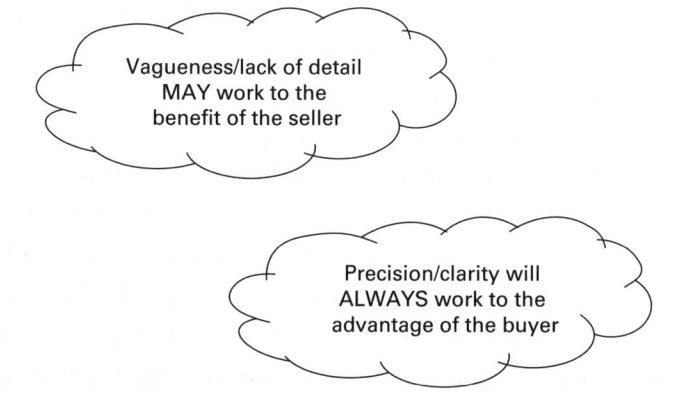

> Vagueness/lack of detail MAY work to the benefit of the seller

> Precision/clarity will ALWAYS work to the advantage of the buyer

NEC3 contract system

This chapter, then, can be thought of as a brief excursus looking at how one particular UK model contract is designed and constructed. Whilst it is not our place to recommend any particular 'model' contract as being more competent than others, we will focus on the UK Institution of Civil Engineers (ICE) model form, which used to be known as the New Engineering Contract. After the model passed its quarter century in use, and had undergone three update revisions, it was simply rebranded the NEC family. The NEC is today a linked and aligned 'family' of contract models that seem to have five principle advantages over all other models:

1 They are modular in construction and so can be assembled as living contracts almost in 'kit' form. The draftsperson simply selects the main elements of the contract to best reflect the required commercial and project strategies.
2 As 'kits', they give users assurance that the various pieces work together and, providing they are not modified in any way to destroy the in-built 'balance', a self-consistent document will emerge every time.
3 They are seen as a tool of project management rather than a block of legalese with which to 'bash' the contracting counterparty – NEC's contract management approach therefore adds value and certainty to any project, as well as making certain project management demands of the parties.
4 As far as this author/practitioner is aware, the contract is unique in stating, as part of its preamble, that the parties will operate 'in a spirit of mutual trust and cooperation'. This means, automatically, that any bad or underhand behaviour will immediately place the perpetrator at odds with a fundamental tenet of the contract, against which behaviour will be construed accordingly.
5 NEC uses remarkably plain language which is difficult to misconstrue.

As a 'family' of contracts, and at the date of writing this book, the family consists of:

Works:

Engineering and Construction Contract (ECC);

Engineering and Construction Short Contract (ECSC);

Engineering and Construction Sub-Contract (ECSS).

Services:

NEC Term Service Contract (TSC);

NEC Term Service Short Contract (TSSC);

NEC Professional Services Contract (PSC).

Supply:

NEC Supply Contract (SC);

NEC Supply Short Contract (SSC).

Other:

NEC Adjudicator's Contract (AC);

NEC Framework Contract (FC).

Readers should not go away with the impression that NEC3[1] is solely an engineering form of contract. Although it emerged in the engineering sector (and interestingly it was first trialled in South Africa) it is today being applied across many sectors and (a personal view of the author) the PSC is suitable for all types of professional service activity.

It is sometimes commented that 'Model Conditions' should be contrasted with 'Standard Conditions'. Of course, definitions have to be commonly understood, but generally speaking, model conditions can be defined as being associated with trade bodies and are often the result of negotiations within a trade sector. There is a residual suspicion (not always fair, it must be said) that model conditions are subtly slanted towards the interests of the trade member, and away from those who are not members. Standard conditions, by contrast, are usually associated with a single firm which provides its own 'standard' contract for whatever subject matter. Standard conditions may, then, be subtly slanted in favour of the firm that has devised them and tries to impose them upon its trading operations. The NEC family, by contrast, seems to be generally even-handed between the counterparties, and simply demands good, conscientious and competent behaviour from each party.

How, then, is the NEC assembled in kit form? We will not try to do anything here, other than summarize the process. A certain level of training is typically required to become competent in the drafting and use of NEC3 but, like riding a bicycle, once learned it is never forgotten. Essentially, the contract drafter will select from one *main option*, which describes the type of contract. This is backed by nine *core clauses* which feature in every contract (they are non-optional). Choices are then made between 20 *secondary option clauses* which can be used in any combination. These are in turn supplemented by agreed *contract data* – to be provided by both counterparties – and finally there is a separate scope document, which is broadly a technical specification (or scope of work) in a traditional contracting format. Readers who want to consider NEC3 in greater detail might start with a simple Google search. NEC certainly seems to be afflicted with fewer court disputes than other model contracts, suggesting that it is working well in practice, as a truly 21st-century *contracting mechanism*. Figures 6.3a and 6.3b summarize the overall 'shape' of an NEC contract, in terms of laying the foundations and then assembling the superstructure (or 'filling in the details').

Figure 6.3a Assembling an NEC contract – options

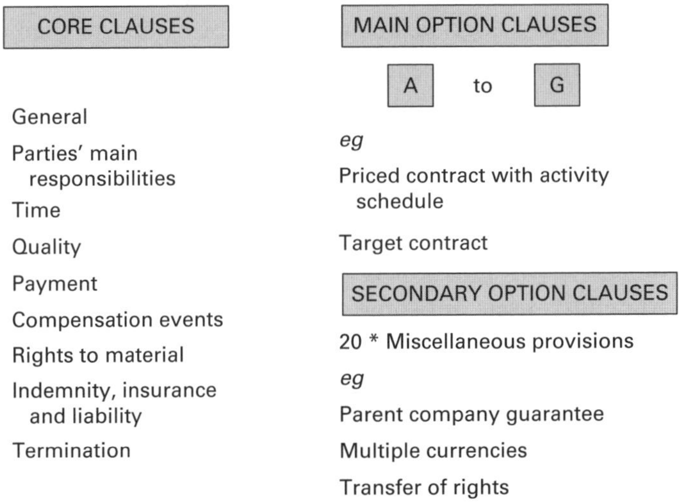

CORE CLAUSES

General
Parties' main responsibilities
Time
Quality
Payment
Compensation events
Rights to material
Indemnity, insurance and liability
Termination

MAIN OPTION CLAUSES

A to G

eg
Priced contract with activity schedule

Target contract

SECONDARY OPTION CLAUSES

20 * Miscellaneous provisions

eg
Parent company guarantee
Multiple currencies
Transfer of rights

Figure 6.3b Assembling an NEC contract – data

CONTRACT DATA	THE SCOPE
Basic information provided by both parties: • PART 1 Data provided by the employer • PART 2 Data provided by the contractor (Key 'variables' of the contract)	This is equivalent to the 'Specification' or 'Statement of Work' document found in traditional contracts

Old-fashioned lawyers

In summary, contract design is not for the complete novice! It can be helpful to go back to first principles and to consider just what it is that we want to achieve in a particular project strategy, and how this commercial ambition 'fits' with our broader commercial strategy. A standardized form of contract may well be adequate for our general purposes – certainly as a starting point in contract design – and perhaps 'tweaked' in some way to match it with particular project demands and objectives. If using an external legal counsel, then try to ensure they take a realistic approach to contractual *risk distribution*. Surprising as it may seem, there are still today old-fashioned lawyers who think that an attempt to offload all contractual risk to the counterparty is good business, and best reflects their client's needs! Rather, this is a recipe for protracted pre-contract negotiations and potentially sets off the contractual relationship on the 'wrong foot' from day one!

Finally, an organization should have some formalized understanding of its own attitude to commercial and contractual risk. This, in turn, will colour its approach to contract negotiations and contract design. Appendix 3 sets out some considerations in terms of commercial risk appetite, as specifically applied to contract design. A periodic review and restatement of risk appetite is surely a valuable exercise and helps us to approach our markets, whether sales or purchase, with a useful degree of commercial nous and commercial reality.

Endnote

1 At time of writing, NEC3 is the third major iteration of the NEC family of contracts.

Mobilization   07

Getting started

Figure 4.3 is repeated below but is renamed Figure 7.1. We are focusing now on the period immediately following that (sometimes!) euphoric moment of contract signature when all the hard work of market making, contract development and final negotiation has borne fruit and the parties allow themselves a brief moment of mutual congratulation for having won/awarded business. Both sides[1] now need to make good on their promises.

By the term 'mobilization' (perhaps more correctly, *contract mobilization*) we mean, simply, the tasks initiated by each party to issue internal instructions to commence work, including, where necessary, the detailing of personnel to perform specific tasks, the establishment of budgets and budget systems to handle payments, and associated allocation of overheads. Linked to this might well be the placing of sub-contracts and purchase orders with sub-tier suppliers. Mobilization is different from *contract execution*[2] – carrying out the contractual tasks. As its name implies, mobilization is about initiating tasks and overcoming the potential for inertia, with the associated possibility of starting (and finishing) late.

Typically, in any such *mobilization phase*, there will be three sub-workstreams, which we have highlighted as 7a, 7b and 7c in Figure 7.1. There will always be technical tasks to be undertaken and delivered, whether the contract is for a physical supply (or goods or other physical items) or for the provision of services under contract. Those technical tasks must, of course, be carried out by technically competent and experienced people.

A word for suppliers at this point: assembling the right project team is an important task. Do not leave it too late. Your author was once involved in a project where there was significant mobilization delay. Why? Because having won the contract, the supplier was unable to

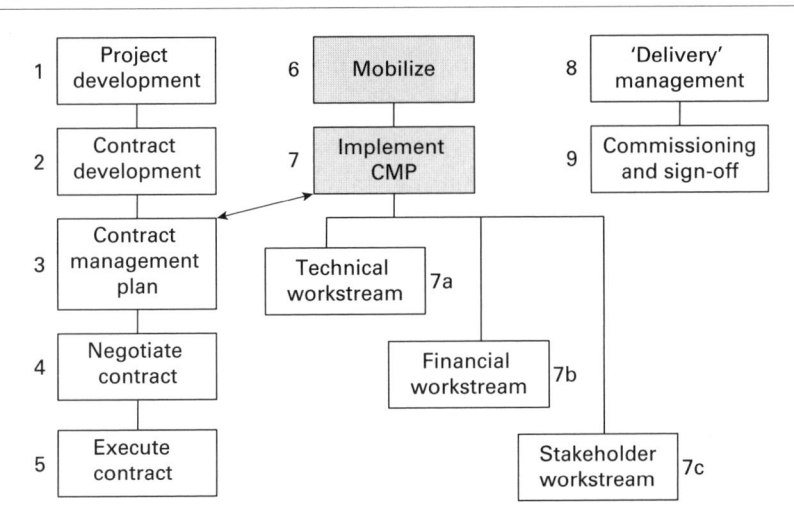

Figure 7.1 Contract management life cycle – workstreams

```
1. Project development
2. Contract development
3. Contract management plan
4. Negotiate contract
5. Execute contract
6. Mobilize
7. Implement CMP
   7a. Technical workstream
   7b. Financial workstream
   7c. Stakeholder workstream
8. 'Delivery' management
9. Commissioning and sign-off
```

find the right personnel to actually do the task – possibly because they had successfully bid for more work than they were expecting to win. This resulted effectively in a short-term skills shortage.

A word for buyers at this point: if mobilization looks in any way challenging or complex, ask the supplier, before the contract is signed, to detail their mobilization plan. Consider it. Challenge it. Monitor it. Ensure that mobilization tasks planned are carried out in practice. Consider incorporating the mobilization plan into the contract documentation[3].

The *financial workstream* (7b in Figure 7.1) is really about two things: *first*, that we have sufficient money allocated to fulfil our contractual obligations and *second*, that we monitor money in and money out during the life of the contract. It may be that the finance department will be solely responsible for this task; however, if the finance department is really a bill-paying operation and little more, then the Contract Manager or project manager (however defined) may need to take a more proactive interest in financial matters, especially that payments are made/received at the right time under the terms of the contract.

The *stakeholder workstream* (7c in Figure 7.1) will perhaps be the most variable across different projects. Some contracts will have virtually no stakeholder engagement beyond the budget holder (or demand manager) on the buying side and the delivery manager on the selling side. By contrast, complex or high-value projects, or politically sensitive transactions, may have numerous stakeholders and a view must be taken (during the *project development* phase, Stage 1 in Figure 7.1) as to how much effort we will apply to stakeholder mapping, engagement and ongoing stakeholder management.

Mr or Ms 2 per cent

It is sometimes said that the 19th-century Armenian oil magnate Calouste Gulbenkian was called 'Mister 5 per cent' because of his ability to retain 5 per cent of the shares in the oil mega-deals that he masterminded. Whilst it is unclear that there is much empirical evidence behind it, there is a popular suggestion in commercial circles that the cost of managing a contract will typically be 2 per cent of the value of the contract itself. If true, this is an interesting statistic. The cost of administering and managing contract tasks will plainly consist of personnel time allocated, with a smaller allocation (usually absorbed in general overheads) of progress meetings, communications, travel and so on. The financial workstream also represents the overhead of time – mainly – within the finance department.

Managers in any organization, though, should be aware that the successful delivery of any contract will be critically dependent on the competence of the *contract management team*. We will not get proper contract management on the cheap! CFOs and project directors should be aware that proper investment needs to be made in the overall contract management task – and this will entail the allocation of a named and dedicated Contract Manager, certain support staff and ad-hoc expenses around travel and communications. A figure of 2 per cent is probably the right order of magnitude for this expense. All senior managers, therefore, need to be aware of this collateral investment and should ensure they achieve concomitant value for money.

In return for their 2 per cent, they should expect as a minimum:

- timely management reports that highlight progress;
- early warning of issues that might prejudice contract delivery;

- work-arounds to practical problems (ie proactivity, not reactivity – or solutions rather than problems);
- a competent understanding of the terms of the contract – and an understanding that delivers practical benefits rather than debating points;
- a competent understanding of the technical issues associated with the contract – although this may fall short of being a technical expert in the subject matter. We employ a *Contract Manager* rather than a technical expert.

> **LEARNING POINT**
>
> Senior managers – do you think of your contract administration and management in terms of a fraction of the value of the contract? Is 2 per cent meaningful in your context?

We're underway!

As Figure 7.2 suggests, there are in fact two workstreams associated with mobilization, once the contract is signed. Each party to the contract must initiate their activity. The amount of 'swapping' of information about what each side is doing under this workstream must, again, be a judgement call. As noted earlier, there may be disadvantages to incorporating mobilization plans into the contract terms (eg as a separate document, see Endnote 3). We do not want the contract bogged down in what must be secondary (if not extraneous) detail. On the other hand, if time or technology is critical, or if the contract is in any other way *material* to our organization, then

Figure 7.2 Mobilization – two sides of one coin

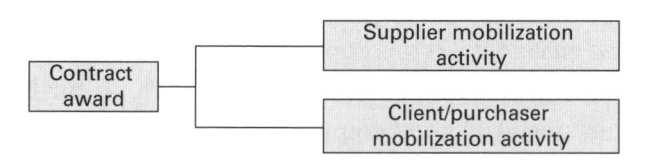

Contract award
- Supplier mobilization activity
- Client/purchaser mobilization activity

it is almost a dereliction of duty to be ignorant of (or blind to) the mobilization activity.

What, then, can we say are the typical supplier mobilization tasks? These will boil down to the appointment of people and ensuring that materials or provisions will be available when required. Below is a reasonably exhaustive sample:

- Contract Manager (CM) or Customer Relationship Manager (CRM) appointed;
- sub-contracts placed and/or supplier procurement team engaged and market testing commences;
- contract delivery team assembled and team governance notified;
- manufacturing and/or operational plan is put into effect;
- senior/internal stakeholder manager/director appointed;
- internal progress reports initiated;
- internal risk reports initiated;
- external progress reports planned and initiated;
- testing/QA regime implemented.

It is, perhaps, beyond the scope of this book to detail how a prime contractor should appoint its sub-contractors – or indeed how to control them. Suffice to say that some prime contractors get themselves into a terrible pickle about awarding sub-contracts, insisting that they cannot place sub-contracts until they have been awarded the prime contract. This, however, is precisely the time at which their bargaining strength vis à vis their sub-contractors will be lowest! It is arguably better to place sub-contracts *in advance* of being awarded the prime contract, providing of course that the end client's specification is sufficiently firm to make the technical/operational solution that is required a reasonable certainty: these sub-contracts should be placed under a *conditions precedent* clause which states that the sub-contract will be affirmed on the achievement of the (preceding) condition that the prime contractor is itself awarded the main contract *by a given date*. If this condition precedent is not achieved by that given date, then the sub-contracts lapse with no further obligation on either side. Any good commercial lawyer will know all about conditions precedent and how they are used in contracts. If your lawyer does not know this, then consider getting a different lawyer!

What are the supplier's key objectives in this mobilization phase? Really, they are the same as its objectives throughout the contract, which are:

- the contract is profitable;
- client relationships are maintained and enhanced;
- supplier reputation is affirmed/enhanced.

In other words, that the contract is profitably and satisfactorily delivered.

What is the equivalent client/buyer-side mobilization activity? These tasks are typically:

- Vendor Manager (VM), Contract Manager (CM) or Supplier Relationship Manager (SRM) appointed;
- contract logged on *'contract management system'*;
- copy of contract to finance department and other key stakeholders (or at least payment schedule to the finance department) – distribution of copies of contracts is, of course, a sensitive issue as they contain commercial and other confidential information;
- contract mobilization meeting – key stakeholders present;
- key 'milestones' scheduled;
- payment plan scheduled;
- project communication system implemented.

What are the buyer's/client's key objectives in this mobilization phase? Really, they are the same as their objectives *throughout* the contract. That is:

- the contract commences in a controlled, expeditious manner;
- deliverables are fit for purpose;
- there is no delay;
- the client is enabled to fully utilize the deliverables;
- the client has 'quiet enjoyment'[4] of the deliverables.

The primary objective at mobilization is to ensure that the transition from theory to reality happens in an orderly way, matching any contract promises made regarding the mobilization task. If mobilization is carried out as planned, then we have greater confidence that the remainder of the contract will also be carried out effectively. If there is a separate *contract management plan* (see Chapter 4 and Stage 7 in Figure 7.1) then this will become the guiding document in terms of mobilization tasks.

> **LEARNING POINT**
>
> Senior managers – how well geared up is your organization in terms of the mobilization phase? Do you need to strengthen this aspect of your governance structure?

Monitoring performance – what do we monitor?

This book is about contract management and is meant for both buyers and sellers. Once mobilized, the focus turns very much towards day-to-day administration. Buyer and seller will need to determine precisely how much effort will be devoted towards administration activities – plainly the more important the contract, the more attention will be paid to administration with a view to full and mutually satisfactory delivery. Buyers and sellers have a slightly different, albeit similar, way of understanding the relative importance of business to their organizations. For buyers, a spend–risk analysis is the basic tool. Created by Peter Kraljic and first appearing in the *Harvard Business Review* in 1983, the universally recognized Kraljic Portfolio Purchasing Model (also known as the Portfolio Analysis Tool) remains a popular and useful model used in companies worldwide.[5] Its purpose is to help buying organizations maximize supply security and reduce costs by making the most of their purchasing power. In doing so, procurement moves away from being a transactional activity towards a strategic activity – because, as Kraljic said in 1983, 'purchasing must become supply management'. At its simplest, the model attempts to characterize and plot suppliers on a grid in terms of their spend value (from low to high) against supply risk to the organization – where loss of supply represents a risk (again from low to high). Low-cost, low-risk supplies can then be differentiated from high-cost, low-risk supplies and high-cost, high-risk supplies. This, in turn, helps us to assess whether the balance of negotiating power lies with the customer or with its suppliers. Once we have a good sense of this, we can select an optimized purchasing strategy. The model, in simplified form, with recognized supply titles and associated characteristics, is depicted in Figure 7.3 below.

Figure 7.3 Kraljic Portfolio Purchasing Analysis Matrix

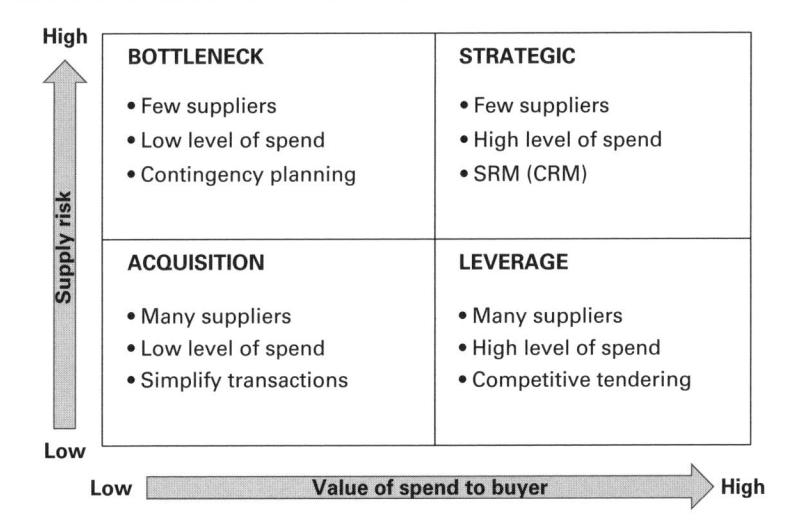

Supply risk (Low → High)	**BOTTLENECK** • Few suppliers • Low level of spend • Contingency planning	**STRATEGIC** • Few suppliers • High level of spend • SRM (CRM)
	ACQUISITION • Many suppliers • Low level of spend • Simplify transactions	**LEVERAGE** • Many suppliers • High level of spend • Competitive tendering

Value of spend to buyer (Low → High)

For buying organizations, the normal distribution of expenditure (the 80/20 rule, or 'Pareto Rule') means there will be a high concentration of expenditure (80 per cent) with relatively few suppliers (20 per cent). On account of this, it is likely that many suppliers and contracts will be of relatively low value/criticality and accordingly need lighter management than others. Contract and supplier administration tasks cost money. As well as the supplier's cost built into the contract price, contract administration will cost the buyer about 2 per cent of the contract's value, as we saw earlier. For selling organizations, there is also an attempt to characterize their sales contracts, usually along analogous axes to the Kraljic model – where *value of income* (or profitability) will replace 'spend' and *account attractiveness* will replace 'risk' – but the underlying rationale is broadly similar, and some sales contracts will accordingly receive greater management scrutiny than others.

Both sellers and buyers need to know their contracts are 'on track' to deliver. Each side keeps a weather eye on whether any contract liabilities are emerging. For buying organizations, however, and especially where they have multiple contracts to monitor, there needs to be a systematic approach to contract administration activities. There is no hard-and-fast rule about which characteristics of the product or supplier should be measured or how many measures there should be. In general, however, there should be as few measures as possible (since monitoring costs money) and key performance indicators, if used, should normally be linked to end-user or consumer experience. Factual and objective information about performance (particularly in relation to the product or service) can often be obtained from the supplier's or buyer's IT systems. Examples could include:

- how often delivery is *in full* and *on time*;
- project milestones delivered on time and to cost;
- level of non-conformance, eg rejects;
- invoice accuracy;
- number of customer complaints/returns or rectification costs;
- flexibility (ability to respond to changing needs);
- levels of waste, CO_2 emissions or landfill disposal.

Supplier performance characteristics, especially in service contracts, require the objective views of internal customers or other stakeholders. In these types of contracts, key performance indicators (KPIs) may be devised as a stand-alone measure specifically to ensure that monitoring of performance over time can be achieved, and that the supplier maintains service levels within acceptable boundaries – this recognizes that 100 per cent performance 100 per cent of the time is rarely achievable, so we determine parameters within which we will grant that the service level is acceptable. Measures may relate to perceived value for money, satisfaction with the product or services, responsiveness of the supplier, or the quality of people or ancillary support services (such as call centres). Both buyer and seller need to consider carefully the measures to be applied, and just how difficult it may be to apply them. Mechanisms to collect relevant data might include:

- Use of customer/stakeholder **surveys** that can be distributed and collated electronically.

- Periodic customer/stakeholder **interviews** using a pre-determined set of questions. These could be face to face or via the phone, but need to be sufficiently interactive so that the interviewer can pull out more detail when required. Often commitment is required from stakeholders such as engineers in the field to maintain records of their experiences of working with a supplier in order that factual and objective data can be used.

- Periodic practical **verification** such as supplier self-assessment reports. This might be part of a product or supplier audit and might involve direct sampling of the product or service (for example as a 'mystery shopper') or by auditing the supplier's management and control systems. This verification can be a contractual obligation and so paid for by the supplier – but remember they may charge an overhead to the customer for this element of the work!

Reverting to the Kraljic Portfolio Analysis Tool for a moment, we can see that proper thought must be given to what will be monitored. The contract performance monitoring action plan suggested in Figure 7.4 overleaf may be considered as a suitable model at least to devise a bespoke model for particular contracts.

Note that some of the review characteristics above have been amended by this author, and the model in Figure 7.4 is not as originally published in the UK trade journal *Supply Management*. The strength of the approach set out overleaf, however, is that it links, in a simple manner, the types of contract monitoring activity to the different Kraljic supply characteristics as set out in the Portfolio Analysis Tool. Contract performance information should be reviewed formally with the supplier at intervals. The frequency of this will depend on the duration and complexity of the contract or relationship. Many organizations will adopt quarterly business reviews for major outsourced contracts, and that is your author's practical experience of these types of arrangement. Otherwise, twice a year for more complex contracts would be a minimum. Such reviews, probably using a pre-agreed and

Figure 7.4 Contract performance monitoring action plan

CONTRACT PERFORMANCE MONITORING ACTION PLAN

Monitoring Tasks – Kraljic Supplier Positioning (review case by case) M = mandatory D = desirable E = exception	Segment according to Kraljic Model			
	Routine	Leverage	Bottleneck	Strategic
Routine Contract Management Tasks				
Monitor contract compliance	M	M	M	M
Manage disputes / dispute resolution	M	M	M	M
Develop a contract management plan	E	E	D	M
Performance Management Tasks				
Measure supplier performance	M	M	M	M
Undertake supplier performance reviews	D	D	M	M
Agree improvement initiatives/targets	E	M	D	M
Seek formal stakeholder feedback	E	D	M	M
Undertake benchmarking	E	M	E	M
Risk Management Tasks				
Monitor supplier risk	E	D	M	M
Prepare business continuity plan	E	E	M	M
Relationship Management Tasks				
Appoint senior relationship officer	E	E	D	M
Develop a relationship strategy and action plan	E	E	D	M
Agree joint initiatives with the supplier	E	E	D	M

pre-published review agenda, should cover a range of performance parameters, including:

- assessment of KPIs and associated trends;
- analysis of non-conformance events and any follow-up investigation, with associated report;
- significant changes to the supply situation (supplier or market);
- changes within the buyer organization;
- progress against improvement or efficiency targets;
- progress against cost-reduction targets;
- assessment of relationship-type issues or relationship-appraisal findings;
- identification of opportunities to further improve innovation, efficiency and quality.

Contract correspondence

It is important that correspondence is handled carefully from the outset, and in a manner that does not inadvertently risk amending the terms of the contract. At mobilization, it is prudent to ensure that both parties understand how correspondence should be handled. First, a couple of principles are set out in Figure 7.5. There are six fairly obvious things that correspondence should achieve, so that each party is crystal clear about what is to be done. And as we correspond, we should similarly bear in mind our underlying commercial and operational objectives. So, our correspondence must be:

1 clear;

2 concise;

3 accurate;

4 relevant;

5 complete;

6 precise.

If we abide by these principles, hopefully we will avoid the temptation (for some people) to write unduly extensive or 'flowery' or even

Figure 7.5 Contract correspondence

Principles	Objectives
1. Clear	COMMERCIAL OBJECTIVES
2. Concise	Maximize profit(ability)
	Optimize cash flow
3. Accurate	Secure further orders
4. Relevant	Protect ideas (IPR)
	Minimize risk
5. Complete	OPERATIONAL OBJECTIVES
6. Precise	Ensure each party understands what is required

irrelevant prose, instead being factual and concentrating on what really matters. In addition, our broad commercial objectives will always be to:

- maximize profit(ability);
- optimize cash flow;
- secure further orders;
- protect ideas (IPR);
- minimize risk.

At a practical level, your author has found the so-called Project Memo system to work well, as it involves the discipline of single points of contact and rigorous monitoring. This may be an overly rigorous approach for a simple, immaterial contract where correspondence is likely to be light. But on complex projects where there are many stakeholders and possibly multi-disciplinary teams with potentially hundreds, if not thousands of communications, then the Project Memo system is ideal. Refer to Appendix 4 for a sample Project Memo format, and to Appendix 5 for detailed notes on how the Project Memo system is managed in practice.

Notices of poor performance and variations

Without getting too bogged down in the details of the administration of a contract, or its precise terms, we should note that from the start (from 'mobilization') some communications issued may be considered as being of greater 'weight' than others. There may be circumstances where performance under the contract is in some way deficient, and we wish formally to bring this to the notice of the counterparty. A Project Memo may not be the optimum mechanism through which to make such a formal 'Notice' to the other party. Furthermore, the terms of the contract may include a provision along the following lines.

> **Service of Notices**
>
> 1 Any Notice to be given to the Contractor under the terms of this contract shall be served by sending the same by post to, or leaving the same at, the Contractor's address for correspondence (or in the event of the Contractor being a company to, or at, its registered address).
>
> 2 Any Notice to be given to the Purchaser under the terms of this contract shall be served by sending the same by post to, or leaving the same at, the Purchaser's address for correspondence (or in the event of the Purchaser being a company to, or at, its registered address).

In using the above term, it will be necessary to define what constitutes such a 'Notice'. The wording will normally specify that a Notice is a communication issued by one party to the other which is of exceptional importance, requiring the active involvement of someone senior in the chain of command and needing a definite response. It is not, therefore, a normal day-to-day communication. In terms of the subject of this book, where the client side considers that performance of the counterparty overall fails to meet the contractual expectations or commitment, then this unhappy situation needs to be drawn formally to the attention (or notice) of the other. Appendices 11 to 13 provide some wording that may be adaptable where, firstly, performance has fallen short (Appendix 11), where there is a proper remedy of the shortfall (Appendix 12) and where subsequently performance deteriorates again (Appendix 13). These template letters provide a graduated response, but seek to allow the counterparty to remedy the defect. Each such communication suspends the 'injured' party (typically the buyer/client side) from use of the full weight of the contract to compel compliance. They make use of the phrase 'without prejudice' so as to hold open the reality that there are other terms of contract that may subsequently be applied with full vigour. Where the contract document does specify 'Notices' and how they are to be served (and bear in mind it may be better to not specify the use of such written devices, but rather to leave their use unspecified) then it is essential that the handling of such communications meets the specific requirements of the associated contractual clause. Failure to do so may prejudice a party's rights and remedies, should the dispute later go to arbitration/court – as the argument will be raised that a 'Notice' was not properly 'served' on the counterparty. Appendix 14 provides a little more background on this difficult subject.

Many contracts will require amendment (or 'variation') during their term. Requirements may be added or subtracted, and/or timescales altered. It is important that the variation letter (sometimes called a change order) is precise, and that it makes clear the exact implications of the change. The key operational elements to be considered are:

1 **Scope**: the principal changes need to be spelled out.
2 **Price**: any increase to or deduction from the previously agreed price must be specified.
3 **Programme/term**: any change to key dates must be specified.

Appendix 10 provides a useful template that can be adapted or used as a benchmark to readers' own template documents. Needless to say, as much care needs to be taken over the variation document as was applied to the original contract document.

Endnotes

1   'All parties' might be a better phrase. Remember there may be more than two parties to a contract!
2   The term 'execution' in some circumstances means physically signing (executing) a contract document. In the broader context, it means doing all the things required – as in executive/execution, or carrying out – under the terms of the contract.

3   It is debatable whether the incorporation of such plans within the body of the contract is advisable. This really must boil down to 'horses for courses'. Incorporate the mobilization plan if it genuinely adds value to the project. If it does not, then make the document separate from the contract documentation, but also make it clear that the mobilization plan will be monitored and will 'inform' the discussion should there be delays or difficulties around the mobilization task.

4   This is a legal concept, and indicates that a buyer is expected to be able to take a benefit from their investment, and not enter into a struggle to see those benefits materialize.

5   The original *Harvard Business Review* article can be found at: https://hbr.org/1983/09/purchasing-must-become-supply-management.

When things go wrong 08

Why contracts need to be managed

Often in business life we hear the old adage, *once the contract is signed it is never referred to again.* This is a nice sentiment as it suggests we are not going to adopt a confrontational or 'contractual' attitude towards the other party (or parties), but instead we will work with them in a spirit of mutual respect and trust, seeking win-win solutions. The contract document, then, is not to be allowed to get in the way of practical solutions to practical problems – so we will adopt a *can-do* attitude to ensure things happen as planned. We will be pragmatic at all times! Lawyers take a somewhat different view, and not because they are unduly confrontational. They will point out, quite reasonably, that if we do not pay due attention to, and place due weight upon, the contract document, and instead act in ways outside its specific terms, then we may inadvertently amend the contact such that, in the event of a later dispute, a guilty party might be able to argue that the innocent party had agreed/assented to changed terms and that therefore the original obligations either no longer apply, or they apply in a modified form. This is a real danger. This chapter helps us to think through why and how we manage contracts in a practical manner, leaving a suitable audit trail of decisions.

The first question we need to consider, without stating the obvious, is that there are common, and indeed universal, reasons why any contract needs *managing*. Just because a contract is clearly defined in written form, and executed (signed) between the contracting counterparties, that does not mean it will simply happen, irrespective of any other factor. People are fallible. Mistakes will happen. There are perhaps four key, universal, reasons why contracts need proactive management:

- rapidity of business change;
- things go wrong!
- people lose interest/focus;
- to create (archive) an audit trail.

Rapidity of business change

Things happen so quickly that tomorrow's circumstances may not match today's expectations. A contract that was profitable when signed, may later decline in profitability and so tempt us towards cost cutting – or even corner cutting – to the detriment of one of the counterparties. Natural or man-made disasters can upset the economic objectives of a contract in a way that requires active remedy. One or more of Porter's Five Forces[1] may shift in such a way that original economic objectives are no longer relevant, or sustainable, causing a loss of interest in a particular contract. Under Kraljic[2] Supplier Positioning, a contract relationship that was once considered to be core becomes downgraded and the resource and energy originally applied to create it later look profligate. Each of these is a reason why circumstances and perceptions change and a once-favoured contract becomes a burden.

Things go wrong

If the tasks under a contract for whatever reason cannot be fulfilled in accordance with the contract, again its attractiveness as an economic bargain may change markedly. What things can go wrong?

- delay;
- force majeure;
- latent defects;
- cost escalation;
- unexpected conditions that vitiate the original contract;
- fails to meet specification.

Within the operations undertaken to fulfill a contract, once again, things can go wrong:

- health and safety incident;
- third-party liability incurred;
- PR incident (reputation damage);
- IPR infringement;
- fraud/corruption;
- inability to meet our obligations under another contract(s).

Whilst none of these circumstances must, of necessity, bring a premature end to a contract, they might severely impact profitability and so one or more party may reallocate valuable resources to the detriment of the future performance under this contract.

People lose interest/focus

People are only human! Some may lose interest, perhaps because they are pursuing different career opportunities. Or once the bulk of the contract has been discharged, people begin to consider their next career move or next contract, and so begin to neglect the current one.

Create (archive) an audit trail

It is necessary to manage a contract in order to create and maintain an accurate audit trail of decisions and associated contract changes ('amendments'). This is important so as to be able to debate and if necessary challenge any demand from the counterparty that the terms or obligations have wittingly changed to their detriment.

Each of these four reasons suggests that both parties need to be assiduous in focusing on the performance of the contract, not allowing deliverables and obligations to 'slide' in an uncontrolled way.

Things have a habit of going wrong in commercial life. The excitement of the pre-contract discussions, where we flourish our negotiation skills and demonstrate how commercially astute we are, gives way to BAU, *business as usual*. People can lose focus. Are people concentrating on finding solutions to today's problems or are they emotionally focused on 'the next big deal'? This may be especially true of sales personnel. Furthermore, competing projects or customers may render *this* contract relatively less attractive to one (or both) parties. I would suggest that it is the buyer (client) who is potentially exposed to most strategic risk in this regard. The seller very often is on the lookout for their next big deal and *may* rest on their laurels with regard to already-won business, especially if the profitability of other customers, projects or contracts looks better than today's contract – the profitability of which may already be compromised for multiple reasons.

Sammons' Five Forces!

Taking a metaphorical leaf out of Professor Michael E. Porter's book, we can say there are five forces conspiring to undermine any contract. Perhaps 'forces' might be putting it too strongly, but there are definitely five risk areas which predominate as a catalyst to contract disputes – whether or not those disputes go on to a legal resolution (as opposed to a commercial resolution). What are they?

- Cost increase.
- Time delay.
- IPR infringement.
- Force majeure/disaster recovery.
- Performance shortfall.

Let us review them in turn.

Force 1: Cost increase

Costs to either party, but particularly to the seller, may rise for any number of reasons! Typically, these cost increases coalesce around material or labour input increases, possibly occasioned through a materials supplier or sub-contractor. Energy costs or other major utilities or regulatory costs tend to rise over time. The time taken to complete tasks may overrun on programme estimates. A technical task may prove simply to be more complex than originally anticipated. Each of these potential difficulties should, to a large extent, be ameliorated through good planning and good cost build. At the end of the day, a supplier may simply have to absorb cost increases, but may try to find ways to surreptitiously pass on those increases to their customer, or be tempted to cut corners on some other aspect of the project, in order to recover some of those lost costs.

A cost increase occasioned through a contract change from the customer may also be encountered. In these cases, it is normal for some compensation to be provided by the customer and cost indices, rates and options prices may be written into the contract. The buyer should be aware of the possibility that such changes might be exploited by the seller if he is encountering cost difficulties elsewhere; bluntly, the seller may try to offset some losses via enhanced claiming against the contract change. Vigilance on both sides is important, but this one is very much down to *caveat emptor* – let the buyer beware!

Force 2: Time delay

Either party might encounter unplanned or unforeseen circumstances that cause programme slippage. This, in turn, can impact either the end date, final delivery date or might incur additional costs for a whole host of reasons. An early determination of where the liability (blame) for this situation lies is important. Further, an early discussion of the impact of time delay is essential, as there may be other time dependencies that are impacted. We think, for example, of the idea of a critical path in project planning. If a delay impacts the critical path, then it is very likely that a cost will be incurred by one or both counterparties. As they say, 'time is money'!

Force 3: IPR infringement

In today's complex business environment, where competitive advantage lies so much in know-how, bespoke technology, or a 'lock' on patents, the likelihood of some form of IP infringement looms ever larger. Many organizations, particularly those that hold patents, will vigorously defend their rights. Compensation for infringement may be pursued by an aggrieved IPR holder and it is vital to establish liability as quickly as possible. The drafting of clear and enforceable contract terms to cover this eventuality is important, as is the establishing of any *pre-existing rights* that need to be ring-fenced from the contract deliverables, and associated with free, perpetual licence to use such pre-existing rights without the necessity of paying further royalties simply in order to use the 'foreground rights' created under the contract. Once again, it is important that both parties to a contract have clarity about these issues, which can be expensive to resolve if they arise in practice. Typically, each party will indemnify the other against claims arising from a dispute with a third party over the misuse of intellectual property. Such difficulties may be insured under professional indemnity insurance (PII), but if this issue is vital to your company, then you may need to delve into the terms of the PII to ensure that the limit of indemnity adequately protects your organisation.[3]

Force 4: Force majeure/disaster recovery

Unforeseen or unforeseeable events can arise. These, in turn, can impact the parties' ability to fulfill their part of the bargain. It is important for both parties to undertake sufficient *risk analysis* in the pre-contract (or 'project development') phase so that potential risks are managed and ameliorated. There will always remain, however, the possibility that events happen that could not be planned for. These are within traditional English contract law, dealt with under the doctrine of *frustration of contract*. Frustration is a well-worn concept under English contract law and there is a sound argument for remaining silent on the whole subject, allowing the courts to determine in the event that agreement on liability cannot be reached. In the past 25 years (within the English legal system), increasing use has been made of the continental civil law preference for using 'force majeure' clauses. The difficulty with these clauses is that they attempt to undermine the traditional English law doctrine of Frustration (and largely succeed). Arguably, then, force majeure clauses introduce a measure of uncertainty, which is presumably what their authors intend. The pressure on sellers, generally, is to draft such clauses as widely as possible, so as to 'capture a wide range of circumstances that give them the ability to avoid their liabilities'. In contrast, the pressure is on buyers to negotiate such clauses narrowly, so as to reduce the allowable range of situations that allow the counterparty to escape their obligations.

Irrespective of the drafting of contract clauses or the use (or non-use) of the English law doctrine of Frustration, such unplanned events are a cause of friction between the parties and accordingly need to be carefully thought through in advance of contract signature. An organization's risk appetite will also influence their attitude to handling force majeure-type events (Appendix 2 explores this subject).

Force 5: Performance shortfall

By this word 'performance' we mean that the deliverables from the contract activity do not live up to contractually expressed expectations and that accordingly the economic purpose of the contract is undermined. It may be that a piece of technical equipment does not meet its defined performance characteristics. In the situation of something less tangible, such as software, it may mean a preponderance of 'bugs' that have to be retroactively 'fixed'. In the provision of professional services, it might mean that tasks were not carried out with the application of 'reasonable care and skill', as should reasonably be expected to be applied by a professional person. Performance shortfall may show up immediately, for example in performance testing of commercial equipment, and it is likely that the terms of the contract will include provisions for putting things right in these situations. Some performance issues will not emerge until time has elapsed, however, and these may be dealt with, for example, through 'latent defects' terms within contracts. Irrespective, performance shortfall, however it manifests itself, is a regular 'suspect' in the Contract Manager's list of 'public enemies'.

Remedies

Sooner or later in any Contract Manager's life, they will encounter contractual problems. These may be fundamental problems, which destroy the original economic intentions of the parties, or they may be (and more likely will be) more mundane day-to-day issues. The first point to note is that it may be possible for the parties to reach an amicable and essentially non-contractual solution to the problem that needs only to be recorded within the audit trail. In this situation, both parties recognize the reality of the problem and move rapidly to resolve it, and generally the party most at fault will pick up the economic consequence. However, where there is a more definitive 'blame' leading to a more serious economic consequence, it is important that a contractual remedy is formally discussed and agreed upon, and recorded as a contract change. Figure 8.1 summarizes the most likely options.

Figure 8.1 When things go wrong – likely remedies

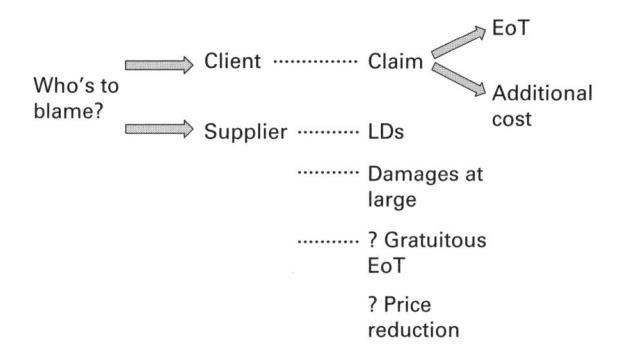

```
                          ┌──→ EoT
Who's to  ══⇒ Client ····· Claim
blame?                    └──→ Additional
          ══⇒ Supplier ····· LDs       cost

                    ····· Damages at
                          large

                    ····· ? Gratuitous
                          EoT

                          ? Price
                          reduction
```

In Figure 8.1 the abbreviated terms are defined as follows:

LDs = liquidated damages.

EoT = extension of time.

Once outline liability has been established – and hopefully this will be a simple question of fact – then the most obvious remedies are suggested above. So, if the liability rests with the client (buyer) then probably the seller will typically make a formal contractual 'claim' under the relevant provisions of the contract. If there are no such predetermined contractual provisions then the parties will enter into good faith discussions 'subject to contract and without prejudice' in the expectation of reaching a mutually satisfactory agreement on a circumstance which is, to all intents and purposes, an extra-contractual issue that neither party foresaw. If the contract basis is a fixed price, *fixed deliverable*, then the seller may in these circumstances simply have to accept the additional costs to his account and suffer the associated loss. It is where the contract makes provision for the distribution amongst the contracting parties of additional costs and/ or delays, that a 'claim' situation might arise.

If a claim is made against the client and providing it is fair and substantiated (as set out in the contract) then the benefit conferred on the seller will be either or both of (1) an extension of time; (2) additional costs as assessed and agreed. If the liability ('blame') rests with the seller, then there will typically be four basic remedies available to the buyer:

- **Liquidated damages** – a pre-agreed assessment of the likely cost of delay, performance shortfall or other performance delinquency on the part of the seller. Liquidated damages are usually levied on a per day, per week or per event basis and are capped at a given percentage of the contract value. In the event of continued performance delinquency beyond the cap, usually the next recourse is to levy unliquidated damages (normally called *Damages at Large*).
- **Damages at Large** – are any and all additional financial costs that can be demonstrated. Unlike liquidated damages which can simply be levied, the person seeking Damages at Large will need to 'prove' the extent of the damages claimed in some tangible way, and this may lead to debate and argument.
- **Extension of time** – if the contractual problem is of low detriment to the buyer and is only in fact a delay, he may simply grant an extension of time under the contract. This, in fact, will be an amendment to the contract and accordingly must be granted under the change control provisions of the contract – it needs to be done formally. No further remedy will be available for that delay. Further time delay would be negotiated (and dealt with) separately as a fresh issue under the contract. An extension of time becomes a *gratuitous extension of time* where there is no compensating price reduction. The extension is gratuitous – a 'gift' to the seller. Typically, an extension of time should be approved via a formal written amendment to the contract.
- **Price reduction** – in the event of a supplier delinquency under the contract, to compensate the buyer for delay or loss of performance

(or whatever the delinquency may be) a negotiated reduction in price may be a fully acceptable remedy. Or it may be combined with one of the other three remedies above. Typically, a reduction in price should be approved via a formal written amendment to the contract.

Summary of actions in the event of a contractual issue arising between the parties

The first order of business when anything goes wrong is to establish liability. This may be straightforward, or may require 'detective work' to determine. Then we check the detailed terms of the contract to see if the issue has been anticipated and the remedy has already been agreed. We should avoid confrontation if possible. At this stage, we are on a fact-finding mission. The 'blame game' can be postponed to a later date. We need, then, to establish liability and seek to leave an audit trail that accurately reflects any decisions agreed between the parties. We should try to implement remedial actions at a practical level that do not involve strictly 'contractual' remedies – hopefully both parties will be operating in a spirit of mutual trust and cooperation. Accordingly, we should seek win-win solutions wherever possible, being aware of mutual business interests and client account attractiveness (seller)/supplier positioning (buyer) to help to inform decisions and commercial approaches. Discussions should be unashamedly 'subject to contract' and 'without prejudice' in these sorts of situations, as both parties try to find acceptable solutions that do not involve contractual confrontations.

When delinquency becomes a claim

Many contracts are designed to place design and delivery performance liability largely, or solely, on to one or the other party. Whilst liabilities and indemnities across a range of subjects might be equitably distributed amongst the parties under the terms of the contract, very often the client (buying) organization will take the view, quite reasonably, that they are paying for the privilege of another party supplying a good or a service, and that this other party is an expert in their own field, whereas the client (buyer) organization may not be an expert. In this situation, the parties might agree upon a fixed price for fixed deliverables – with 'delivery' risk falling very much upon the supplier. However, where the client changes the details of the requirement, or there are unforeseen circumstances that are designated as *shared risks* within the contract document, then the selling side might consider they have a legitimate claim against the buyer either for an extension of time or additional costs – or both. We began to explore this in Figure 8.1. Whilst 'delinquency', in a contractual sense, may be considered a very strong word, we should note that changed circumstances might also give rise to unforeseen expenses and therefore an unexpected financial burden on a party that is not itself to blame for that circumstance arising.

Where, however, the contract allows flexibility for the parties to raise compensation demands against the other party (or parties), providing certain specified circumstances have arisen, then this process is usually described as a contract 'claim'. In these situations, and without necessarily apportioning 'blame' for the situation, the contract terms may well specify a 'claims procedure' allowing an injured party to request additional compensation. The aggrieved or injured party demonstrates some form of contractual delinquency upon the other and proceeds to demonstrate the financial (or other) demand upon the other through the claims procedure. We should note that it is usually the seller that makes a claim upon the buyer.

How are these sorts of 'claims' typically managed? What are the typical 'steps' we need to go through? Without being overly definitive in this, we can trace a typical and well-defined claims process as depicted in Figures 8.2a and 8.2b.

In Figure 8.2a we can see that the initial steps are to identify that something has gone wrong – for example a defect is discovered in an engineering contract. This should be, quite simply, a question of fact. The 'defect' being considered, however, may be some form of service or communication failure on the part of the counterparty – this claims process is never restricted to engineering technicalities. The immediate next step is to determine whether the contract documentation actually caters for this particular situation. As we suggested

Figure 8.2a Initiating a claim

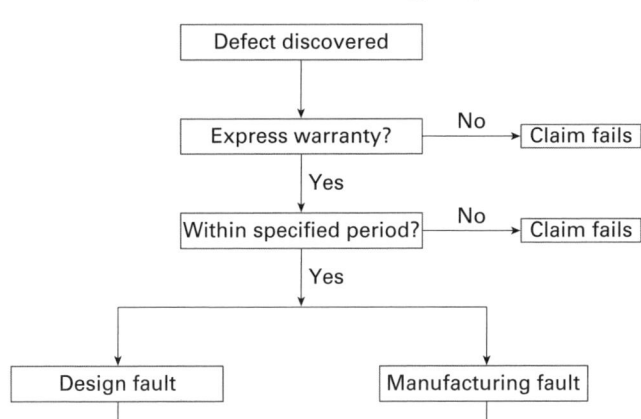

'Claims' under the terms of a contract – typical process (1)

```
                    ┌─────────────────────┐
                    │  Defect discovered  │
                    └──────────┬──────────┘
                               ↓
                    ┌─────────────────────┐   No   ┌─────────────┐
                    │  Express warranty?  │───────→│ Claim fails │
                    └──────────┬──────────┘        └─────────────┘
                               │ Yes
                               ↓
                    ┌──────────────────────────┐  No  ┌─────────────┐
                    │ Within specified period? │─────→│ Claim fails │
                    └──────────┬───────────────┘      └─────────────┘
                               │ Yes
                    ┌──────────┴──────────┐
                    ↓                     ↓
           ┌─────────────────┐   ┌──────────────────────┐
           │  Design fault   │   │  Manufacturing fault │
           └────────┬────────┘   └──────────┬───────────┘
                    ↓                       ↓
```

rather prosaically in Figure 8.1, 'who is to blame'? Is there an express warranty within the contract covering this matter? By 'express warranty' we mean *is something written (expressed) in the contract covering this matter?*

The next question of fact will be, are we still within any time limit for making claims, especially the sort of claim that can be characterized as being caused by a latent defect, or some other delinquency that only comes to light after a period of time has elapsed? If the answer to this question is 'yes', then we may well be able to proceed to make a successful claim.

In Figure 8.2a we are exploring a decidedly technical/engineering claim, but similar considerations might apply in a service-type contract. Essentially, we must work through the various implications of a particular situation to establish that the claim will 'hold-up' under the terms of the contract. Only then should we formally initiate a 'claim' under the terms of the contract.

A well-designed contract should provide for the parties to have a legitimate compensation route in the event of unusual (and normally specified) extra-contractual circumstances arising. A party should not unfairly be left out of pocket in such circumstances, providing the contract documentation makes specific provision for changed

Figure 8.2b Exploring the extent of a claim

'Claims' under the terms of a contract – typical process (2)

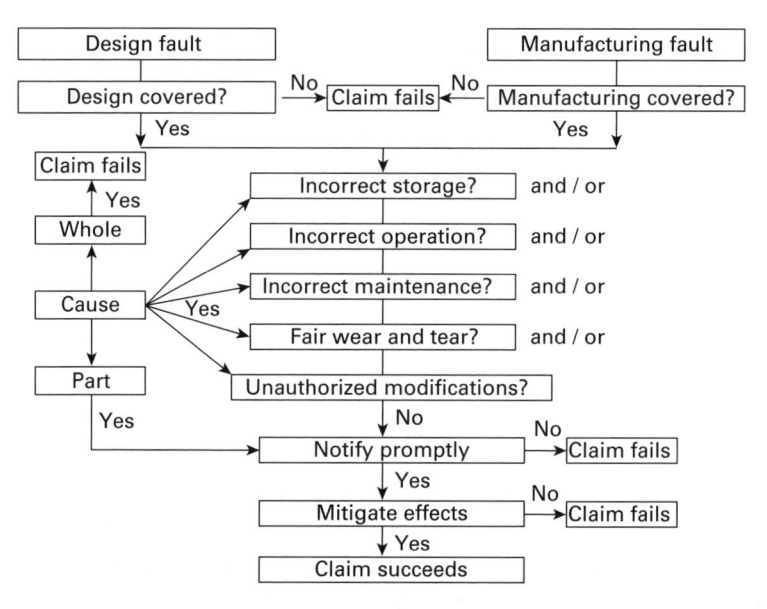

```
                Design fault                              Manufacturing fault
                     |                                             |
            Design covered? ──No──► Claim fails ◄──No── Manufacturing covered?
                    Yes                  ▲                        Yes
                     │                   │                         │
             ┌───────┴───────┐           │                         │
             │ Claim fails   │           │                         │
             └───────▲───────┘           │                         │
                    Yes                  │                         │
             ┌───────┴───────┐           │                         │
             │    Whole      │           │                         │
             └───────▲───────┘           ▼                         │
                     │          Incorrect storage?    and / or     │
                     │                                             │
             ┌───────┴───────┐  Incorrect operation?   and / or    │
             │    Cause      │── Yes ►                              │
             └───────┬───────┘  Incorrect maintenance? and / or    │
                     │                                             │
                     │          Fair wear and tear?   and / or     │
                     ▼                                             │
             ┌───────────────┐  Unauthorized modifications?        │
             │     Part      │                                     │
             └───────┬───────┘            │ No                     │
                    Yes                   ▼                No      │
                     └────────────► Notify promptly ───────► Claim fails
                                          │ Yes
                                          ▼                 No
                                   Mitigate effects ───────► Claim fails
                                          │ Yes
                                          ▼
                                    Claim succeeds
```

circumstances. The claims procedure allows the parties to negotiate and recompense in an orderly, controlled manner that takes some of the heat out of a situation that might otherwise become a bone of contention between the parties – and in this sense to drive adversarial behaviour.[4] Where the buyer believes there has been some breach of a contract, then normally they have the ability to levy liquidated damages,[5] or damages at large.[6] That is in distinction to a claims procedure, which is typically included to protect the seller.

> **LEARNING POINT**
>
> Senior managers – how well geared-up is your organization in terms of the managing of contractual claims?
>
> Do you have in place the contract management competencies to effectively manage the issues set out in this chapter? If not, do you require specific resource?

Pulling the levers!

In the event of problems occurring and after determining probable liability, an initial assessment will be made of the contractual levers available to us. We might say that there are generally two 'levers' that we might use – certainly in an English Law (Common Law) context: they are (1) *express terms* in the contract document/agreement itself and (2) contract law generally. The second lever is a subject well beyond the scope of this book, and professional advice may be necessary. If we are in a dispute that looks as though it might end up in court, then contract law will kick in and case law may have a bearing on the outcome. The first 'lever', those *express terms* of the agreement, will help to determine what was in the minds of the parties when they entered into the contract. The express terms are the first port of call in understanding what the contract was all about. Without getting too technical about this we can make the following summary.

Contracts managers should keep this distinction in the back of their minds. A Contract Manager does not need to be a legal expert or even a paralegal by training, but a broad overall appreciation of contract law can only be of value. A Contract Manager should, however, be well acquainted with the express terms of the contract document they are managing – that is, all those things that are expressed as being the key issues and remedies between the contracting counterparties. Indeed, senior managers will rightly look to the Contract Manager to be their company's expert in this particular

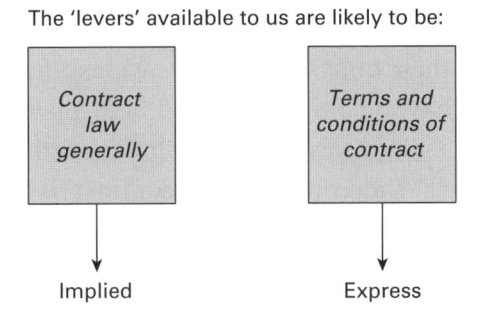

Figure 8.3a   Time delay or performance shortfall

The 'levers' available to us are likely to be:

Contract law generally	Terms and conditions of contract
↓	↓
Implied	Express

Figure 8.3b Time delay or performance shortfall

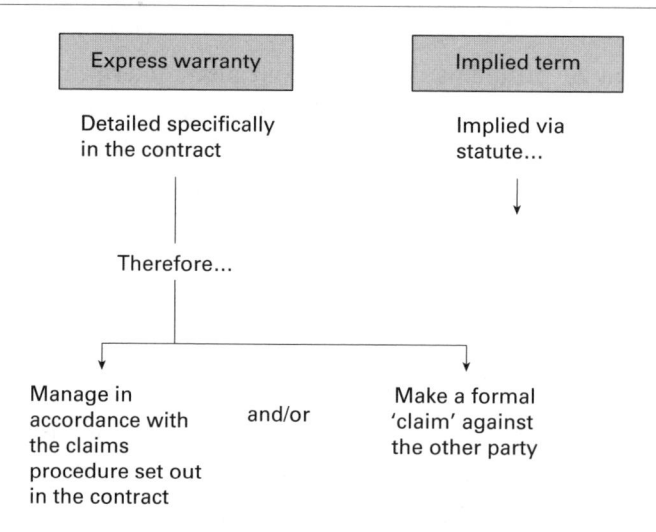

```
         ┌─────────────────┐              ┌─────────────────┐
         │ Express warranty│              │  Implied term   │
         └─────────────────┘              └─────────────────┘
          Detailed specifically            Implied via
          in the contract                  statute...
                                                │
                                                ▼
                     Therefore...

          ┌──────────────────┐              ┌──────────────────┐
          │ Manage in        │              │ Make a formal    │
          │ accordance with  │   and/or     │ 'claim' against  │
          │ the claims       │              │ the other party  │
          │ procedure set out│              │                  │
          │ in the contract  │              └──────────────────┘
          └──────────────────┘
```

contract. In the event of a contractual 'difference' emerging between the parties, an early question to resolve is: 'is this a breach of an implied warranty (something implied by commercial law generally) or is it a breach of an express term – something actually expressed in the contract document?'

We can see in Figure 8.3b above that the preparation for making an official 'claim' against the counterparty needs to reflect this basic question. If the subject of the dispute is set out ('expressed') clearly within the terms of the agreement then we should be able to manage the question within those terms – as set out. We might have the additional option, however, of determining to make a formal 'claim' against the counterparty. The contours of the discussion then take on the character set out in Figure 8.3c. We approach the counterparty in a formal manner to advise them that we consider that they are in breach of their obligations to us. We ask for a resolution of the problem we have identified. But we hold open the reality that the discussions remain (to use a legal technical term) 'privileged' and 'subject to contract'. Indeed, 'subject to contract' is a term we should use until such time as the matter is resolved, probably by formal amendment to the contract document. In terms of the documentation, we should also advise the counterparty that the remedy agreed 'shall be without prejudice to any other remedies available under

Figure 8.3c Time delay or performance shortfall

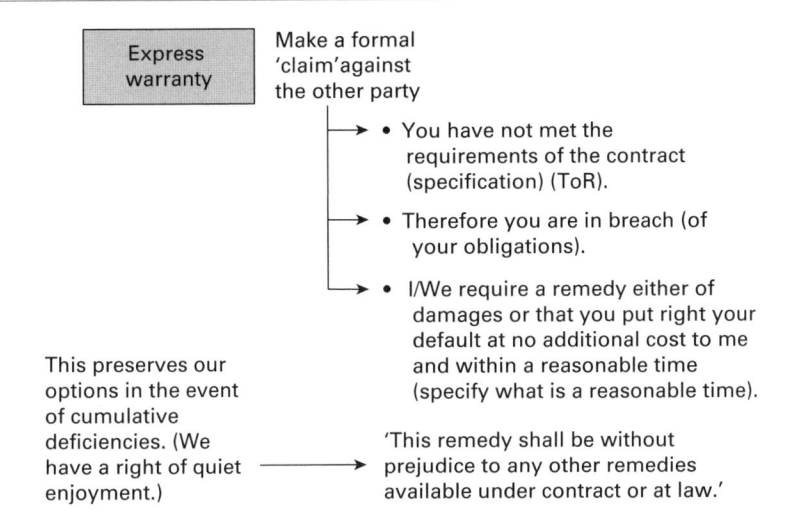

```
                 ┌─────────────┐   Make a formal
                 │   Express   │   'claim' against
                 │  warranty   │   the other party
                 └─────────────┘
                                  → • You have not met the
                                      requirements of the contract
                                      (specification) (ToR).

                                  → • Therefore you are in breach (of
                                      your obligations).

                                  → • I/We require a remedy either of
                                      damages or that you put right your
                                      default at no additional cost to me
    This preserves our                and within a reasonable time
    options in the event              (specify what is a reasonable time).
    of cumulative
    deficiencies. (We              'This remedy shall be without
    have a right of quiet    →      prejudice to any other remedies
    enjoyment.)                     available under contract or at law.'
```

contract or at law'. Why do we hold open this reservation? We hold it open because a delay or performance shortfall may in isolation appear to be containable within the remedy agreed by the parties, but later some further performance deficiency may, cumulative with the earlier deficiency, begin to seriously undermine the purpose of the contract, at which point the 'injured' party may need to reconsider all of the options at their disposal. We do not, therefore, want to close those options off.

Up the escalator!

In everything we have discussed so far in this chapter, we may have assumed, or perhaps may have given the impression, that remedies will be found written on a piece of paper, or within the 'fine print' of the contract document. We did of course state the clear caveat that we MUST ensure that we DO NOT act in ways that are in contradiction to the requirements expressed in the contract itself. But, having said that, we need to remember that, at a practical day-to-day level, we have business and commercial relationships between differing organizations (contracting counterparties) and that these relationships have a real value. In 90 per cent – or more – of cases, the counterparties

Figure 8.4 Potential remedies – escalation

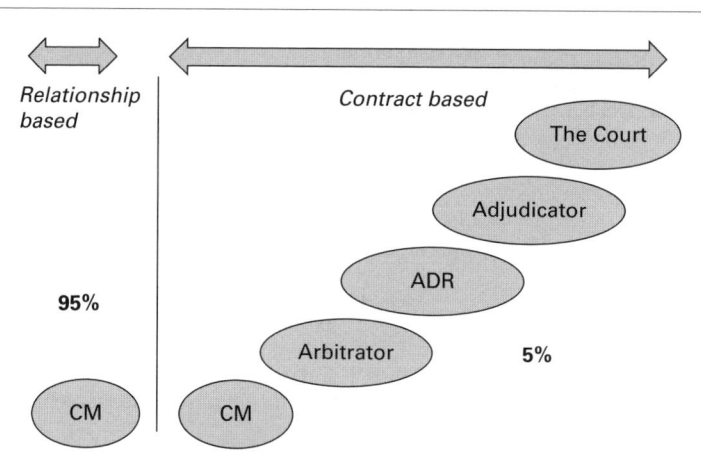

```
Relationship          Contract based
based
                                      The Court
                                 Adjudicator
                            ADR
     95%
                       Arbitrator    5%

     CM        CM
```

will want to find essentially non-contractual resolutions to problems. If both sides value the relationship then they will do whatever is necessary to reach mutually satisfactory outcomes. Figure 8.4 above flags up that there will be a hierarchy of steps in most contracting dispute situations, leading from essentially self-resolution, through to resolution via the court.

Once again we must be clear that what is depicted above is not 'science'. Not all 'cases' will be handled in this escalation manner, but as a general statement it is broadly true that 95 per cent of effort and 95 per cent of activity should be handled by the Contract Managers in each organization, with practical resolutions found based upon the value of the relationship. Even where the 'issue' between the parties becomes 'contractual' and both parties are formally focused upon it, still even here it may well be within the competence of the Contract Managers to formally resolve the question(s). We can think of that as being at the bottom of the escalator. Dependent on what is expressed in the contract about conflict resolution, so there may be a hierarchy of steps leading towards a definitive resolution through the court.

Arbitration may be the first 'port of call' for some organizations, especially where arbitration is a well-recognized and well-understood mechanism within their sector. It is true that arbitration can be expensive and is not always quick. Accordingly, some businesses try to avoid arbitration. It is possible, also, that an arbitrator may make an arbitrary decision (play on words here!) which one or both of the parties feel is at variance with the facts of the situation as they see it. In other words, bluntly, they may consider that the arbitrator got it wrong! And of course, an arbitrator cannot enforce their decision and so if one party determines to ignore the arbitral verdict, then the parties may still have to go to court in order to enforce the arbitration! On that basis, they will then have paid twice for a resolution! Taking these difficulties into account, there are some major organizations that adopt the pragmatic view that they will never use arbitration because the outcome is uncertain and they may yet end up in court. So why not go straight to court?

ADR (Alternative Dispute Resolution) and adjudication share some of the drawbacks of arbitration, although both ADR and adjudication are generally speedier than full arbitration and accordingly less expensive. Each remedy has its fans and its detractors. The approach to be adopted will be influenced by a number of factors, not least of which is the level of your organization's risk appetite. Appendix 2 may provide some pointers.

Endnotes

1 Porter's Five Forces analysis. Developed by Professor Michael E Porter (Harvard), this is a framework that analyses the level of competition within an industry and assists with business strategy development. It identifies five 'forces' that determine competitive intensity and therefore attractiveness of an industry. Attractiveness in this context refers to overall industry profitability. An 'unattractive' industry is one in which the combination of Porter's Five Forces acts to drive down overall profitability. A very unattractive industry would be one approaching 'pure competition', in which available profits for all firms are driven to normal profit.
2 The Kraljic Portfolio Purchasing Model was created by Peter Kraljic and it first appeared in the *Harvard Business Review* in 1983. Its purpose is to help purchasers maximize supply security and reduce costs, by leveraging their purchasing power. In doing so, Procurement moves from being a transactional to a strategic activity – because, as Kraljic said, 'purchasing must become supply management'.

3 Note that insurance firms will often 'invest' their funds in defending their client against the claim, not in actually paying compensation to the aggrieved party.
4 Some economists call this a 'zero-sum game'. See game theory.
5 Liquidated damages – a genuine estimate as to what costs will arise in the event of certain specified events occurring, such as delay. If the event occurs, then the liquidated damages are applied up to the limit set out in the contract. Loss does not have to be proved for the damages to be applied.
6 Damages at Large – any ascertained actual additional costs. The party claiming damages at large has the burden of proving the loss. Damages at large are normally un-capped.

Managing for success 09

Core style versus adaptive style

What really makes the difference between failure and success in terms of contract management? By now we will have seen that by laying the right commercial foundations, we position ourselves to best exploit the opportunities presented by the contract – whether we are a buyer or a seller. We now understand that there are many business 'drivers' that influence commercial strategy, and a sound contract will have taken due account of economics, technical performance elements and competitive rivalry (and opportunities). In addition, a formalized mobilization activity will initiate the contract in a visible, controlled and energized manner. We close this short book with three further thoughts:

- the person description of the archetypal good Contract Manager;
- the need to stay on top of detail;
- planning for exit.

Figure 9.1 (repeated overleaf from Chapter 4 for convenience) reminds us that the 'life' of any contract will involve certain tasks and activities. The Contract Manager is the person who sits 'at the centre' of all these tasks and who should be the main point of contact for any query related to the contract. We saw in Chapter 4 the main contract management tasks – in the brief exploration of the Contract Manager's main objectives, roles and responsibilities. As senior managers determine the task/role and delegated financial authorities of any Contract Manager, they will also 'design' a job specification that encompasses many of the activities identified in Figures 4.5a to 4.5j (Chapter 4).

Figure 9.1 Contract administration phase

Conception	• Corporate strategy • commercial strategy • need identification • budget allocation • contract strategy
Gestation	• Market test (buyer) • negotiation • business case • bid (seller)
Birth	• Drafting • negotiation • 'execution' (signature) • copies to key stakeholders
Life	• Mobilization • contract management plan • progress monitoring • changes to scope or duration • dealing with problems • SRM • CRM • progress payments • transfer of legal title • progress meetings • project memo system for communications
	• Final delivery • final payment • final 'sign-off' (issue certificates)
Death	• expiry of warrantees/guarantees • latent defects period • IPR provisions expire • archival of documentation • document retention and destruction policy

Plainly we are not looking for 'superman' (or superwoman) in terms of the manager appointed to handle specific contracts. Some employees will be assigned a contract only on an ad-hoc basis. These will be handling, generally speaking, lower-value or lower-'materiality' contracts – not contracts that might sink the firm if they go wrong. Other employees may be appointed to manage a group of contracts, where their management tasks take up a larger proportion of their day-to-day activities. Yet other employees will be virtually full-time Contract Managers, perhaps handling one or a few major contracts on behalf of their employer. These are often contracts associated with major outsourcings that are of critical importance to the day-to-day operation of the firm. These types of manager are often called 'Vendor Managers', indicating that their primary role is to manage a specific supplier ('vendor') on a major outsourcing.

> Note these descriptive terms have no generally accepted definitions, so businesses will need to devise their own job titles and job specifications.

What is critically important here is that people know what is expected of them and have appropriate training and delegations. For some roles, a genuine level of personal gravitas will be essential, as they face off to powerful suppliers that are well aware of their own strength and the over-arching business context. For other roles, a relatively junior person might be appointed as Contract Manager, and many employers consider that a temporary period in such a role is an excellent way to bring on a commercial employee and give them really valuable experience that stretches them personally as well as rapidly maturing them as well-rounded commercial and professional employees.

Is there such a thing as a perfect mindset or skill set that guarantees consistent and successful Contract Manager performance? Your author considers that the answer to this is 'no'! Plainly the Contract Manager must be moderately intelligent and moderately mature. For some roles, a reasonable 'technical' knowledge of the subject matter will be an essential prerequisite. So, a manager with responsibility for a major payroll outsourcing arrangement in a larger firm would probably have past experience of HR and associated hands-on payroll activity. Indeed, such a Contract Manager might well report to the HR director and be a part of the HR team.

Plainly we are being a little tongue in cheek in Figure 9.2. However, there is an element of truth there, especially for more senior Contract Managers. In *adjudication*, we reflect that a manager in this role will from time to time have to make judgement calls and even be regarded as their company's decision point on certain contract issues. In terms of acting as an *arbitrator*, a larger project may well have multiple stakeholders and a good Contract Manager will need to be able to

Figure 9.2   Traits of a Contract Manager

                    Adjudicator   Arbitrator

                              World's
                              greatest
         Accountant   Contract   Juggler
                              Manager

                  Contract expert   Diplomat

keep them focused on the same (right) objectives. Where there are 'zero sum game' differences between stakeholders, then the Contract Manager again may be considered the 'obvious' person to make an initial assessment and to *adjudicate* on the subject dividing them. That in turn may require mature *diplomacy* skills. The juggling aspect reflects the realization that any sizeable contract will have multiple stakeholders, workstreams, communications, meetings, decision points and so on. All this detail has to be managed – or *'juggled'*! Inevitably, to a greater or lesser extent, the Contract Manager is also the contract *accountant*, keeping a weather eye on the flow of money, both in and out. And lastly, he or she will be considered to be the *contract expert* – the person who knows both the minutia of the written terms, as well as how things work out on a day-to-day basis.

It is not the purpose of this book to advise organizations on how they identify and appoint Contract Managers. By now readers may well have formed their own opinions as to the sort of skill sets and personal attributes required for their own business sectors. We would, however, observe this: most people have a personal *core style* and *adaptive style* – a factor known well to industrial psychologists. The core style, as its name suggests, is what lies at the heart of an employee – what really makes them tick. These core styles are a product of many factors, including:

- personality;
- beliefs, attitudes and values;
- education and upbringing;
- national culture;
- role or function (marketing, procurement, engineering, personnel, etc);
- past work experience.

Our overall 'style' as employees can be thought of as the way we 'come across' and the impression we make, as well as the way we are likely to react in any given situation. Generally, style consists of two components. A 'core' style, which is the larger part (roughly 80 per cent) and an 'adaptive' style which is the lesser (roughly 20 per cent), and which we can manage in the short term to cope with particular situations.

These ideas are sometimes explored in the art and science of negotiation techniques, where a thorough self-awareness, in concert with an ability to assess the core style of our negotiating opponents, is a valuable technique, enabling us to anticipate personality-driven moves by the other party. But the same lesson applies to contracts management, where a Contract Manager will have a core and an adaptive style. The four personality 'styles' in business have been identified as:

- warm;
- tough;
- numbers;
- dealer.

The basic idea is that we each have a core and an adaptive style. Both core and adaptive comprise both typical strengths and typical weaknesses, so we need to be aware of our own style, play to our strengths and make due room for known weaknesses. A person with any two of the 'styles' above should be a perfectly competent Contract Manager, although I would express a personal opinion that the core style of 'numbers' (a focus on and respect for detail) and an adaptive style of 'dealer' (a willingness to give and take, and to spot and exploit opportunities) would make a particularly strong candidate. 'Tough' and 'warm' core styles are pretty much mutually exclusive, but a good Contract Manager should be empathetic and able to see other points of view. In the same way, being a *people-type person* will help to get the best out of teams.

> **LEARNING POINT**
>
> Reader – do you have any idea of your own core and adaptive styles? Can you recognize these traits in other people?
>   Senior managers – do you try to take into account peoples' personality traits as you identify and empower Contract Managers?

With the above thoughts in mind, there are two job descriptions for *Vendor Managers* in Appendices 7 and 8. These are fairly self-explanatory and arise from job role specifications for personnel whose jobs 'major' on the management of external service providers, ie the typical Vendor Manager whose primary role is to look after an outsourced service. Readers are recommended to review the two Appendices and to use them as a benchmark for any role profiles or job descriptions their organizations presently use for Contract Managers, however defined. Perhaps the most important consideration in all this is not to appoint people whose personality traits will not support them in their tasks. Someone who is immature, and/or uncomfortable with detail and/or uncomfortable with people will not, in all probability, make a good Contract Manager, whatever other compensating strengths they may have. A bluntly lazy person will be no good, either!

Details, details, details!

If we can be sure of one thing in virtually any contract management situation, whether we are talking about *contract administration* or contract management (in the terms we explored in the Introduction to this book) then it is that *a lot of detail will emerge that needs to be archived and presented as evidence in the event that there are later issues, difficulties, misunderstandings or, in extremis, disputes.* Earlier in the book, we recommended that the use of a Project Memo system will be helpful and eminently trackable for any moderately complex contract. See Appendices 4 and 5 for guidance on this.

The other aspect of this is managing documentation. A good filing system is important, together with the ability to safely archive documents, meaning they can be accessed again in the future. The various documents typically to be looked after are:

- contracts;
- contract amendments;
- specifications;
- service level agreements;
- correspondence;
- guarantees.

What else might we need to know about contracts? Plainly the financial aspects – what payments are to be made (or received) and when? What are the key dates for delivery? When is completion due? When do latent defects provisions expire? When do IPR/copyright provisions expire? And crucially, when do contracts themselves expire and what notice period are we obliged to give? This latter may also involve the vexed question of automatic renewals – or 'evergreen' contracts as they are sometimes known. If your organization is small (ie an 'SME' – small to medium enterprise) and you have relatively few contracts, then in all probability a good filing system and proper diary system will suffice. Today most small organizations will reflect and manage the detail on a simple spreadsheet that tracks detail under various headings relevant to their situation, possibly backed up by diary entries via, for example, a Microsoft Outlook office management system. Figure 9.3 reflects this idea. We are tracking money in, the detail of the contract(s) and money out. In addition, start and end dates and so on will be reflected in the spreadsheet.

A further key problem for SMEs is that organizational 'delegated authorities' and controls to enter into contracts tend to be lax. So potentially (and very often in practice) a multitude of managers enter into contracts and information about contract ownership is rarely maintained in a common accessible format or location. When a senior manager leaves, often a lot of the information is lost. The result? Contracts on 'rollover' terms are not cancelled, and numerous agreements remain in place covering equipment and services that are no longer required.

The tracking and monitoring issues and problems are multiplied, however, for larger organizations, such as large enterprises, blue-chip organizations and virtually all public-sector organizations, each of which is likely to have hundreds, if not thousands, of contractual relationships ongoing simultaneously. And these, in addition, may vary between sales- and purchase-type commitments! The control problems here are considerable and it is a blunt fact that many organizations are simply not coping adequately with the detail. Figure 9.4 illustrates these ideas and adds three simple questions that any business has to answer.

Figure 9.3 Record keeping – small companies

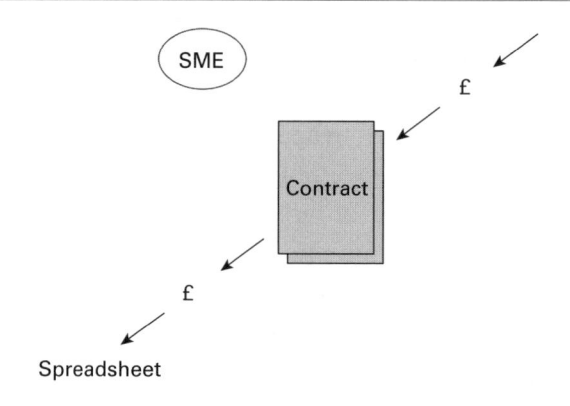

Figure 9.4 Record keeping – complex businesses

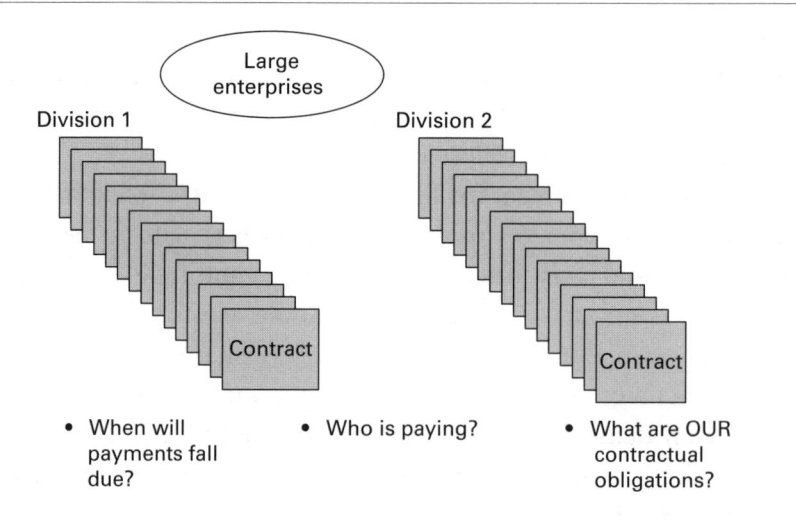

- When will payments fall due?
- Who is paying?
- What are OUR contractual obligations?

These considerations bring us inevitably to the requirement for properly designed IT-based contract management systems. There are two basic types of system currently available: (1) those based around ERP (enterprise resource planning) systems; and (2) free-standing dedicated contract management software. ERP systems are system intensive and often based around the needs of finance departments – they are in fact extended budgetary control systems. The contract management functionality of these systems tends to be bolted on as an afterthought and designed by non-specialists. They can also be quite counter-intuitive in operation or downright awkward to use for non-specialist business users – and often these are the very people who actually manage contracts on a day-to-day basis! Too often, it is primarily finance personnel who have access to the relevant IT system, and yet their people are rarely responsible for the practical administration of a contract.

To follow the thought depicted in Figure 9.5, we might add this: not only do complex businesses typically have multiple divisions and multiple budgets but, depending on the type of business, they may take differing approaches to the need for cash-flow forecasting. Figure 9.5 may be a slight over-simplification, but it is probably true to say that public-sector organizations and those heavily dependent on public expenditure (such as defence) and indeed utilities, are mission focused and their budgets are set in advance – sometimes a long way in advance. They are perhaps somewhat less focused on the liquidity question and are more focused on mission-critical contract outcomes.

By contrast, organizations that are trading and highly dependent upon interim or progress payments, and are also managing sub-contracts alongside their main sales contracts, are somewhat more focused on the need for cash flow forecasting. These ideas are simplified in Figure 9.5. For these organizations, perhaps, ERP-type controls loom larger in their day-to-day activity. Any company should consider the advantages of a dedicated contract management system. It is well beyond the scope of this book to 'specify' what an

Figure 9.5 Record keeping – complex businesses

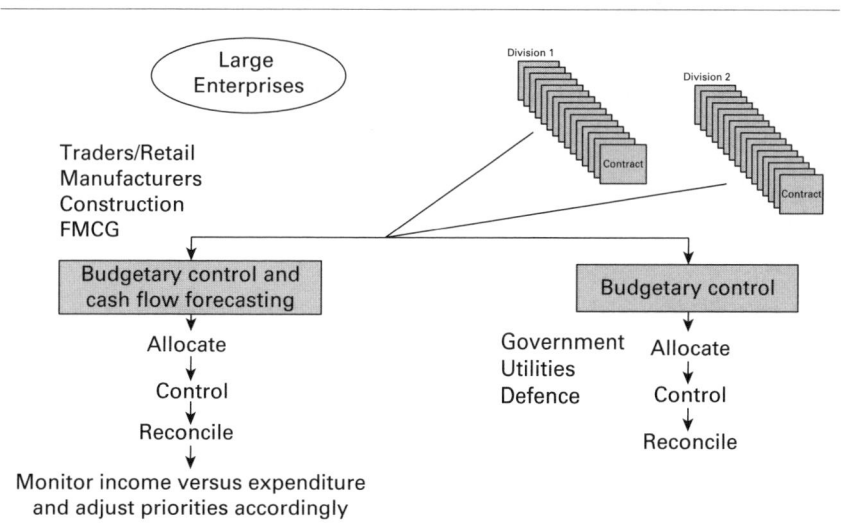

organization should look for in such a system. Suffice to say, we can highlight the main attributes of such systems and recommend that readers undertake their own further research. Today, the five overlapping functions of an IT-based contract management system are:

- **ability to store electronic versions** of signed documents, tagged with various attributes of the documents to identify and classify them;
- **ability to trigger reviews** against contractual milestones, log status and associated narrative;
- **ability to search against various attributes**, in full text, to retrieve the contracts saved in the system;
- **ability to send an automatic date-triggered e-mail** to the relevant business contact reminding them of an upcoming right or obligation;
- **ability to track 'next actions'** such as interim deliveries, progress meetings or renewals, including allowing sufficient time for renewal via the sourcing (procurement) process.

A typical list of basic functional requirements is suggested below:

- **Manage legal risk** through a searchable register of all material contractual obligations that a business (a) is required to comply with, (b) needs to remain aware of, and/or (c) should be enforcing against third parties.
- **Ability to input full scanned copy of a final document** or agreement for electronic storage.
- **Scanned copy inputted to be full text searchable** from the system (not just within the pdf reader).
- If searching for a word in a document, the search output can **highlight where the word is found in the document pdf**, rather than just bringing up the whole pdf.
- **A straightforward record of obligations** with a structure to ensure all such obligations are recorded.
- **Drag and drop e-mails** from Microsoft Outlook (or equivalent e-mail system).
- **Connect up 'attachments'**, ie all documents held/tagged together for one amended contract.

- **Automatic flagging of deadlines/time-specific obligations,** etc (software automatically sends e-mail to business owner). Ideally has ability to input/output multiple dates – 60 days prior, 30 days prior, deadline date, 30 days after, etc.
- **Reminder e-mail if initial e-mail doesn't get a response.** Escalation ability if no reply. Out-of-office functionality (desirable).
- **Simple search and report functions** (search by date of agreement, date of obligation, type of agreement, type of obligation, etc).
- **Ability to merge Excel data** into system.
- **Ability to set different levels of access** – eg read only, edit, administrator.
- **Ability to configure functions to behave differently for different user groups,** eg contracts added by one business unit may have different attributes to those inputted by another business unit.
- **Ability to report on recent changes** – audit trail of what has happened to a contract document/who has looked at it/who has amended terms.

The basic data requirements, then, for such a dedicated system would include:

- contract number;
- business owner;
- contract reference (linked to soft copy which will be stored in register software);
- key contractual obligations;
- parties;
- type of agreement;
- effective date;
- term;
- business contact;
- searchable free text box to include overview of contract, and possibly key words.

The very good news for readers is that these days there are excellent and flexible systems available relatively inexpensively. Where

ERP-type systems used to have major licence fees attached to them, and were very labour intensive, requiring major business-change projects to implement them (and sometimes took on the characteristic of 'a tail wagging the dog' in terms of the practical demands made upon business users) today, a dedicated system can be licensed on a relatively low headcount basis. Licence fees can be based on a fee per employee with direct access to the system, and this can be as low as a few hundred dollars equivalent per employee. Modern systems also tend to be much easier to use than the old ERP systems. Your author is agnostic on whether these systems could or should be Cloud-based – that is a matter of fundamental corporate (IT) policy, again, well beyond the scope of this book[1].

All good things come to an...

It was stated in Chapter 2 that senior directors in any organization are obligated to be able to provide an accurate picture of the liabilities attached to the business, and one key liability area is that of external contracts, whether sales or purchase. Senior directors have legal obligations to investors/shareholders, creditors, directors and stakeholders for the correct management of contracts along the value chain and for ensuring that obligations/risks are adequately recorded so that we can ascertain a reasonably accurate understanding, at any given point in time, of our current liabilities. Contracts can, of course, be interlinked, so problems under one contract might impact other, possibly unrelated, contracts; therefore, a reasonably effective contract repository is a key aspect of normative, prudent business management. If directors cannot lay their hands on their company's legal obligations, then they are failing to discharge their director duties adequately and with due diligence. This has become ever more important with the greater penetration of outsourcing and third-party management generally. Figure 9.6 reminds managers of two simple truths: a contract repository (however we define that, and we have made the case for IT-based systems for all but the smallest companies) needs to tell us what our sales and purchase obligations are – at the very least for those contracts that are *material* to our organization.

Figure 9.6 Tracking and monitoring

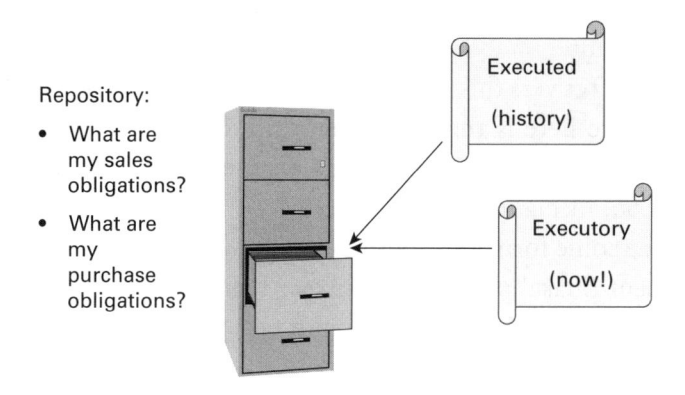

Repository:
- What are my sales obligations?
- What are my purchase obligations?

Executed (history)

Executory (now!)

Like this book, all contracts reach a conclusion sooner or later. In Chapter 8 we considered the issue around contract problems and disputes. If these are not resolved to the mutual satisfaction of the parties to a contract, then an early termination may be triggered. So there are two types of exit to be considered under any contract – planned (or natural) exit and unplanned exit, occasioned through significantly changed business circumstances or some fundamental dispute that the parties are unable to resolve through the process of negotiation.

In Chapter 4, we reviewed the question of whether a contract management plan is required. The planning around exit may well be detailed in that document. Some organizations (and this is perhaps a growing trend) are today preparing separate exit plans, either stand-alone or as an appendix to their contract management plan. Such plans are certainly prudent for those contracts that are material to our organization (see Chapter 2) and/or represent considerable operational or reputational risk, should they go wrong. Appendix 9 in this book is a thorough consideration of exit planning and readers are encouraged to work through this and consider the need for such specific planning for their organization, and to what sort of contracts it should be applied. In Chapter 3, Figure 3.1 (Kraljic supplier positioning) and its equivalent for sales organizations in Figure 3.2 (Client positioning from a seller's perspective) we recognized that some contracts are more risky and/or rewarding, and/or represent bigger opportunities to drive profit. It is these types of contract, perhaps, where exit planning is more important. Indeed, we could simplify this and say that where risk and spend are highest, or third-party dependencies greatest, then exit planning becomes steadily more important.

Appendix 9 covers this subject in greater detail. The only additional point to make here is that planning for exit should almost become an *organizational mindset* from the very earliest stage in contract planning. So, in Figure 4.3 (Chapter 4) we suggested that there will typically be some form of 'project development phase' and a 'contract development phase' prior to a contract being entered into. Looking at Figure 4.3 we might consider that in fact phases 1 to 4 provide the natural opportunity to consider, in detail, the need and opportunities to exit the contract. Exit planning, then, should really become part and parcel of the planning for any *material contract* and any contract that would cause to us significant difficulty should it go wrong. Furthermore, depending on the situation leading to the exit, there should be a contractual requirement on the parties to work together in a spirit of mutual cooperation so as to bring the contract to a close and properly manage the outstanding contractual obligations on both sides. Standard clauses in most *model contracts* cover this, but particular thought should be given to what ongoing tasks might need to be carried out, and whether there should be a requirement for an existing contractor *to assist in transitioning to a new contractor*. This is the position in many typical outsourcing type arrangements, where the operational, day-to-day tasks will continue, irrespective of the contractor actually carrying them out. A good commercial lawyer will be able to advise on these matters.

Endnote

1 It is not the purpose of this book to recommend bypassing IT governance! However, for some business departments the Cloud option might well bypass IT (depending on governance rules) and licensing arrangements can sometimes be set within departmental discretionary budget approval. One software firm advised the author that 95 per cent of their contract management deployments were Cloud-based. They commented that 'it is the easy option that removes most of the historical barriers of capital software purchases and IT involvement!'

Practical tools and checklists

APPENDIX 1
Preparing specification documents: an approach to support client–supplier contract negotiations

1 What is a specification?

What is a specification? A dictionary definition is: 'specification – act of specifying; detailed descriptive statement of contract or patent. Specify – make particular mention of; include in specification.' To say a specification is 'specifying what you want' is clearly inadequate! The best definition of a technical specification is contained in BS 5760.

Specifications: BS 5760 – a definition

Specification: 'means of communicating the requirements or intentions of one party to another in relation to a product, service, material, procedure or test.

Specification – function: 'to provide the basis of understanding between two parties so that both agree on the criteria to be met.

In spite of the general clarity as to what a specification is and what it is designed to do, it appears very often in commercial contracts that client-side (buying) organizations fail to achieve their objectives when they buy in high technology or specialist goods and services. It may be that their expectations are unreasonable or insufficiently thought through. But it may be that they are failing to specify clearly what they want to buy. Specifications are important because they assist or hamper these buying organisations in acquiring what they need to fulfil their commercial objectives.

Whilst it is often the buying side that prepares the Specification, sellers also have a practical interest in the document. It contains all the technical and commercial 'promises' that they must meet. If the seller prepares the Specification, then it represents their 'public' statement of what they are capable of delivering, and their confidence in meeting all their contractual promises.

2 General principles

Specifications can be in varying levels of detail ranging from a simple performance/functional description, through to a fully detailed exposition of how a process, system, or equipment is to be analysed, designed, procured, manufactured, delivered, installed, commissioned, operated and maintained, or a service carried out.

UK Supply of Goods and Services Act 1982

How does the Act define a 'contract for the supply of a service'? ... *'In this Act, a "Contract for the supply of a service" means... a contract under which a person ("the supplier") agrees to carry out a service.'* The Act goes on to state that a contract is a contract for the supply of a service *'whether or not goods are also transferred or to be transferred, or hired'*.

- It should be recognized that, in general, the greater the level of detail in a specification, the more constraints this imposes on the contractor/supplier with consequent effects on costs and price levels.
- Greater detail in specifications does not always lead to increased price, but added detail often provides an opportunity to 'gold plate' the goods or services being supplied. This is especially true where the Specification requires the contractor to vary their normal capacity, methods, practices or resources. Moreover, if what is sought is not in fact obtained, the contractor may be able to avoid liability by demonstrating that it has followed the 'letter of the Specification'.
- It is generally more satisfactory to describe the required final result rather than the methods by which the results should be obtained.

The contractor/supplier may be able to offer alternative, more cost-effective proposals, so to constrain them via a detailed specification may be counter-productive.

- Detailed specifications can lead to sourcing limitations and 'one-off specials' which are likely to cost more in purchase and through-life costs.
- By comparison, to specify simple **performance/functional requirements** can reduce costs, including the engineering and project management costs associated with the purchaser/user activities, and enable a wider choice of suppliers. These suppliers may well be able to offer existing commercially available items.

Specification writers **must be clear in their descriptions** of the items or services required, to avoid inconsistency between one part of the document and another, or between the technical specification and the contractual documentation that must accompany it.

3 Determining the extent of detail required

To decide the extent of detail for inclusion in the Specification, the specification writer first establishes the extent of the following risks to their organization:

- technical;
- operational;
- safety;
- commercial.

4 Specifications: basic considerations

- What is the purpose/function of the component, equipment or system within the overall company activity?
- What is its relative importance?
- Are there statutory or mandatory requirements to be met?

- Are there personnel, plant or public safety requirements?
- What level of quality is necessary?
- What is life expectancy?
- What are the interfaces to be considered?
- Are there physical/spatial limitations?
- What are the user's operational and maintenance requirements?
- Are there any future spares requirements to be considered?
- What is the extent of coordination/project management to be undertaken by the purchaser?
- What is the proposed contractor/supplier experience and capability for the required work?
- What are the likely consequences of default by the contractor/supplier?
- In what environmental conditions will the product be used?

5 Special requirements for specifying R&D and consultancy services

- What we have considered above is particularly relevant to the purchase of equipment, although the general principles hold true for the purchase of services as well.
- If a specifier concentrates on the outputs required rather than on the detailed activities needed to achieve the outputs, the proposed contractor will be more likely to use their professional judgement in determining the best methods to achieve those outputs, taking into account any technology, environmental or budgetary constraints.
- When specifying research and development services (and indeed other 'consultancy' services) the following headings may provide a helpful framework.

R&D/consultancy specifications – basic headings

- Background to requirement – why are we doing the work?
  - economic objectives;
  - technical objectives.
- Alternative methods of research considered and why rejected.
- History of requirement.
- Overall goal of the project – simple language.
- Primary objectives.
- Secondary objectives.
- Major innovations on which the work is to focus.
- Project description – project tasks:
  - timescales and milestones;
  - project management/administration;
  - format of results required;
  - documentation to be provided;
  - technical liaison required.
- Quality requirements.
- Reporting requirements.
- References – other specifications, published works, etc.

Some R&D specifications, written principally in scientific terms, may be unintelligible to the layman. This has two disadvantages:

1 If a lawyer cannot understand the requirements, then any legal problems could be unduly difficult (and expensive) to resolve.
2 It undermines the contribution of the non-technical contract writer who may be prevented from understanding what are the most appropriate commercial terms to apply. Having a 'plain language' summary project description should prompt the contract writer to ask further questions which will themselves contribute to the specification drafting process.

The important point to bear in mind is this: **if the technical specification is not clear to an intelligent non-specialist (eg a lawyer) it may be difficult to decide what the Specification *really* meant** in the event that there is a serious dispute as to interpretation. In these circumstances, a court or arbitrator will have to employ (expensively) an expert in the field to interpret what the Specification actually meant.

6 General guidelines

- Where possible, technical specifications should be presented in functional or performance terms, allowing contractors to take on design and development risk and offer what they believe will best achieve the required results.
- Where appropriate, quality standards should be cited.

To avoid limiting competition, [Client Organization] may consider using in its invitation to tender document a statement which encourages tenderers to be creative in responding to the technical requirement. A typical commercial clause inviting creative responses:

> The tenderer may submit proposals based on standards equivalent to any standards referred to in this Specification. In such event, the tenderer shall identify the standards proposed and demonstrate their equivalence to the stated standards. If the tenderer wishes to submit for consideration proposals on an alternative basis, he shall submit a tender in accordance with the stated requirements and in addition shall submit an alternative tender or tenders.

Performance specifications are probably most suitable in situations:

- where there are minimal *interface risks* between the contractor/supplier and [Client Organization];
- where the direct/consequential costs and other risks of default are recoverable from the contractor.

At the other end of the spectrum, where there are complex or critical interfaces and the direct/consequential costs and other risks of contractual default are not adequately recoverable from the contractor, then a detailed technical specification may be more appropriate.

7 Specification writing – some do's and don'ts

Do:

- consider the purpose;
- evaluate what is important – eg safety, quality, reliability, maintainability, public confidence;
- avoid the use of proprietary components/equipment where a choice exists, as well as reference to brand names;
- describe clearly what is required, avoiding meaningless words;
- prepare the technical specification with competitive bidding in mind.

Do not:

- copy a description or quotation from one company;
- refer to specific trademarks, patents, product names, brand names;
- use vague or subjective terms;
- over-specify or needlessly impose special standards or 'one-off' requirements;
- develop a design which limits the choice of components where a specification has to be a detailed, descriptive specification.

8 Checklist for detailed equipment specifications

- Scope.
- Design parameters.
- Manufacturing methods.
- Installation.
- Commissioning.
- Construction methods.
- Performance requirements:
  - ratings;
  - overall performance;

- life;
- reliability;
- consumables.
- Physical requirements:
  - materials;
  - dimensions;
  - weight;
  - finish;
  - interface;
  - accommodation;
  - interconnection/interfaces.
- QA levels.
- Relevant standards.
- Safety requirements.
- Inspection and testing.
- Acceptance tests.
- Packaging and marking.
- Storage and handling.
- Installation.
- Drawings.
- Spares.
- Maintenance requirements.
- Information to be provided by the contractor.
- Handling.
- Case history/lifetime records.
- Independent assessment.
- Services to be supplied by purchaser and other contractors.
- Timescale/programme.
- Use of copyright drawings, patents and software.

APPENDIX 2
Supply contract risks: an approach to support client–supplier contract negotiations

Contents

Executive summary
Commercial reality
Summary of recommendations

1. Definitions
2. Purpose and scope
3. Background
4. Project sourcing phase
5. Risk identification
6. Risk mitigation
7. Contract risk evaluation framework
    7a – Typical project risks
    7b – Special project risks
8. Evaluation of risks
9. Insurance of supply risks
10. A rationale for risk distribution between contracting parties
11. Contract negotiation
12. Conclusion

Executive summary

A growing number of *client* organizations – ie those that buy in goods and services from third-party suppliers – are exploring opportunities to offset contract risk against price. This provides a new opportunity to deliver bottom-line savings, but without increasing client risks in an unstructured or non-deliberative way.

Directors of companies and public sector bodies should have a good appreciation of any risks to their business that could impact the way that they interact with their key stakeholders – especially customers. Special risks arise as a result of supply/procurement activity. The purpose of this Review is to identify common risks in supply/procurement contracts, whether capital buys, direct services or outsourcing, and to suggest methods for addressing and managing those risks.

Review purpose is NOT to define a new approach to contract risk conditions. It is to enable client organizations to evaluate contractual risk in a general way so they can assess, on a case-by-case basis, whether there are commercial and/or economic benefits to be gained from reassigning the contractual ownership of *project* risks in a substantial way. Risk transfer could be either by transferring risk to the supplier or, conversely, by the client organization itself absorbing contract risk in a controlled manner. If the client accepts risk, it needs to put in place *risk mitigation* and *risk management* strategies.

Commercial reality

It is a basic principle of contracting that 'risk should lie where risk is best managed'. The party best able to manage a risk therefore carries that risk under the contract unless there are compelling reasons for another party to carry the risk.

> It is stressed that *risk management* is not the same as *risk elimination*.

Summary of recommendations

- Client organizations should identify in a formal way those projects to which systematic *risk* review shall be applied (**Recommendation 1 (R1)**).

- Identified risks should be listed in a *risk register* which should be appended to, or referenced in, the *financial business case* (**R2**).
- A contract *materiality* review should be undertaken by client organizations at the commencement of any *project*, and repeated as necessary during the life of the *project* (**R3**).
- Under a formal Contract Risk Evaluation Framework (CREF), *risk registers* should be created in a systematic way for proposed contracts, so enabling the client to have a good appreciation of the risk profile of the *project* (**R4**).
- Where insurance cover by suppliers is written into a *contract*, clients should obtain a copy of the relevant insurance certificates (**R5**).
- Contractual loss recoverable from suppliers under low- or medium-*materiality* contracts should be capped at fee + 25 per cent. Highmateriality contracts should be considered on a case-by-case basis (**R6**).
- Client organizations should define *materiality* on supply contracts, taking due account of any sector-specific regulations covering 'outsourcing'. This will help with overall *risk* assessment, putting it into a regulatory context (**R7**).

1 Definitions

Note: in this Review, defined terms are shown in bold where singular, not plural.

- **Risk** – a risk is an adverse event that may happen, as opposed to an issue, which is an adverse event that has happened. Typical client-side risks will be risk of failure of the contract relationship, and risk of regulatory breaches.
- **Risk elimination** – a situation where identified risks no longer exist.
- **Risk mitigation** – things done to reduce effects of risk should an issue emerge.
- **Risk management** – control, evaluation and monitoring of risks, including risk mitigation and issue management. Use of risk logs/registers is a key element of risk management.

- **Risk register** – a list of risks and issues.
- **Financial business case** – (a) the document in whatever form used as the rationale for entering into a supply contract. May also include audit trail of management approvals. (b) A document that expresses the rationale in financial terms, being direct and indirect costs as well as 'savings' achieved and/or revenue earned as a result of the *project*.
- **Financial close** – normally the time when all the contracts associated with the *project* are signed and the contractual liabilities are assumed.
- **Issue** – a risk that has happened in practice, so becoming an issue to be resolved.
- **Client** – an organization buying in goods and/or services.
- **Materiality** – the importance of a *project/contract* to a client organization measured in a consistent way against five key dimensions: contract value; market concentration risk; risk of partner change during contract; legal risk; reputation risk.
- **Project** – a plan to develop and implement some financial opportunity, which may include the need to meet a regulatory requirement.
- **Project developer** – the person who is responsible for putting together a project plan, often including the business case.
- **Project manager** – the person who implements the project, carrying responsibility for its effective completion.
- **Contract** – complex supply involving, for example, planning, project development, design, execution (service delivery or supply of goods of some type) and possibly after-sales support (or enduring post-contract obligations, eg to secrecy).
- **Vendor manager** – person in the client organization who is charged with providing technically competent client control of supplier operations, and especially specification-compliant delivery, or SLA-compliant delivery. Usually this is someone in the sponsoring group with appropriate technical knowledge. It is generally not someone in 'procurement'. Procurement departments often provide a Supplier Relationship Manager under their generic Supplier Relationship Management programme.

2 Purpose and scope

The purpose of this Review is to suggest for *client* organizations a common way of evaluating and describing generic procurement/supply contractual risk, and a common framework for addressing those risks within the supply contract.

This Review applies to *client* organizations generally, as well as to procurement or supply management organizations.

3 Background

In developing a *project* that involves external supply/procurement, the *project developer* needs to evaluate the additional risks that the supply/procurement element of the *project* entails. Having identified special risks in the supply/procurement element, the *project manager* must institute *risk mitigation* or *risk management* measures to address those risks as far as reasonably practicable. Although supply–procurement risks will be only a part of the risk profile attached to any *project*, for the purposes of this Review, supply–procurement risks are considered in isolation, as though they are the sole risks that impact the *project*. In practice, there will be other *project* risks.

In developing any *project* and the contractual structure within which it will operate, the *project manager* must develop a risk-sharing package that is acceptable to the parties, normally the client and a single contractor acting as 'supplier'. In some projects, there may be other (third) parties that have an interest in the way that risks are distributed. *Client* organizations must make due allowance for this.

The risks discussed in this Review are those that normally affect high-cost and high-complexity contractual arrangements. Some of the risks described will apply to simple purchase orders. But *risk* evaluation, measurement and control measures will normally be applied only to 'contracts' for 'supply' ('supply' includes the supply of services), whereby *project* scale or complexity risks tend to be magnified in their potential effects. We define a *contract* as being complex supply involving planning, development, design, execution (service delivery or fabrication of some type) supply, and possibly after-sales support.

Unless their costs are high or delivery failure implications particularly acute, we ignore 'purchase order'-type risks in this Review.

> Client organizations should identify in a formal way those projects to which systematic risk review shall be applied (R1).

A *project* contract structure should normally balance risks in such a way that the party best able to price and to manage specific risks ultimately bears them under the contract. In this way, supply costs are optimized and returns for the client organization's stakeholders maximized. It is occasionally necessary for clients to accept risks that they would not otherwise wish to, for example in order to enhance returns from a *project* or simply in order to make a *project* happen. In these cases, it is doubly important that risks are identified, mitigated, monitored and managed through the life of the *project*.

> Identified risks should be listed in a risk register which should be appended to, or referenced in, the financial business case (R2).

4 Project sourcing phase

Any *project* that is being developed will move through a number of sub-phases up to the signing of contracts (the 'sourcing phase'). See Table A2.1. During these different sourcing sub-phases, our appreciation of risks will develop and evolve. Although all projects are different, it is suggested that the following minimum sub-phases are likely to be undertaken, and in the order shown. The 'percentage complete' column suggests a typical sourcing *project* and the cumulative time spent on its various phases up to the 'completion' of *financial close* – normally the time when all the contracts associated with a *project* are signed and the contractual liabilities are assumed.

5 Risk identification

The *project* needs to be broken down into discrete activities and risks identified against each activity. See Table A2.2. In the early stages, it is vital to identify the scope of risks to which the client organization

Table A2.1 Project sourcing – sub-phases and risk considerations

Project sourcing phase	Risk management	Percentage complete*
Concept	Initial risk identification – highlight 'show stoppers'.	5
Evaluation**	Detailed risk identification, categorization and initial evaluation, including due diligence.	15
Tender/offer	Risk evaluation and strategy to transfer or mitigate risks. Assessment of risks is a critical element in tender evaluation.	50–70
Negotiation	Negotiate risk mitigation, negotiate contractual terms.	70–90
Financial business case	Final approval of risk distribution and risk management strategies.	95
Financial close	Completion of risk identification and risk distribution between contractual parties.	100
Implementation	Ongoing management of risks.	n/a

* This is a suggestion for a typical sourcing project. 'Completion' of sub-phases is impossible to measure with such precision.
** This means proof of concept – basic steps to ensure that further work on the *project* is unlikely to be wasted.

may be exposed. A key aim of the proof of concept phase is to identify any risk so severe as to be a potential 'show stopper' and which would make further investigation pointless. Such risks could have the effect of terminating a *project* at that stage.

During later phases of a project, as the overall project is being implemented, it is best practice to continue to monitor risks and try to identify new risks that may be emerging.

6 Risk mitigation

It is vital to understand that risks do not go away because a contract document states that they are shouldered by someone else (normally the supplier). Certainly, for high-*materiality* projects, risks must be monitored and controlled. Should risks materialize and become

Table A2.2 Sourcing phase – risk identification

Project sourcing phase	Risk identification	Percentage complete*
Concept	What are the biggest risks to this concept?	5
Evaluation**	What new risks or risk mitigation strategies are identified?	15
Tender/offer	Have we already established in principle which risks the supplier will shoulder? Do the terms of contract under which tenders are invited appropriately distribute risks?	50–70
Negotiation	Clarify that risks are appropriately distributed in the draft contract. If using, for example, the NEC family of contracts (or equivalent), does the supplier understand the implication of the idea that the client accepts only the risks listed as *client risks* and that all other risks are shouldered by the supplier?	70–90
Financial business case	Have we set out adequately the risks and do budget/sponsor managers understand them?	95
Financial close	Have any risks changed? Does the financial business case need to be amended or re-approved?	100
Implementation	Monitor risks identified as at financial business case and identify and mitigate any new risks that emerge during implementation	n/a

* This is a suggestion for a typical sourcing project. 'Completion' of sub-phases is impossible to measure with such precision.
** This means proof of concept – basic steps to ensure that further work on the *project* is unlikely to be wasted.

issues, then there could be knock-on consequences to the client. These consequences may themselves become new risks. Prior to a contract being concluded, the client's focus on risk issues will be directed as suggested below:

- **Tender/offer**: the emphasis in this phase is to exploit as far as reasonable the client's power as 'buyer'. The opportunity should be taken to define the terms of the contract in detail, thus converting *risk* distribution from a negotiation factor into a part of the client's specification. The specification then describes what is wanted and the terms on which they are wanted (usually the technical specification supported by the contractual terms and conditions).
- **Negotiation**: in this sub-phase, the client organization should achieve an overall understanding of project/contract risks and how they may be assigned under the contract(s).

Contract negotiators need to be realistic. Risk mitigation, which aims to offload all risk to the other contracting party, may achieve this outcome only at an uneconomically high price, thus undermining the *project* concept. Offloading all risk may encourage the supplier to become overtly 'contractual' in their dealings with the *client*, to the overall detriment of the concept/*project*.

7 Contract risk evaluation framework

Investment opportunities, whether capital investment, revenue expenditure, new business opportunities or outsourcing, where they involve external expenditure with a third party (or the assumption of risks as in a joint venture or contractual collaboration) must set out clearly the *project* risks and uncertainties and how they will be managed during the life of the *project*. A formal risk assessment is therefore required for each *project*. The higher the *materiality*, the greater effort to be invested in *risk* assessment.

A valuable and simple step is to undertake a basic contract materiality review which measures the impact of any proposed contract against five key dimensions: contract value; market concentration risk; risk of partner change during contract; legal risk; reputation risk. By doing such a simple and quick step (around 10 minutes for a low- to medium-materiality contract) our organization achieves a consistent view of the importance and possible impact of a *project/*

contract. This in turn suggests the extent of due diligence to be undertaken by our organization before entering into the contract.

> A contract *materiality* review should be done by client organizations at the commencement of any *project*, and repeated as necessary during the life of the *project* (R3).

See Appendix 6 on pages 153–57.

A *risk* assessment framework, the Contract Risk Evaluation Framework (CREF) can be designed for use in conjunction with the *financial business case*. A CREF can provide a structured method to establish the contract *risk* profile. A CREF also enables projects to be considered and compared on a consistent basis. Table A2.3 provides a simple mechanism for listing and measuring contract risks.

Client organizations should decide, in their own context, the 'score' ranges where aggregate contractual *risk* is considered acceptable/unacceptable and/or where senior management sign-off is required before contracts can be entered.

CREF *risk* registers, as above, enable *client* organizations to prepare mitigation strategies and keep *contract* and *project* risks in view throughout the *project*. They also enable clients to have reasonable confidence that proposed conditions of contract properly anticipate the contractual effects should a *risk* become an *issue*, and that those risks are properly assigned between the contracting parties.

> Under a formal Contract Risk Evaluation Framework (CREF), *risk registers* should be created in a systematic way for proposed contracts, so enabling the client to have a good appreciation of the risk profile of the project (R4).

7A – Typical project risks

- cost overrun;
- completion delay;
- failure to meet performance guarantees;
- environmental risks;
- force majeure risks;

Table A2.3 Contract Risk Evaluation Framework (CREF) – risk table

Risk description	Person responsible	Mitigation strategy	Dependencies	Weight	Score	Weight x score

Weight: eg L = 1, M = 2, H = 3. Score range: eg 1–10. So, the higher the score, the greater the *risk*.

- credit worthiness of supplier/contractor;
- after-sales support delinquency;
- client's business needs change during implementation;
- adverse legal changes;
- adverse exchange rate movements;
- price inflation;
- environmental risk.

7B – Special project risks

- Reputation risk;
- client risk;
- intellectual property rights – risks;
- regulatory risk.

Clients should assess whether a particular *project* will encounter heightened/special risk within the typical risk areas above. If 'yes', then this will suggest where *risk mitigation* activity will add most value. It will also assist in discussions with insurers should project specific insurance be required.

8 Evaluation of risks

The CREF can become the key mechanism for evaluating *project* risks. It is useful to consider *contract risk* in the context of risks versus rewards. At the end of the day, why do we run risks? A *risk/reward matrix* can help to put some perspective around *project* risks. Both supplier and buyer are vitally concerned about the allocation and management of risks. Their respective motivations as they discuss a proposed contract are suggested in Table A2.4.

Under a CREF, an organization should track – at least for high-*materiality* projects – overall *risk* exposure to third-party supplier risks. If a decision is taken by the *client* to absorb more contract *risk* in return for other benefits in a particular *project*, it may become

Table A2.4 Risk–reward motivation

Role	Risk	Reward
Buyer/client	Revenue expenditure on supply.	The contract deliverable and its contribution to corporate objectives.
Buyer/client	On T&M/target priced contracts – risk of cost overrun.	A mechanism for easily tracking costs.
Buyer/client	Regulatory compliance.	Regulations drive best practice.
Buyer/client	Third-party client interests.	Doing deals with the client.
Buyer/client	Intellectual property rights – leakage to rivals.	Develop new knowledge or competencies.
Supplier	Fixed price contracts – cost overrun.	If effectively priced and adequate margin, fixed price is always attractive to clients.
Supplier	Performance guarantees.	A mechanism to limit the client's demands.
Supplier	Timeliness of delivery.	Enhance reputation.
Supplier	Supply pipeline.	Being part of the client's 'team'.
Supplier	Sub-contractors.	The ability to offload non-core activity to specialists.
Supplier	Cost inflation.	Profit.

necessary to ensure that, across a range of current key projects, the client is not over-exposing itself to aggregated risks. Note that risks, if encountered in combination across a range of projects, could potentially impact the client organization should those risks materialize and become issues. Taking on too much contract *risk* could potentially invalidate or reduce a client's insurance cover.

9 Insurance of supply risks

Many supply-type contracts are not sufficiently complex or risky to justify separate insurance of the risks. For exceptionally risky projects the following insurances, either with the client organization as the insured, or the supplier as the insured (and covering the client organization against claims) may be necessary:

- **Professional Indemnity**: covers professional negligence – generally incorrect advice leading to client direct or indirect loss, or poor design leading to performance shortfall.
- **Construction All Risks**: provides protection against physical loss or damage to the permanent or temporary works, materials during construction and commissioning. It also provides some defects liability cover.
- **Consequential Loss**: provides protection against financial consequences of loss of anticipated revenue as a result of delay following insured loss.
- **Third-Party Liability**: protection against legal liability for compensation for bodily injury, property damage, nuisance and sometimes pollution.
- **Business Interruption**: protection against loss of revenue as a result of insured physical loss or damage at client organization premises and/or at supplier premises.

Where insurance cover by suppliers is written into a contract, clients should obtain a copy of the relevant insurance certificates (R5).

As a general negotiating question, some reasonable limit should be placed on contractual loss recoverable from suppliers. A decision should be made as to whether 'professional indemnity'-type risks should be considered separately from other possible losses – and if so, separately specified in the *contract*. Otherwise, it is suggested that the indemnity limit should be set at *contract* value plus a percentage figure that liquidates a measure of losses likely to be encountered should particular risks become issues.

> **LEARNING POINT**
>
> Contractual loss recoverable from suppliers under low- or medium-materiality contracts should be capped at fee + 25 per cent. Higher materiality contracts should be considered on a case-by-case basis **(R6)**.

10 A rationale for risk distribution between contracting parties

There are 'red-line' risk issues for most organizations. These are issues on which they cannot compromise, eg for an airline, safety in transport operations. The areas where they cannot compromise will always include areas where criminal liability attaches to board-level directors for failure.

It is important that client organizations understand which areas are red-line. Attempts to make every issue non-negotiable will ultimately fail and may be counter-productive (a bad argument undermines a good one in negotiations). Red-line areas do not have to be flagged up for public discussion, but it is vital that contract negotiators are clear about where true 'red-line' areas lie for their organization. If it is necessary to trade-off risks, then negotiators need to understand which are important and then assess that risk in the context of the contract being contemplated. For example, intellectual property rights may be irrelevant in the supply of food-related services.

Client organizations should periodically validate in a systematic way what are red-line areas in their context. The following simple framework may be helpful.

Table App 2.5

Client red-line issues	Why?

Issues not listed should be considered as potentially negotiable, providing the benefits to the client are compelling. Many client organizations use 'standard' or 'template' forms of contract. It is not unduly difficult to reassign contract risks in a CREF-managed environment and it should be possible to make speedy decisions on requests to reassign risk for specific projects.

However strongly we feel about a particular contractual clause, it is potentially 'tradeable' for other benefits. Specific legal advice will only be required for decisions to renegotiate red-line areas and/or for high- and exceptional-materiality projects. The overall package of risks needs to be balanced so that the economic benefits of the project are not undermined by risks that may happen, so becoming expensive issues.

> **LEARNING POINT**
>
> Client organizations should define materiality on supply contracts taking due account of any sector-specific regulations covering 'outsourcing'. This will help with overall risk assessment, putting it into a regulatory context **(R7)**.

11 Contract negotiation

The client organization will enhance its negotiating position if it carefully evaluates risk at the beginning of the project and sets out its technical requirements in a technical specification document and its commercial requirements in a carefully drafted form of contract. The two documents taken together can be seen as the client's overall requirements specification.

The client may be helped if it uses an industry standard form of contract – sometimes called model conditions – where such model conditions are recognized (but always bearing in mind that trade association-based contracts are often weighted unduly in favour of the supplier). An alternative approach is to use the client's own template form of contract, assuming that this has been drafted taking into account the principles set out above, and especially observing the basic rule that contractual risk should lie where risk is best managed.

Having appreciated any red-line risk areas and invited offers ('Proposals') based upon the client's requirements specification, the client can be open to requests to redistribute contract risks in exchange for other benefits. Alternatively, where a particular clause has become a deadlock factor, the client can offer to concede in return for a realignment of contract risks elsewhere; or they can hold the line on the deadlocked issue, but propose concessions on other contract clauses that could be of tangible benefit to the other party.

Providing that red-line areas are not breached, the overall integrity of the proposed contract should remain intact. Where re-balancing risks it will be necessary to discuss with in-house or external legal advisers to ensure that they understand the overall context. It may be necessary to debate/resist legal protests that the risk balance has shifted adversely and therefore should not be allowed. Providing the client has an overall Basic Contract Materiality Review, and works within a CREF environment for monitoring and managing risks, the client should be on safe grounds to adjust risk distribution.

Where concessions are made from standard positions, the reasoning should be flagged and a clear statement given that this should not be interpreted as setting a precedent for future contract negotiations. Significant concessions should also be flagged in the financial business case.

12 Conclusion

There are potential financial benefits in evaluating contract risks and maintaining an open mind on reassigning risks between contracting parties. The starting point should always be that risk should lie where risk is best managed. It is best practice, and certainly good business, to have a risk management strategy, and for this purpose a CREF to review and monitor risks is a practical, simple and effective tool.

APPENDIX 3
Contract management plan

Example contract management plan (CMP) for a large-scale (or complex) procurement

Table A3.1 is devised from a customer's or purchaser's viewpoint, but is illustrative of what might also be of interest to the seller, who would develop something analogous from their viewpoint. The table, then, would be the key elements of a CMP for large or more complex procurement task; it could be used by the Contract Manager as the basis for developing a CMP. The amount of detail required for any section used would be adjusted to reflect the complexity of the contract, the level of risk associated with it, and the internal processes of the organization preparing the plan.

Table A3.1 Example contract management plan

Section	Outline	Detail
Title and purpose	Title and purpose and version control	Devise a title for the plan and summarize its overall purpose. Include details of name and date of the person(s) approving the plan, including arrangements for reviewing and updating the plan.
Contract summary	Contract structure	Summarize key contract details such as: contract number, commencement date, contract term, procurement process (eg panel, open tender), key personnel details, authorized users of the contract, estimated contract value, reporting obligations specified (yes/no).

(Continued)

Table A3.1 *(Continued)*

Section	Outline	Detail
	Background	Summarize the procurement process leading to this contract. Include purpose, objectives, scope and key deliverables. Note: information should be detailed enough to allow a person with no prior involvement in the contract to have a clear understanding of its background.
	Documentation	List all documents relating to the contract that are held by the contract management team. This may include, for example, transition plans, tender evaluation reports, risk management plans, etc, and identification of their location and when they were last updated.
	Contract term and extension options	List contract start and end dates and contract extension options, if applicable.
	Pricing	Total contract value, pricing arrangements and fee variations. If applicable, a fee schedule may also be included.
Roles and responsibilities	Contact details	At a minimum, the Contract Managers for both the buying entity and the supplier entity should be listed with their contact details.
	Identified roles and associated descriptions	List key stakeholders, where they come from and their major responsibilities in relation to the contract. In some contracts, there will be a number of parties with varying levels of contractual, financial and reporting involvement. A 'map' of these relationships may be useful for illustration purposes.
	Key stakeholder management and communication tasks	Identify key methods to be used for liaison, reporting, signalling issues to, and building relationships with, key stakeholders identified above.

(Continued)

Table A3.1 (Continued)

Section	Outline	Detail
Conditions of contract	General conditions	Specify if any standard/published form of contract is used.
	Special conditions	List any special conditions that are not covered elsewhere in this plan. For example, warranties, intellectual property ownership, etc.
	Contract variations (price, product/ services or other)	Highlight any management approvals, authorization requirements, etc, that need to be met in order to implement a variation. This should be consistent with the specific provisions in the contract.
	Insurance	Record details of currency and adequacy of insurance certificates. Specify procedures for obtaining evidence from the contractor of future currency.
Financial considerations	Payment conditions	Insert any clauses from the contract on payment conditions. The payment schedule should also be described. For example, the schedule may provide for monthly payment, or payment on completion of deliverables, or a mixture of progress and time-based payments.
	Incentives or rebates	Specify any incentive arrangements included in the contract and how they are to be calculated.
	Liquidated damages, 'penalties' or disincentives	Note: under English law, 'penalties' are illegal, so be very careful in using such a term! Specify any financial remedies incorporated into the contract and how they are to be calculated and applied.
	Invoicing	Specify and detail the invoicing requirements for the contract.

(Continued)

Table A3.1 (Continued)

Section	Outline	Detail
Performance measurement	Key performance measures	Specify key performance measures/indicators to be used for measuring the performance of contract. These should be consistent with the performance measures identified in any associated tender documentation and the contract. If there is a separate 'service level agreement' then this will be specified.
	Non-financial performance incentives/disincentives	Specify any non-financial performance incentives or disincentives that are applicable to the contract and the key performance indicators that trigger them.
	Performance monitoring	Specify the data collection and analysis methods to be used for monitoring and assessing performance (eg user surveys, third-party accreditation, benchmarking. In addition, specify who will undertake such performance monitoring. Include: responsibility for collecting and analysing data; how frequently monitoring will take place; the reporting arrangements; and any processes to review the arrangements.
Contract administration	Seller's (contractor's) obligations	Specify all contractor obligations for which the supplier is responsible. This will probably include: goods or services to be provided; any other 'deliverables' covered by the contract; timeframes to be met; insurance arrangements; specified key personnel; reporting requirements; provision of equipment and/or operatives; and back-up arrangements.
	Buyer's obligations	Specify all obligations of the buyer (client) under the contract. This is likely to include: access to premises; security arrangements; information to be made available to the contractor; equipment to be provided; accommodation; feedback and satisfaction reporting; scheduling of meetings.

(Continued)

Table A3.1 (Continued)

Section	Outline	Detail
	Product or service standards expected	Specify requirements included in the contract relating to product or service standards and how they are to be administered.
	Compliance management	Specify relevant procurement policies and obligations that the buyer and the contractor are required to comply with and how these will be managed. Note: the Contract Manager is responsible for the correct management of these obligations. It may be useful to include these as an attachment to the CMP.
	Transition	Include here arrangements for managing any transition and attach transition strategies or plans.
	Reporting requirements	Specify the reporting requirements, for example what is to be reported and the frequency and format of reports.
	Audit requirements	Detail any requirements for both internal and independent audits, and the elements of the contract to be audited. The timeframe for the audit, along with resources required (in-house or external) should also be identified.
	Meetings	Provide a schedule of meetings specific to the contract and the process for inviting and reminding relevant parties.
BCM and risk assessment and management	Project risk plan	Include details of earlier risk planning conducted for earlier procurement phases and highlight any risks that carry through to the contract management phase.
	Contract risk plan (risk log or risk register)	Insert details of contract risk planning, risks and mitigation strategies. Attach the completed contract risk plan to this CMP.
	Business continuity management (BCM) plan	In the event of a significant contractor failure, what work-around options do we have?

(Continued)

Table A3.1 *(Continued)*

Section	Outline	Detail
	Contract reviews	Outline regular reviews (for example, quarterly, annually). Detail how they will be conducted, including what data needs to be collected and by whom.
	Issue register	To record any issues (realized risks) that may arise and how they are to be managed, including by whom. At contract commencement, the creation of such a register is important.
	Dispute resolution process	Detail the trigger point(s) at which formal contract review becomes necessary due to under-performance. Detail any associated clauses specified in any tender documents and/or the contract. Detail procedures for addressing any dispute.
	Termination	Detail any clauses in the contract which may give rise to termination and detail the termination process to be followed.
Contract expiry	Renewal or extension	Outline the process to be followed in assessing whether to renew or extend a contract and the steps that need to be followed as the contract nears expiry. Keep in mind any termination notification requirements.
	Contract closure	List the tasks that are required to successfully complete and close the contract. For example, recovery of buyer-side material and equipment; handover procedures; security and access closure; contract evaluation, including the process and resources required (in-house or external); documentation of lessons learned; and notification to stakeholders.
Attachments	Numbered list of attachments to contract document	Depending on the type and scope of the contract, a variety of attachments may be required. Examples include compliance management, risk management plans, transition plans, invoicing and payment schedules, service level agreements, and user/client survey questionnaires.

APPENDIX 4
Project Memo format

PROJECT TITLE

PROJECT MEMO – COMMERCIAL, IN CONFIDENCE

TO: ....   PROJECT MEMO # ....

VIA: ....   PAGE 1 of ....

FROM: ....   Reply Requested?   YES   NO

DATE: ....   Date Reply Required ....

SUBJECT: ....

FAX No:/E-MAIL TO: ....

This message is not a Contract Variation/change authorization. Contract changes (changes to Contract Specification, scope, programme, prices etc) must be made in accordance with the terms of the Contract.

----

1 REFERENCES

2 DISCUSSION

3 ACTION REQUIRED

4 ATTACHMENTS

APPENDIX 5
Project Memo system – guidance notes

All formal communications between the parties on *technical* and *programme* issues are sequentially numbered and sent to a single point of contact in each organization, who will:

- maintain a register of incoming and outgoing Project Memos;
- distribute Project Memos to any internal addressee;
- ensure that Project Memos are properly actioned;
- make a monthly report of 'unclosed' Project Memos.

For incoming Project Memos, the register records the sequential number of the memo and date received, the addressee and the subject. The equivalent register of outgoing Project Memos records the sequential number, the date sent, name of originator, name of addressee and the subject. If this is strictly adhered to there is no possibility of communications going astray or being forgotten. Where Project Memo numbers indicate that some previous memos are missing, these are immediately requested and an effort made to discover why they were received out of sequence.

Project Memos are particularly useful in complex projects where both the buyer and seller have several team members who need to interact with each other regularly on technical issues. Simpler projects should use the same system as it represents 'good housekeeping' and is good training for junior staff on project management techniques and communication discipline. Whether commercial correspondence should be included is a matter for each organization to decide, *but with this important caveat*:

THE PROJECT MEMO CANNOT UNDER ANY CIRCUMSTANCES ALTER THE SCOPE OR COST OF THE PROJECT OR THE CONDITIONS OF CONTRACT. FOR THESE TO BE ALTERED, THE 'CONTRACT CHANGE' PROCEDURE SET OUT IN THE CONDITIONS OF CONTRACT MUST BE ADHERED TO.

An example Project Memo is given in Appendix 4. Note very carefully that the Project Memo format given uses words similar to those immediately above. Through *course of dealing* (an English contract law concept) it is difficult, but not impossible, for either party to point to a Project Memo and argue that it was in reality a contract change notice and that they 'acted' upon its instructions.

It might be appropriate in a project office environment for the memos to be sent as PDFs to a single point of contact via e-mail (or even faxed, although this technology is no longer widely used). Via this mechanism, the e-mails and attachments themselves are easy to archive.

Alternatively, these messages can be sent as formatted e-mails and electronically registered under sequential number. Indeed, this is the more likely approach in today's 'virtual' world.

APPENDIX 6
Basic Contract Materiality Review

Tab 1: Materiality review

BASIC CONTRACT MATERIALITY REVIEW (BCMR)		© Buy Research Limited 2008
Project Information Project Ref No: .... Proposed contract partner: (name) .... Planned commencement date: .... A) Sale: Goods or Services or both (G, S or G + S) .... (select A, B or C below) B) Purchase: Revenue OMGS expenses or Capital expenditure (R or C) .... C) Special: (detail)	**Assessed Materiality:**	**MEDIUM**
	Copies of BCMR, together with supporting text (see Tab 2) to be retained on project risk file for audit purposes. If high risk, relevant director or board member to be briefed and to countersign prior to contract entry.	

Five dimensions of Materiality

1) Contract Value: Income value/spend value = over £50M ○ Income value/spend value = £10M to £50M ○ Income value/spend value = £1M to £10M ○ Income value/spend value = up to £1M ●	**4) Legal Risk – contract/performance failure will expose our company to:** High damages, regulatory non-compliance, loss of advanced funding, loss of intellectual property. ● Moderate damages, possible regulatory issues, possible loss of funding or IPR. ○ Minor and containable impact. ○
2) Market Concentration Risk: Only one or two contract partners can deliver the benefit. ● There are a number of potential contract partners. ○ There are many potential contract partners. ○	**5) Reputation Risk – performance failure would involve:** Industry wide damage and/or make customers / other (third) parties cease commercial / trading relations with our company. Negative public comment and/or make other (third) parties reconsider their position re trading relations with our company. ● Limited dissatisfaction within customer / stakeholder community. ○
3) Risk entailed in Partner change during contract: Major risk to our company in changing contract partner. ○ Medium risk to our company in changing contract partner. ● Minor risk to our company in changing contract partner. ○	

BCMA Assessor (name) .... (Date) ....
Director (name) .... (Date) ....

Summary comment on reviewed materiality (free text)

Tab 2: Assessment notes

ASSESSMENT NOTES

© Buy Research Limited 2008

Assessors must provide below commentary to support their election on the five key dimensions on Tab 1. This helps to clarify thought, enables quick checking by company seniors and provides an audit trail.

Contract Value:

Legal Risk: contract/performance failure will expose our company to:

Market Concentration Risk:

Reputation Risk: performance failure would involve:

Risk entailed in Partner change during contract:

Notes on special aspects of risk or materiality not covered elsewhere:

Tab 3: Calculations

Dimension	Option	Materiality score	Selected		
1					
	a	50			
	b	15			
	c	10			
	d	5	4	Total question 1	5
2					
	a	15			
	b	5			
	c	3	3	Total question 2	3
3					
	a	20			
	b	10			
	c	5	3	Total question 3	3
4					
	a	25			
	b	15			
	c	10	1	Total question 4	25
5					
	a	25			
	b	15			
	c	5	2	Total question 5	15
Total score		53	**Materiality as a percentage**		25.75%
Materiality	MEDIUM				

Instructions for customization of document

Tab 1

All dotted lines can be double clicked and replaced with your desired text. Or they can be left and written on by hand on a print out, eg signatures.

For each of the five dimensions, only one radio button should be selected. If using Microsoft Office this should be enforced for you.

Tab 2

All dotted lines can be double clicked and replaced with your desired text.

Tab 3

The mathematics are relatively simple and allow for questions to be changed, eg for question 1 all the numerical values can be scaled down or up to match the size of your organization. But they must retain the same ratio; for example, all values could be reduced by one-third but you could not just reduce or increase the value for option A(50m). You could change one value but you must then change the materiality score to reflect this. (These values should not be changed unless you understand the consequences and mathematics behind them.)

APPENDIX 7
Vendor Relationship and Contracts Manager – job description

JOB TITLE: VENDOR RELATIONSHIP AND CONTRACTS MANAGER

REPORTS TO: HEAD OF [DEPARTMENT]

LOCATION: GRADE: DATE EVALUATED:

JOB PURPOSE: (1) Provide comprehensive and autonomous vendor and contract management of those contracts under his/her control and (2) promote and manage their development and operation through [Company]

KEY ACCOUNTABILITIES	MEASURES	DIMENSIONS
• Develop and manage performance against KPIs. • Resolve strategic and operational issues. • Liaise with vendor in a timely manner on relevant [Company] and contract developments. • Develop and manage continuous improvement programmes in line with Operating Company requirements. • Manage [Company] compliance. • Communicate to all stakeholders in a timely manner on all matters relevant to the contract. • Liaise with various [Company] corporate functions, eg HR, Tax, Legal, Finance, on developments/issues related to the contract. • Work with Global Supply Management on global opportunities and developments as required.	• Delivery of bottom-line savings and individual KPIs as agreed with Operating Companies measured through the benefits tracking system. • Expressed satisfaction of key stakeholders including [Company] senior managers and vendors measured through customer surveys and other feedback. • [Company] buy-in and compliance to contracts under his/her control measured through tracking of leakage and non-conformance reporting. • Demonstrates effective use of and compliance with [Company] processes and methodology.	**Financial:** Total contracts value in excess of £ [ ] per annum. Role has total responsibility and authority for managing contracts and vendors under his/her control. **People reporting:** None **Key relationships:** • Head of Corporate Services • Relevant vendor(s) • Operating Company • Procurement Department and other relevant internal stakeholders **Management Committees:** N/A

(Continued)

(Continued)

LEGAL REQUIREMENTS	SKILLS AND EXPERIENCE
Contracts and procurement processes used must comply with [state appropriate regulatory body] regulations.	**Education:** Graduate calibre or equivalent. Professional membership of the [Chartered Institute of Procurement and Supply]. **Skills:** Strong communication, negotiation and presentation skills. Excellent analytical skills and innovative in problem solving. Proficient in use of Microsoft tools. **Knowledge:** Detailed knowledge of contracts and vendor management processes. **Experience:** Minimum of 10 years' experience in Procurement, at least two of which have been gained in vendor management, preferably with blue chip companies. Experience in managing at least one of the following: ● outsourced fleet services; ● travel agency services; ● couriers or stationery.

Appendix 7 | Vendor Relationship and Contracts Manager

ROLE PROFILE OF ....

NAME OF JOB HOLDER ....

SIGNATURE OF JOB HOLDER ....

NAME OF LINE MANAGER ....

SIGNATURE OF LINE MANAGER ....

DATE ....

NAME OF HR DIRECTOR ....

SIGNATURE OF HR DIRECTOR ....

DATE ....

APPENDIX 8
Vendor manager – job description

JOB TITLE: VENDOR MANAGER

REPORTS TO: HEAD OF [DEPARTMENT]

LOCATION: GRADE: DATE EVALUATED:

Table App 8.1

JOB PURPOSE: Manage day-to-day supply relationships for [Department] to optimize value, ensure deliverables are fit for purpose and, where targeted, to deliver cost savings

KEY RESULTS	KEY PERFORMANCE INDICATORS	SKILLS AND EXPERIENCE	CORE BEHAVIOURS

• Manage relationships with supplier(s) to ensure service delivery and cost reduction in line with business strategy.
• Deliver maximum value and satisfaction to the customer from third-party suppliers.
• Lead day-to-day negotiations with supplier on an ongoing basis to maintain service and ensure contract deliverables are fit for purpose.
• Continually challenge operational requirements and supplier spend, identifying and critiquing cost and contract amendments.
	• Delivery of cost savings.
	• Supplier satisfaction – care, support and efficiency.
	• Supplier performance.
	  – Quality
	  – Cost
	  – Delivery
	• Regulatory requirements met [specify] for all contracted arrangements.
	• Contractual compliance.
	• Personal goals delivered.
		• Junior management-level experience in a commercial environment.
		• Sufficient knowledge of company management processes [specify], procurement concepts, and techniques including supplier performance metrics.
			Energize
			Coaching for exceptional performance
			Provoking extraordinary commitment
			Holding people accountable
			Building belief
			Mobilize
			Creating the future
			Focusing on customers
			Adopting quickly to change
			Drive
			Driving to win
			Being brave
			Demonstrating integrity

(*Continued*)

(Continued)

- Design and implement measures, KPIs and management reports to demonstrate supplier performance and value added.
- Ensure effective knowledge transfer.
- Benchmark services, collecting and analysing information on supplier(s), competitors and service/product innovations in order to inform strategy and negotiations.
- Where targeted, report and provide evidence to the Head of [Department] of cost savings and other financial or technical benefits delivered through the effective management of the supplier.

- Organizational ability.
- Load and update/maintain contracts on company contract database [specify]
- Understanding of process management methods and approaches.

Basic requirements:

- Project management skills.
- Commercial awareness.
- Analytical skills.
- Presentation, influencing and commercial negotiation skills.
- Internal relationship management and consulting skills.

Dimensions: Manage third-party supply relationship with a total influenceable spend of circa £ [   ] contract value. Influence key stakeholders and, where relevant, senior executives across [Company]

APPENDIX 9
Outsourced services: exit management – planning guidelines

Introduction

This Appendix helps commercial managers to consider and plan for contract exit. The principles explored will be relevant to both buyers and sellers, but this is written very much from the client (buyer) viewpoint. This Appendix:

1 explains the rationale for comprehensive exit planning at the appropriate step(s) of the process;
2 provides guidance on formulating an exit plan, including the identification of barriers to exit;
3 suggests methods of removing or minimizing barriers to exit;
4 explains the importance of contingency planning to strengthen preparedness for an unplanned exit (eg where the supplier goes bankrupt).

Referencing back to Figure 4.1 in Chapter 4, the optimum time for exploring these questions and determining our exit plan will be during the first three stages in the life of a contract, which we called 'Conception', 'Gestation' and 'Birth'.

In this Appendix, the terms Vendor Manager, Contract Manager, and Supplier Relationship Manager are used interchangeably. We bear in mind that some larger organizations will call their day-to-day controller of an outsourced service a 'Vendor Manager'. Whilst this Appendix has in mind larger 'outsourcing' arrangements, its principles are equally applicable to any strategic supply contract. Sales managers and other commercial managers will have their own perspective on 'exit' from a selling contract, and the issues this will entail.

Rationale for exit planning

Client-side sourcing/outsourcing arrangements, even those where these are likely to be long-term contracts, are essentially temporary in nature. However attractive a commercial proposition may be, subsequent changes in business requirements, or in the regulatory environment or changes in the marketplace, will eventually drive [Client Organization] to seek alternative supply arrangements. If business changes slowly and the supplier is responsive, this transition may take a long time. Poor supplier performance, however, or major business changes such as mergers and acquisitions, and the potential for bankruptcy in times of financial uncertainty, may accelerate the need to exit. For critical supply requirements and/or those where the market is limited to few competitors, it is vital to plan for exit and also to consider contingency planning to reduce the risk of a negative business impact if a supplier fails.

Purpose

The exit plan will:

- identify and manage all key risks associated with exit;
- minimize disruption to [Client Organization] operations due to a planned or unplanned exit from a sourcing arrangement;
- smooth the transition to any new supply arrangement;
- drive the exit activities in accordance with [Client Organization] agreement with the supplier;
- facilitate stakeholder engagement and communications;
- ensure the retrieval of [Client Organization] property from the supplier;
- ensure the return of the supplier's property from [Client Organization].

Responsibilities

We noted in Chapter 2 (and Figure 2.1) that there may be multiple people with responsibilities to 'deliver' a contract. Typically, however, when it comes to exit planning (especially in larger organizations where these roles may be highly defined), there are two managers who will assume greater day-to-day responsibility for planning the exit strategy:

1 **Sourcing Manager**: creates and signs off the initial exit plan. If the exit plan is created at the sourcing phase of an outsourcing project, then the Sourcing Manager will normally undertake this task using their market knowledge and understanding of the dynamics of this particular market, how many alternative suppliers there may be, and just how difficult it could be to 'procure' an alternative.

2 **Supplier Relationship Manager/Supplier Manager**:
   - develops the exit plan with contingency planning as required;
   - ensures that the exit plan details remain up to date;
   - ensures the exit plan is communicated to key stakeholders;
   - maintains the change log for the exit plan and updates copies with each change.

It is assumed that the SRM or Contract Manager will be closer to the practical details of how the contract works on a day-to-day basis, so will be well positioned to think through, and remain abreast of, these questions.

Note [Regulatory] requirements: The [Regulator] requires adequate exit strategies and contingency planning for all material outsourced activity. The plans must enable [Client Organization] to set up new arrangements as quickly as possible, minimizing service disruption. (NB: Not all organizations are governed by regulators in this way.)

Preparing an exit plan: exit barriers – due diligence

The optimum time to plan and agree exit arrangements is before the contract is signed. The analysis conducted during the early stages (as depicted in Figure 4.1 in Chapter 4) will help to identify the options available following contract exit, for example:

- re-source the services from an alternative supplier (identify and list potential alternative suppliers);
- transition to a managed service (list potential suppliers);
- bring the service back in-house (quantify in-house capability);
- re-negotiate with the existing provider.

Pre-contract due diligence on exit

Pre-contract due diligence will identify issues that may potentially drive early exit from the contract. For example:

- financial stability of the supplier;
- cash flow;
- strategic alignment;
- performance record;
- staff turnover;
- adequate controls (and fraud protection measures);
- adequate provisions for business continuity.

To be workable, an exit plan must:

- identify and minimize barriers to exit;
- create options for different exit routes (transition to a new supplier, transfer back to an in-house service etc);
- be workable under all likely scenarios including a dispute with the supplier, and an unplanned exit due to supplier termination or bankruptcy;
- be embedded into the initial contract, binding the supplier to support [Client Organization] exit.

The exit plan and the contract document must ensure that ultimate control over any critical business process always remains with the client organization.

The analyses undertaken during the conception, gestation and birth phases of a contract help us to assess potential barriers to taking the ultimate step of exiting from a contract. The barriers to exit are typically:

Financial barriers

- cost of re-sourcing or termination;
- one-off migration costs due to technology or other significant change;
- need for investment capital to bring a service back in-house.

Operational barriers

- impact of service disruption during transition;
- dependence on the supplier's infrastructure and services (especially those which are unique);
- lack of retained expertise within [Client Organization] (if outsourced);
- issues of ownership of intellectual property, or other unique or critical assets;
- ability to deal with management complexity;
- potential TUPE[1] issues (consult HR legal department).

Removing barriers to exit

There is considerable scope for creativity (and indeed flexibility) in the approach to removing exit barriers and for tailoring the exit plan to the specific circumstances of each proposed new contract. It is best practice to ensure that during the initial approach to the market (eg Request for Proposals (RFP) or Invitation to Tender (ITT) phases, which would typically take place in what we earlier called the 'gestation' period of a contract (see Figure 4.1)) we explore exit issues and deal with these in the subsequent pre-contract commercial negotiations.

Financial barriers

Some (but not all) financial barriers can be removed. A client organization can:

- secure the rights to buy back any assets required at a pre-determined price (link to the timing of exit and the cause);
- avoid penalties for early exit, considering the benefits of negotiating for all services to co-terminate with the master agreement;
- secure the rights to assume any subcontracts (step-in rights, assignment rights);
- secure the rights, at no charge, to information (data, IPR) required to maintain the service;
- agree the charges payable for the supplier's support through exit as part of the initial agreement;
- avoid fixed-volume commitments such as forward buying.

Operational barriers

Service disruption caused by migration can be reduced (but not avoided). A client organization can:

- ensure the supplier is contractually bound to provide access to everything required to maintain the service, such as intellectual property, manuals, assets, circuits, configuration information etc;
- retain, or buy in, the expertise required to manage the transition;
- avoid highly customized or proprietary solutions;
- avoid exclusivity clauses – retain the ability to use other sources of supply;
- ensure that service boundaries and ownership issues remain clear throughout the contract term;
- plan for exit well in advance (where the exit is a planned exit). Consider the practicalities of implementation timescales when planning the exit.

Other considerations

Confidence in our ability to manage termination and to switch suppliers can be enhanced by including well-crafted 'termination' provisions and associated key clauses in the contract. These clauses should cover as a minimum:

- right to terminate for non-performance – tailored closely to [Client Organization] service requirements;
- naming specific individuals or skill sets that are considered critical, and giving the right to terminate should they move off the account.

These elements should be agreed and specified in the contract. Clearly, once the contract has been signed and is underway, the supplier no longer has the incentive of active competition. In addition, it is preferable to factor reasonable exit costs into the contract pricing. This can best be done before the contract is signed.

Unplanned exit – contingency planning

Exit can also be forced upon us – and at relatively short notice – if service performance levels fall off dramatically or if there is a major business change affecting either [Client Organization] or the supplier. Where the service provided is critical, a contingency plan must be in place for such circumstances. The skills used to plan for this possibility are analogous to those used in BCM (business continuity management) planning.

Ongoing risk registration and associated due diligence throughout the contract term will assist identification of situations likely to necessitate early exit. This will help to give us additional time and early warning of the need to invoke the exit plan. The exit plan and any contingency arrangements must, periodically, be formally reviewed and updated in response to:

- due diligence findings – specifically business intelligence about changes in the marketplace;

- significant changes to [Client Organization] business strategy;
- changes to business or regulatory requirements;
- significant contract amendments that undermine the original business rationale of the contract.

Examples of such changes are:

a) consolidation in the marketplace, eg the supplier acquires major competitors, reducing the attractiveness of the re-sourcing option;

b) gradual customization of the service through the term of the contract which results in substantially increased switching costs;

c) loss of retained in-house capability which effectively removes the option to bring the service back in-house, or makes that option significantly more costly.

Other typical options to consider in contingency planning are to:

- discontinue the service (viable where the business impact is low);
- transfer the service to an alternative supplier (where alternative sources are available);
- retain sufficient in-house capability to replicate the service internally – either temporarily or permanently.

Further options may be available for individual sub-sets of the overall requirement. It is important to understand:

- **The time to implement**: for each of the contingency options, establish a reasonable timeline for invoking the option, and review this against the potential business impact of service disruption.
- **Cost implications**: assess the full cost of each contingency option. Include the service costs, costs associated with service disruption and any potential sanctions or penalty charges associated with each (eg regulatory penalties, late settlement charges or contractual costs).
- **Risk profile for each option**: assess any risk factors, including reputational risk, associated with a disruption in service. Perform a risk assessment for each option.

Exit planning: conclusion

A Client Organization's ability to exit a contract, especially a critical/major outsourced arrangement, where inevitably they have lost an element of control and/or reduced internal head count and skill base (and possibly TUPE'd the associated personnel across to the new service provider) means that they need to consider carefully the practicalities and risks associated with closing off the contract. We need to bear in mind that the need to exit may be forced upon us – so to have a practical plan to deal with the situation is really just good, old-fashioned, sound management! What follows below ('exit plan template') is a potential template that readers should be able to envision and adapt in their own business situation. As with all the materials in this book, it is necessary to think through how things work in your organization and in your business context. As a crib sheet, however, the exit plan template is a useful starting point to brainstorm what is appropriate in your context. Note that the text is designed with a major outsourcing in mind, in a highly regulated environment, where an external Regulator takes a practical interest in outsourcing arrangements within its regulated sector.

Exit plan template

Proposed Contract:

Proposed Supplier:

Version Control Detail:

Date of Issue:

Table of contents

Introduction	Section 1
Completed by Sourcing Manager	
Alternative Suppliers	Section 2
Completed by Sourcing Manager. Refreshed/updated periodically by Vendor Manager (Contract Manager)	
Retained in-house capability	Section 3
Completed by Sourcing Manager. Refreshed/updated periodically by Vendor Manager (Contract Manager)	
Factors and circumstances that might lead to termination	Section 4
Completed by Sourcing Manager. Refreshed/updated periodically by Vendor Manager (Contract Manager)	
Roles and Responsibilities	Section 5
Completed by Sourcing Manager. Refreshed/updated periodically by Vendor Manager (Contract Manager)	
Task List and Accountabilities	Section 6
Compiled and periodically updated by the Vendor Manager (Contract Manager)	
Communications Plan – external	Section 7
Completed by Sourcing Manager. Refreshed/updated periodically by Vendor Manager (Contract Manager)	
Communications Plan – internal	Section 8
Completed by Sourcing Manager. Refreshed/updated periodically by Vendor Manager (Contract Manager)	
Key Stakeholders – external	Section 9
Completed by Sourcing Manager. Refreshed/updated periodically by Vendor Manager (Contract Manager)	
Key Stakeholders – internal	Section 10
Completed by Sourcing Manager. Refreshed/updated periodically by Vendor Manager (Contract Manager)	

1 Introduction

[Company Name] proposes to enter-into a contract with [Supplier Name] for the supply of [Services, Goods] during the period [dates].

Under BCMR (Basic Contract Materiality Review) this contract has been assessed as [Exceptional] [High] [Medium] [Low] materiality. This plan has been prepared to consider the issues around contract exit, whether planned or unplanned.

The purpose of this plan is to identify:

- alternative potential suppliers for the services;
- contact points for an in-house capability if applicable;
- roles, responsibilities and contact points for core internal exit management team;
- activities that will be required in the event of both planned and unplanned exit, highlighting those that need to be completed on 'day one';
- stakeholders for communications cascade, both internal and external.

In addition it is to provide an outline communications plan for completion in event of decision to exit being taken.

2 Alternative suppliers

In the event of an exit decision being taken, it may be possible and appropriate to engage other external suppliers. The key contact points in each potential alternative supplier organization are:

Supplier name	Contact name and title	Telephone number and e-mail	Current supplier manager (if applicable)

3 Retained in-house capability [delete if inapplicable]

Where decision is taken to exit, it may be most appropriate to bring the services provided back in-house. If in-house capability is an option, the key internal contact details are identified below.

Contact name	Organizational area	Telephone number and e-mail

4 Factors that may lead to termination

Stated here are the factors identified as potentially giving rise to the need to exit the contract. This list is as exhaustive as we can reasonably make it, but focuses on issues that might impact service delivery. It takes into account what we know about market dynamics (business intelligence).

Also considered are factors that might lead the supplier to terminate the contract and/or to allocate to it a lower status within their organization (which might lead to poorer performance under the contract).

5 Roles and responsibilities

The Vendor Manager (Contract Manager) determines who is in place to take up key roles and responsibilities in the event of a decision to exit. These are listed overleaf.

Role	Name of individual	Telephone number and e-mail
Exit Manager	[Normally the Vendor Manager]	
Communications/ stakeholder management		
Legal and commercial		
HR (if required, eg for TUPE implications)		
Others		

6 Task list and accountabilities

The following two tables list tasks that are to be completed in the event of first an unplanned, then a planned, exit. At the time when the exit plan is invoked, the Vendor Manager should review the appropriate list, review the task list and plan timescales for completion of each task.

Unplanned exit

Task	Accountable	Timescale [to be completed at exit stage]
Ensure all in escalation path have been notified including *Approved Persons*	Vendor Manager	
Review/update Risk Assessment	Vendor Manager	
Invoke contingency (if applicable)	Accountable Executive	
Invocation of Exit Plan	Accountable Executive	
Engage Commercial Legal support	Vendor Manager	
Engage HR legal for TUPE (if applicable)	Vendor Manager	
Notify internal stakeholders – initiate regular internal communications	Vendor Manager – as per the Communications Plan	
[Regulator] notification via Compliance Department	Vendor Manager	(where relevant)
Engage retained in-house capability (if applicable)	Vendor Manager	
Obtain agreement to Exit from Legal	Vendor Manager	
Engage Procurement Department in order to re-source (if applicable)	Vendor Manager	

(*Continued*)

Contract Management

Unplanned exit (Continued)

Task	Accountable	Timescale [to be completed at exit stage]
Final notice to Supplier and notification of Exit Plan	Vendor Manager (nb: if this is sensitive a more senior person may do this)	
Targeted Communications to external stakeholders per Plan	Vendor Manager	
Ramp up in-house capability (if applicable)	HR Manager	
Engage secondary supplier (if applicable)	Vendor Manager and/or Procurement Department	
Channel new requirements to secondary supplier	Vendor Manager	
Migrate to contingency (if applicable)	Vendor Manager	
Staff Cascade	(as applicable)	
Notify Supplier Manager of sourcing timelines	Vendor Manager	
New Supplier Engagement (if applicable) per sourcing methodology	Vendor Manager and/or Procurement Department	
Agree implementation plan with new supplier (if applicable)	Vendor Manager and/or Procurement Department	
Commence Migration Activity	As applicable	
Exit services from existing supplier	Service Managers	
Retrieve all intellectual and other property from the supplier	Vendor Manager	
Migrate Services to new supplier	Service Managers	
In-scope staff captured by TUPE	Vendor Manager to coordinate with HR Department	
Targeted Communications at completion of Exit Plan	Per Comms Plan	

(Continued)

Unplanned exit (Continued)

Task	Accountable	Timescale [to be completed at exit stage]
Review to capture key learning and feed-back to vendor management community, Legal and Procurement	Vendor Manager	
Debrief exited supplier as appropriate	Vendor Manager	

Planned exit

Task	Accountable	Timescale [to be completed at exit stage]
Recommend non-renewal (if applicable)	Vendor Manager	
Remind escalation cascade of expiry date (if applicable)	Vendor Manager	
Notify [Regulator] Approved Persons	Vendor Manager	(where relevant)
Notice of non-renewal to Supplier	Vendor Manager to engage Contracts team or Legal	
Notify [Regulator] via Compliance	Vendor Manager	
Review/update Risk Assessment	Vendor Manager	
Invocation of Exit Plan	Accountable Executive	
Notify Procurement Department of re-source requirements	Vendor Manager	
Notify all key stakeholders	Per Comms Plan	
[List and detail contract exit provisions with timelines and internal actions]	Vendor Manager	
New Supplier Engagement (if applicable) per sourcing methodology	Vendor Manager and/or Procurement Department	

(Continued)

Planned exit (*Continued*)

Task	Accountable	Timescale [to be completed at exit stage]
Agree implementation plan with new supplier (if applicable)	Vendor Manager and/or Procurement Department	
Commence Migration Activity	As applicable	
Exit services from existing supplier	Service Managers	
Retrieve all intellectual and other property from the supplier	Vendor Manager	
Migrate services to new supplier	Service Managers	
In-scope staff captured by TUPE	Vendor Manager to coordinate with HR Dept	
Targeted communications at completion of Exit Plan	Per Comms Plan	

7 Communications plan – general

The Vendor Manager (Contract Manager) documents all relevant internal and external parties who will feature in any communications cascade, together with the types of messages that will be delivered. The following internal and external communications plan tables should be completed during the sourcing phase and associated contract negotiations. They will be refreshed and updated periodically by the Vendor Manager during BAU. The detailed communication plan table is guidance for the Vendor Manager as to what are the key messages. It will be completed at the time of a decision being taken to exit.

8 Communications plan – internal

Name	Department	Role	Telephone	Comments

9 Communications plan – external

Name	Title	Company	Contact details	Comments

10 Detailed communications plan (example/suggested format)

Communication to/purpose (info or Exit Plan action)	Name	Department/ contact	Date	Comments
All in escalation path notified				Message 1
All approved persons notified				Message 2
Engage Bus Risk Partner(s) – **action**				Message 1
Notify internal Sales or Marketing Department				If the supplier is also a customer of [our company]
Invoke financial contingency – **action**				Message 3
Update escalation path				Message 4
Invocation of Exit Plan – **action**				Accountable Exec
Update all in escalation				Message 5
Engage Commercial Legal – **action**				Message 2 If unplanned
HR legal for TUPE (if applicable) – **action**				Message 6
Comms/PR				Determine whether a reputational issue

(*Continued*)

(Continued)

Communication to/purpose (info or Exit Plan action)	Name	Department/ contact	Date	Comments
Notify other internal stakeholders (eg Risk, Finance) – info				Message 1 (updated)
Regular internal communication				Schedule into plan based on Exit timelines
[Regulator] Notification via Compliance				If applicable
Engage retained in-house capability (if applicable)				Invoke plan if applicable
Obtain agreement to Exit from Legal				If unplanned
Engage Procurement Department				Requirements for sourcing
Exiting Supplier				Termination notice
External stakeholder comms (eg customers, press, unions)				Various – as applicable

Factors likely to lead to termination

1 Unplanned exit

Factors leading [Client Organization] to terminate

Note: The Supplier Relationship Manager/Vendor Manager does not, in most organizations, have the authority to unilaterally terminate a contract or a supplier relationship. Organizations should never terminate a contract early, for any reason, without first engaging the Legal team (or Contracts team as appropriate).

Decline in supplier performance Where the supplier is in breach of the performance requirements in the contract, [Client Organization] will probably have some advance warning. Where performance trends are declining and this is not being remedied, the Vendor Manager must ensure that this is communicated, and that the need for 'unplanned' exit is anticipated. Legal should be alerted to this situation and will provide guidance on what can be done in anticipation of a material breach, without compromising [Client Organization] position.

Supplier discontinues service It is unusual for a supplier to stop a service without warning, but it can happen for a number of reasons. Not all stoppages give [Client Organization] the right to terminate the agreement. Refer to the specific contract provisions prior to engaging the Legal team for guidance on our termination rights.

Generally, [Client Organization] will not be able to terminate if the service disruption is due to circumstances beyond the reasonable control of the supplier (frustration of contract or force majeure), at least until this has continued for an agreed period of time. In this situation, contingency should be invoked.

Change in [Client Organization] business requirements Where [Client Organization] is considering terminating an agreement due to a change in its business requirements, the decision must be made in the context of a clear understanding of [Client Organization] termination rights under the agreement, the termination penalties, and costs which may be incurred for that specific point in time. If [Client Organization] does not have the right to terminate the agreement, then a termination may put us in breach of contract. This may affect all of our other rights, such as the recovery of materials, access to intellectual property etc. All of this needs to be considered and understood. Engage the Procurement and/or Legal team to assess [Client Organization] payment and other obligations at termination.

Factors leading the supplier to terminate

Supplier discontinues service The supplier's refusal to provide service without cause may be interpreted as the supplier effectively terminating the agreement without notice.

Supplier intends to discontinue service If [Client Organization] is told the supplier will discontinue service, or has reason to believe the supplier will discontinue service, and when notified, the supplier does not deny this, then the supplier has effectively terminated the agreement.

[Client Organization] in breach of contract Where the supplier is terminating for breach by [Client Organization], we can expect written notice in accordance with the contract. Guidance is required from the Legal team as soon as possible. The Supplier Manager must follow up the specific breach allegations and engage key stakeholders prior to any decision to invoke the exit strategy. It is also necessary to assess the cost implications and any penalties [Client Organization] is likely to incur.

2 Planned exit

Termination for convenience [Client Organization] may terminate for convenience in accordance with the provisions of the contract with the supplier. The decision to terminate should be taken well in advance of the deadline for serving notice in order to provide adequate time for a smooth transition.

Decision not to renew [Client Organization] may decide not to exercise a renewal option it has under the contract. The decision not to renew should be taken well in advance of the deadline for serving notice in order to provide adequate time for a smooth transition.

Expiration of the contract In the event of a fixed expiration date in the contract, the supplier will also be planning its exit from the service. It is particularly important that the exit plan starts early enough to manage the supplier through a smooth transition.

Time to re-source In developing the timelines for planned exit, ensure that adequate notice is provided to the Procurement Department for the sourcing process. This should reflect the complexity of the services provided.

Key issues

Managing supplier performance

Generally, with a planned exit, the supplier will receive notice well in advance of termination. The Supplier Manager must ensure that performance is maintained throughout the notice period and that key supplier personnel are not migrated to new accounts, where this will negatively impact the service into [Client Organization]. It is recommended that the frequency of performance review be increased during this very sensitive period.

Facilitating transition

In the event of a transition of the service to a new supplier, care must be taken to establish a working relationship between the incoming and outgoing suppliers. Particularly, any negative observations regarding the outgoing supplier, either by [Client Organization] or the incoming supplier must be avoided/actively discouraged. Stakeholder communications are key to the success of the transition.

Endnote

1 A UK-specific Regulation aimed to protect the employment rights of employees. TUPE refers to the Transfer of Undertakings (Protection of Employment) Regulations 2006 as amended by the Collective Redundancies and Transfer of Undertakings (Protection of Employment) (Amendment) Regulations 2014. TUPE rules apply to UK organizations of all sizes and protect employees' rights when the organization or service they work for transfers to a new employer.

APPENDIX 10
Contract variation – letter

Your reference:
Our reference:
Date:

Dear Sirs

Contract Ref No: **********

Variation No: **********

Subject: **********

I refer to our recent discussions relating to .... [and to your quotation/tender/letter dated ....] and confirm acceptance of your quotation/tender/letter. Accordingly, the Contract is hereby amended as follows:

1 Scope

[*Here describe the principal changes which give rise to the Contract Variation.*
Refer as appropriate to any revision to the Technical Specification.]

2 Contract Price

The Contract Price is hereby [increased/decreased] to £[   ] excluding VAT. The revised Contract Price is made up as follows:

Original Contract Price £[   ]

Variation Nos [n] to [n] aggregate £[   ]

This Variation £[   ]

Revised Contract Price £[   ]

3 Programme

The Contract completion date is amended to .... as a consequence of this Variation.

In all other respects the terms and conditions of the Contract remain unchanged. Please acknowledge receipt of this Contract Variation to the undersigned.

Yours faithfully

[Name]
Commercial Representative

Copies to: Commercial File/Supervising Officer/Others

APPENDIX 11
Formal written notification of unsatisfactory contract performance

Your reference:
Our reference:
Date:

Dear Sirs

Contract Ref No: **********

Subject: **********

[Name of organization] routinely assesses performance on all contracts as part of its contract monitoring procedures. It has come to our attention that your company's performance is unsatisfactory in the following areas:

[*Specify performance deficiencies and refer to relevant clauses in the SoW, technical specification and clauses of contract contained in the written contract document. Also specify required improvement activities and expected outputs.*]

We request please your immediate attention to [this deficiency/these deficiencies] and that you mobilize to correct such deficiencies by [date]. [*Note: this date may be influenced by specific clauses in the contract relating to deficiencies and remedies. Alternatively, the date will be whatever is considered to be reasonable in the circumstances.*]

If your company's performance does not reach the required standard within the remedial period specified, then, without prejudice to any other remedies available under the contract or at law, the matter will be escalated to senior management on both sides.

Appendix 11 | Formal Written Notification of Unsatisfactory Contract Performance

Please acknowledge receipt of this Notice and advise your intended compliance with it.

Yours faithfully

[Name]
Commercial Representative

Copies to: Commercial File/Supervising Officer/Others

APPENDIX 12
Formal written notification of improved contract performance

Your reference:
Our reference:
Date:

Dear Sirs

Contract Ref No: **********

Subject: **********

I refer to our letter dated [date] advising unsatisfactory performance under this contract, in relation to [outline previous deficiencies].

I am pleased to advise you that your company's performance now, without prejudice, meets the required standard.

It is of course important that this level of performance is maintained. As mentioned in our earlier letter, our contract monitoring procedures routinely assess performance on all contracts, so we will continue to monitor. [*If it is considered that enhanced monitoring is required for a period, then state this. However, it is assumed at this stage that the contractor has adequately responded to the deficiencies and is now focused on the ongoing task.*]

Thank you for responding to our earlier concerns.

Yours faithfully

[Name]
Commercial Representative

Copies to: Commercial File/Supervising Officer/Others

APPENDIX 13
Formal written notification – repeat of poor contract performance

Your reference:
Our reference:
Date:

Dear Sirs

Contract Ref No: **********

Subject: **********

I refer to previous correspondence dated [list] relating to variable and poor performance under this contract. I must formally draw your urgent attention to the fact that performance has again degraded to an unsatisfactory level.

[*Specify performance deficiencies and refer to relevant clauses in the SoW, technical specification and clauses of contract contained in the written contract document. Also specify required improvement activities and expected outputs.*]

We request please your immediate attention to this repeated deficiency and that you mobilize to correct such deficiencies urgently. [*It may be appropriate to specify a date for resumed satisfactory performance but to keep this vague may assist your negotiating position. If a date is to be given then, once again, it should be a reasonable period but the test of 'reasonableness' may now be at a lower threshold, allowing that this is a repeated delinquency under the contract.*]

In addition, we request an urgent meeting to explore this issue, without prejudice to any other remedies available to us under the contract or at law. We will call you to schedule a date and location.

Please acknowledge receipt of this Notice and advise your intended compliance with it.

Yours faithfully

[Name]
Commercial Representative

Copies to: Commercial File/Supervising Officer/Others

APPENDIX 14
Notices

Notice clauses are contained in many contracts. They specify the types of communication that must be handled in a specific and recordable manner ('Notices'). These clauses require the counterparties to formally notify each other in the event of certain defined circumstances, to give them the opportunity to respond to and deal with these circumstances. Care should be taken with the management of Notices as even a trivial error when giving notice might cause problems later – especially for the party that was relying on the Notice as the precursor to a formal contract claim.

Notice clauses generally allow the counterparties a specified period within which to remedy or deal with the problems/issues identified in the Notice. It is generally the Client/Buyer who issues such Notices, so they need to determine the existence of the problem *in sufficient time* to respond to them. Eternal vigilance is the key here! The Supplier or Contractor, however, can also issue formal Notices, generally where the other party is in default of some obligation on their part. Chapter 7 of this book contains a simple Notice clause for reference purposes.

Notices should make it clear what the counterparty is required to do where it is responsible for an issue such as delay, and consideration needs to be given whether to extend the completion date, or claim additional money. The specific wording of Notice clauses is easy to forget once contract work is underway. Where a contracting party fails to follow the precise terms of the contract document when giving a Notice, it may later find its contractual position is undermined; for example, it may not be entitled to make a formal financial claim on the other. When dealing with notice clauses, be careful to consider:

- giving notice and making claims; and
- practicalities.

Formal Notices

A Notice clause should be precise and unambiguous about what is required. It will typically include:

- what the Notice should look like;
- whether it can be sent by post, fax or e-mail, along with the address, fax number or e-mail address;
- the information it must contain;
- to whom it must be sent;
- the time limit for submitting it.

Contracting parties should comply with every requirement of the Notice clause. If they fail to do so, they are likely to undermine any right to make a subsequent claim.

A condition precedent is a condition that must be satisfied *before* something else can happen under a contract. In the context of claims, an entitlement to extra time and/or additional money can arise. Sometimes clauses use the words 'condition precedent' when describing the significance of a formal Notice, but even if these specific words are not used the clause may still have this effect. Parties should be wary, however, even where giving a Notice is not expressly described as a condition precedent. Failing to give notice in these circumstances may defeat a party's subsequent claim. Sometimes a Contractor may seek a waiver from a Buyer if it has failed to comply with a formal Notice requirement. Whether this will be granted, however, rather depends upon the goodwill of the buying organization!

Practicalities

Bear in mind that failing to give notice as required by the contract may give the counterparty/recipient the opportunity to challenge the Notice. This might prevent an otherwise valid claim from being successful. Other factors to keep in mind:

Notice by e-mail: today it would be surprising if a court decided that Notice by e-mail was not 'in writing'. Notice via e-mail does not have to be physically read; proof of delivery will be enough. However, a contract document could exclude e-mail as a valid form of Notice. Plainly this matter is for the parties to decide in the pre-contract discussions.

Service 'by any effective means': English courts have considered this wording when it has been used in contracts. They have tended to determine that this phrase includes e-mail, post, hand delivery and fax, provided delivery can be proved.

Who should serve a Notice? Notices should be served by a party authorized to do so under the contract. Commercial organizations should take additional care where Agents have the authority to give and receive notices on behalf of a contracting party. Some Agents may not have this authority, even where they think that they do!

Address for service of notice: the contract document should contain a specific address for the service of notices, and the procedure for notifying any changes of this address. The contract should name a company officer, for example the Company Secretary, as opposed to an individual, as the recipient. This allows for the reality of changes in personnel after a contract has been signed. If a contract with a UK company does not contain a notice clause, Notice can still generally be served at the company's registered UK office.

Personal delivery: this means delivery to an individual, which can be anybody at the address for service. It includes, for example, a clerk or receptionist, as opposed to the person who is actually best placed to deal with the Notice. Ensure that the contract document specifies by name the person the Notice should go to, for example the Company Secretary, to help avoid it being lost in the recipient's internal mail!

Delivery by 'registered post': as this mail facility no longer exists it will be sufficient to send a Notice by an equivalent mail delivery service. Remember to retain a proof of delivery!

Deemed receipt: Some modern contracts might specify that a letter, fax or e-mail is deemed to have been delivered once a specified period of time has elapsed from its being sent. This means that, for the purposes of the contract, a Notice has been delivered unless the recipient can prove that this did not happen. Keep in mind that proof of sending is required. Examples of such 'proof' include recorded delivery slips, certificates of posting, fax transmission reports and e-mail delivery receipts. Should there be a proof of *non-delivery* such as the 'return to the sender' of a recorded delivery letter, this will override the deemed delivery.

APPENDIX 15
A dozen things I wish they'd told me when I started

1. Just because it's written in black and white, it doesn't mean it will happen.
2. A dog is a man's best friend; *questions* are the Contract Manager's best friend.
3. Technical expertise on subject matter is helpful – but not essential – for the Contract Manager. But a strategy to cover a knowledge gap is! *('A fool is a man who knows not – and knows not that he knows not...')*
4. Red sky at night, shepherd's delight; red sky at morning, shepherd's warning. Learn to 'read' the signs when business interests/alignment is changing.
5. Knowledge ('know-how') transfer is as important as physical transfer of property (that's what we mean by intellectual property).
6. Communications can become unstructured negotiations – so beware!
7. Just because you have 'penalties' and 'pain' clauses, it doesn't mean you need to use them as a weapon – or a threat.
8. If you have to revert to the contract document details, then your SRM (CRM) has failed.
9. Contract management is not the same as SRM (CRM).
10. Know the contract – but don't blow the contract!
11. Even in litigation, continue to negotiate and settle without going to court – if possible ('without prejudice').
12. If a contract is good it deserves to have a good Contract Manager!

APPENDIX 16
Conditions of contract for purchase

Buy Research 2016: Conditions of contract for purchase

1 Definitions

1.1 'Buyer' means the person, firm or company so named in the Purchase Order.

1.2 'Seller' means the person, firm or company to whom the Purchase Order is issued and is named on it.

1.3 'Goods' means all goods covered by the Purchase Order including raw materials, processed materials or fabricated products and listed on the Purchase Order.

1.4 'Purchase Order' means Buyer's Purchase Order which specifies that these conditions apply to it.

1.5 'The Contract' means the contract between the Buyer and Seller consisting of the Purchase Order, these conditions and any other documents (or parts thereof) specified in the Purchase Order. Should there be any inconsistency between the documents comprising the Contract they shall have precedence in the order herein listed.

2 Quality

In the absence of a specification referred to on the Purchase Order or sample, all goods supplied shall be of satisfactory quality and fit for their purpose.

3 Delivery date

The date of delivery of goods shall be that specified in the Purchase Order unless agreed otherwise between Buyer and Seller. Seller shall furnish such programmes of manufacture and delivery as Buyer may reasonably require and Seller shall give notice to Buyer as soon as practicable if such programmes are, or are likely to be, delayed.

4 Incorrect delivery

All goods must be delivered at the delivery point specified in the Purchase Order.

5 Passing of property and risk to Buyer

The property and risk in the goods shall remain in Seller until they are delivered at the point specified in the Purchase Order.

6 Terms of payment

Unless otherwise stated in the Purchase Order, payment will be made within 28 days of receipt and agreement of invoice.

Value Added Tax, where applicable, shall be shown separately on all invoices as a strictly net extra charge.

7 Loss or damage in transit

7.1 Buyer shall advise Seller and the carrier (if any) in writing, otherwise than by a qualified signature on any Delivery Note, of any loss or damage within the following time limits:

7.1 (a) Partial loss, damage, defects or non-delivery of any separate part of a consignment shall be advised within seven days of date of delivery of the consignment or part consignment. Non-delivery of whole consignment shall be advised within 21 days of notice of dispatch.

7.1 (b) Non-delivery of whole consignment shall be advised within 21 days of notice of dispatch.

7.2 Seller shall make good free of charge to Buyer any loss of or damage to or defect in the goods where notice is given by Buyer in compliance with this condition provided that Buyer shall not in any event claim damage in respect of loss of profits.

8 Acceptance

In the case of goods delivered by Seller not conforming with the Contract, whether by reason of being of quality or in a quantity measurement not stipulated or being unfit for the purpose for which they are required where such purpose has been made known in writing to Seller, Buyer shall have the right to reject such goods within a reasonable time of their delivery and to purchase elsewhere as near as practicable to the same Contract specifications and conditions as circumstances shall permit but without prejudice to any other right which Buyer might have against Seller. The making of payment shall not prejudice Buyer's right of rejection. Before exercising the said right to purchase elsewhere Buyer shall give Seller reasonable opportunity to replace rejected goods with goods which conform to the Contract.

9 Variations

9.1 Seller shall not alter any of the goods, except as directed in writing by Buyer; but Buyer shall have the right, from time to time during the execution of the Contract, by notice in writing to direct Seller to add to or omit, or otherwise vary, the goods, and Seller shall carry out such variations and be bound by the same conditions, so far as applicable, as though the said variations were stated in the Contract.

9.2 Where Seller receives any such direction from Buyer which would occasion an amendment to the Contract Price, Seller shall, with all possible speed, advise Buyer in writing to that effect, giving the amount of any such amendment, ascertained and determined at the same level of pricing as that contained in Seller's tender.

9.3 If, in the opinion of Seller, any such direction is likely to prevent Seller from fulfilling any of his obligations under the Contract he shall so notify Buyer and Buyer shall decide with all possible speed whether or not the same shall be carried out and shall confirm his instructions in writing and modify the said obligations to such an extent as may be justified. Until Buyer so confirms his instructions they shall be deemed not to have been given.

10 Intellectual property rights

10.1 Seller will indemnify Buyer against any claim for infringement of patents, designs or registered designs, trade mark or copyright by the use or sale of any article or material supplied by Seller to Buyer and against all costs and damages (including legal fees) which the Buyer may incur in any action for such infringement or for which Buyer may become liable in such action. Provided always that this indemnity shall not apply to any infringement which is due to Seller having followed a design or instruction furnished or given by Buyer or to the use of such article or material in a manner or for a purpose or in a foreign country not specified by or disclosed to Seller, or to any infringement which is due to the use of such article or material in association or combination with any other article or material not supplied by Seller. Provided also that this indemnity is conditional on Buyer giving to Seller the earliest possible notice in writing of any claim being made or action threatened or brought against Buyer.

10.2 All intellectual property rights in works, goods or materials produced for Buyer by Seller or specifically commissioned by Seller from Buyer shall vest in Buyer and Seller undertakes to execute all documents required to ensure such ownership.

11 Force majeure

Neither party shall be liable for failure to perform its obligations under the Contract if such failure results from circumstances which could not have been contemplated and which are beyond the party's reasonable control. Force majeure does not include strikes or industrial disputes or failures of sub-contractors.

12 Progress and inspection

Buyer's representatives shall have the right to progress and inspect all goods at Seller's works and the works of sub-contractors at all reasonable times and to reject goods that do not comply with the terms of the Contract. Seller's subcontracts shall include this provision. Any inspection, checking, approval or acceptance given on behalf of Buyer shall not relieve Seller or his sub-contractors from any obligation under the Contract.

13 Buyer's rights in specifications, plans, drawings, patterns

Any specifications, plans, drawings, patterns or designs supplied by Buyer to Seller in connection with the Contract shall remain the property of Buyer, and any information derived therefrom or otherwise communicated to Seller in connection with the Contract shall be regarded by Seller as secret and confidential and shall not, without the consent in writing of Buyer, be published or disclosed to any third party, or made use of by Seller except for the purpose of implementing the Contract.

14 Responsibility for information

Seller shall be responsible for any errors or omissions in any drawings, calculations, packing details or other particulars supplied by him, whether such information has been approved by Buyer or not, provided that such errors or omissions are not due to inaccurate information furnished in writing by Buyer.

15 Assignment and sub-letting

The Contract shall not be assigned by Seller nor sub-let as a whole. Seller shall not sub-let any part of the work without Buyer's written consent, but the restriction contained in this clause shall not apply to sub-contracts for materials, for minor details, or for any part of which the makers are named in the Contract. Seller shall be responsible for all work done and goods supplied by all subcontractors.

16 Copies of sub-orders

When Buyer has consented to the placing of sub-contracts, copies of each sub-order shall be sent by Seller to Buyer immediately it is issued.

17 Deterioration

Except where stated otherwise in Buyer's Purchase Order, Seller shall protect any item or part that might deteriorate during transportation or storage.

18 Free issue materials

Where Buyer for the purposes of the Contract issues materials free of charge to Seller, such materials shall be and remain the property of Buyer. Seller shall maintain all such materials in good order and condition subject, in the case of tooling, patterns and the like, to fair wear and tear. Seller shall use such material solely in connection with the Contract. Any surplus materials shall be disposed of at Buyer's discretion. Waste of such materials arising from bad workmanship or negligence of Seller shall be made good at Seller's expense. Without prejudice to any other of the rights of the Buyer, Seller shall deliver up such materials whether further processed or not to Buyer on demand.

19 Warranty

Seller shall as soon as reasonably practicable repair or replace all goods which are or become defective during the period of 12 months from putting into service or 18 months from delivery, whichever shall be the shorter, where such defects occur under proper usage and are due to faulty design, Seller's erroneous instructions as to use or erroneous use data, or inadequate or faulty materials or workmanship, or any other breach of Seller's warranties, express or implied. Repairs and replacements shall themselves be subject to the foregoing obligations for a period of 12 months from the date of delivery, reinstallation or passing of tests (if any), whichever is appropriate after repair or replacement. Seller shall further be liable in damages (if any) in respect of each Purchase Order, provided that such damages and losses were reasonably foreseeable.

20 Insolvency and bankruptcy

If Seller becomes insolvent or bankrupt or (being a Company) makes an arrangement with its creditors or has an administrative receiver or administrator appointed or commences to be wound up (other than for the purposes of amalgamation or reconstruction), Buyer may, without prejudice to any other of his rights, terminate the Contract forthwith by notice to Seller or any person in whom the Contract may have become vested.

21 General conditions in the tender

No conditions submitted or referred to by Seller when tendering shall form part of the Contract unless otherwise agreed to in writing by Buyer.

22 Applicable law and jurisdiction

This contract shall be subject to English law and the parties submit to the exclusive jurisdiction of the English Courts.

23 Notices

Any notice to be sent under this Agreement should be sent to the addresses given on page one and served personally or by pre-paid registered or recorded delivery letter or fax confirmed by first class post. Letters shall be deemed served 48 hours after posting and fax on despatch.

24 Waiver

No delay or omission by Buyer in exercising any of its rights or remedies under this Agreement or under any applicable law on any occasion shall be deemed a waiver of, or bar to, the exercise of such right or remedy or any other right or remedy upon any other occasion.

25 Headings

The headings in this Agreement are for ease of reference and shall not affect the construction thereof.

26 Severance

In the event that any provision of this Agreement shall be void or unenforceable by reason of any provision or applicable law, it shall be deleted and the remaining provisions hereof shall continue in full force and effect and, if necessary, be so amended as shall be necessary to give effect to the spirit of the Agreement so far as possible.

Supplementary conditions

These conditions shall apply only where specifically named in the Purchase Order.

27 Consignment stock

Where Seller delivers and houses stock at Buyer's premises, then Buyer shall use reasonable endeavours to protect and control said stock, but risk in and responsibility to provide insurance for said stock shall remain with Seller.

Where Buyer delivers and houses stock at Seller's premises, then Seller shall use reasonable endeavours to protect and control said stock. Furthermore, said stock shall be clearly marked and identified as being property of Buyer and Buyer shall have the absolute right on giving reasonable notice (two working days, in writing) to enter Seller's premises in order to (a) inspect and stock-check said stock and/or (b) to recover said stock. In this latter case, Seller shall provide suitable assistance to enable Buyer to recover its consignment stock efficiently and without let or hindrance. Unless otherwise agreed in writing, Seller shall insure such stock under its general insurance scheme and shall, if requested, provide to Buyer suitable evidence that said insurance is carried. Buyer shall provide information reasonably required as to the insurance value of any such stock held by Seller.

28 Price indexation

The price for the supply of [material name] shall be the price stated in the Purchase Order. Should the published index price for [material name] move either up or down by more than 2 per cent during the period of this Contract, then the requisite sum shall be added to, or deducted from the Contract Price. The index by which said prices shall be measured is [name of index]. The Base date for calculations shall be [date – as set out in the Purchase Order] [*normally the date of the Purchase Order*].

An example of how such price shall be calculated is given below:

Index price at date of order (base date) = 100.
Index price at date of measurement = 103.
Price increase = 3 per cent.
Accordingly, price or order moves up by 3 per cent.

APPENDIX 17
Master Services Agreement: Buy Research 2016

Note to readers: this appendix, as its title suggests, is a template Master Services Agreement. It might be used, with suitable amendments, in conjunction with Appendix 19 (model Statement of Work); however, the two were not originally designed with each other in mind.

This appendix is included to draw readers' attention to specific terms that the client side (buyer) utilize in order to maintain a good grasp of overall performance. In this regard, clauses 2.2, 2.3, 4.7, 4.8, 6 (all), 7.1, 9.1, 9.2, 10.1, 11.1, 13.3, 16.1, 17.2 and 18.4 are each considered to represent good standard practice in terms of maintaining a proper 'management' stance with regard to the counterparty.

Master Services Agreement

Parties to the Agreement

This Master Services Agreement (hereinafter referred to as the 'Agreement') with an effective date of [Enter Date] ('Effective Date') is made between Buy Research Limited, a company incorporated under the laws of England and Wales (company registration number XXXXXXX), whose registered address is at XXXXXXX (hereinafter referred to as 'Buy Research'), and [Enter Name of Service Provider], a company incorporated under the laws of [Enter Country] (company registration number XXXXXXX), whose registered address is at [Enter Service Provider's address] (hereinafter referred to as 'Service Provider'). Buy Research and the Service Provider may be referred to hereinafter collectively as the 'Parties' and separately as a 'Party'. Unless otherwise specified herein, references to this 'Agreement' shall include any and all related Attachments appended to this Agreement ('Attachments') and Orders as defined below. In consideration of the mutual promises herein contained, the receipt and sufficiency of which are hereby acknowledged, Buy Research and the Service Provider agree as follows:

1 Definitions

Unless the context otherwise requires, the following words and expressions shall have the meanings hereby assigned to them.

1.1 'Affiliate' shall mean any Person that, directly or indirectly, controls, is controlled by, or is under common control with another Person. A Person shall be deemed to control another Person if the controlling Person possesses, directly or indirectly, the power to direct or cause the direction of the management or policies of the controlled Person, whether through share ownership, the power to elect or appoint the board of directors or trustees, by contract, or otherwise.

1.2 'Authorized Buying Entities' shall have the meaning set forth in Section 2.3 hereof.

1.3 'Buy Research's Authorized Representative' shall have the meaning set forth in Section 3.3 hereof.

1.4 'Free-Issue Materials' shall mean all materials or equipment provided by Buy Research free of charge to the Service Provider for use in the provision of the Services.

1.5 'On-Site Personnel' shall mean employees, consultants, subcontractors or other personnel employed or engaged by the Service Provider to perform Services on its behalf at a Buy Research facility.

1.6 'Order' shall mean an order provided by Buy Research or an Authorized Buying Entity to Service Provider for the purchase and delivery of Services to a location specified by Buy Research or an Authorized Buying Entity pursuant to this Agreement. An Order may include, without limitation: (1) a purchase order; (2) a statement of work; (3) a website order; and/or (4) a procurement card order. All Orders shall be accompanied by a corresponding control number and subject to the terms and conditions contained herein, whether such Order references this Agreement or not.

1.7 'Person' shall mean any individual, partnership, corporation, firm, association, unincorporated organization, joint venture, trust or other entity.

1.8 'Service Charge' shall have the meaning set forth in Section 5.1 hereof.

1.9 'Service Provider's Authorized Representative' shall have the meaning set forth in Section 4.5 hereof.

1.10 'Services' shall mean all services to be carried out, or intended to be carried out, by the Service Provider in accordance with the Agreement, as described in Attachment B. Each Order shall contain a full description of the specific services the Service Provider shall provide on a case-by-case basis.

1.11 'Site' shall mean the area within or adjacent to Buy Research's existing plant or any other facility identified in the Agreement where the Services are to be carried out, or any other area that Buy Research may designate as the Site.

1.12 '**Term**' shall mean the Initial Term and all Extended Terms, if any (each expression being defined in Section 17).

1.13 '**Third Party Contractor**' shall mean a subcontractor of any tier, an entity or individual that is not an employee of the Service Provider to whom the performance of any part of the Service has been subcontracted in accordance with Section 18.4.

2 Services

2.1 General. Buy Research hereby retains the Service Provider, and the Service Provider hereby agrees to perform services relating to [*outline/summary description services to be provided*], as fully described in Attachment B. The specific services required of the Service Provider shall be more fully described in one or more Orders referencing this Agreement.

2.2 Orders. The Parties agree and acknowledge that Buy Research shall have no obligation to order or purchase any Services by virtue of this Agreement alone. In the event that Buy Research requires Services hereunder, Buy Research shall issue an Order to the Service Provider stating, at a minimum, the description and quantity of the Services being ordered and the required date(s) for delivery of such Services. The Service Provider shall not deliver and shall not be required to deliver any Services prior to its receipt of a validly executed Order for such Services. In no event shall Buy Research be required to compensate the Service Provider for any Services rendered in the absence of an Order executed by an authorized purchasing representative.

2.3 Authorized Buying Entities. Only Buy Research or an entity listed on Attachment A (each an 'Authorized Buying Entity') may place Orders for Services under this Agreement. An Affiliate may become an Authorized Buying Entity or have its status as an Authorized Buying Entity revoked only by a written amendment of Attachment A signed by Buy Research. Buy Research shall promptly notify the Service Provider of any such amendment to Attachment A. Buy Research warrants and represents to the Service Provider that the Authorized Buying Entities listed on Attachment A are Affiliates of Buy Research. If at any time during this Agreement any entity listed on Attachment A ceases to be a Buy Research Affiliate, Buy Research shall so notify the Service Provider, and such entity shall be removed from Attachment A and shall no longer be an Authorized Buying Entity. Removal of an Authorized Buying Entity from Attachment A shall not, alone, release such Authorized Buying Entity from its obligations hereunder. Buy Research and the Service Provider each acknowledge and agree that the terms and conditions of this Agreement shall apply to all Orders submitted by any of the Authorized Buying Entities during the Term. The placement of an Order by an Authorized Buying Entity constitutes such Authorized Buying Entity's agreement to abide by the terms of this Agreement and the acceptance that the terms and conditions of this Agreement govern such Order. If an Authorized Buying Entity places an Order under this Agreement, the Parties agree that all of Buy Research's rights, licenses and other benefits under this Agreement shall extend to such Authorized Buying Entity with respect to the Services ordered, and that the defined term 'Buy Research' shall be deemed to include such Authorized Buying Entity, as applicable.

2.4 **Ownership of Results.** All specifications, drawings, sketches, text, data, documents and other results (collectively the 'Results'), which are created, developed or delivered by the Service Provider to Buy Research in the performance of the Services under this Agreement, are and shall remain the property of Buy Research. Service Provider hereby transfers all of its intellectual property rights in the Results, including but not limited to copyrights and design rights, to Buy Research, and agrees to sign and execute any document that may be legally required to accomplish such transfer.

3 Buy Research's Responsibilities

3.1 **Site Access.** Buy Research shall, subject to any operational restrictions, allow the Service Provider safe, free and non-exclusive access to the Site for the purposes of carrying out the Services in accordance with the Agreement.

3.2 Free-Issue Materials. If the Order requires Buy Research to provide Free-Issue Materials, facilities or services to the Service Provider in connection with the performance of the Service then such Free-Issue Materials, facilities or services shall be provided at the times specified in the Order, or if no times are specified then at reasonable times having regard to the progress and completion of the Services.

3.3 Authorized Representative. Buy Research shall appoint an authorized representative for the purpose of liaison with the Service Provider ('Buy Research's Authorized Representative') and shall advise the Service Provider in writing of such appointment. Any instructions given to the Service Provider in writing by such representative shall be deemed to have been given by Buy Research.

4 Service Provider's Responsibilities

4.1 General. The Service Provider shall be deemed to have fully understood the nature of the Services to be carried out and to have satisfied itself of the condition and circumstances affecting or likely to affect the Site and/or the carrying out of the Services. Accordingly, no claim by the Service Provider for additional payment or extension to time will be allowed on the grounds of any matter relating to misunderstanding or misinterpretation in relation to the provision of Services, nor shall such ground release the Service Provider from any contractual obligations.

4.2 Performance. The Service Provider warrants that during the Term, all Services provided to Buy Research shall be performed in a timely manner and in accordance with all the terms and conditions of this Agreement and any Order issued hereunder. If the Service Provider anticipates any delay in the performance of the Services, the Service Provider shall promptly notify this to Buy Research in writing, indicating at the same time the reason(s) for the delay.

4.3 Instructions. The Service Provider shall promptly comply with instructions, authorizations and notices given by Buy Research's Authorized Representative.

4.4 Resources. Unless it is expressly stated in the Order that Buy Research is to provide Free-Issue Materials, the Service Provider shall provide all supervision, labour, materials, equipment and other resources (including financial resources) required for the timely execution of the Services.

4.5 Authorized Representative. The Service Provider shall appoint an authorized representative ('Service Provider's Authorized Representative') for the purpose of liaison with Buy Research and shall advise Buy Research in writing of such appointment. The Service Provider's Authorized Representative shall be an appropriately qualified and experienced member of the Service Provider's staff and shall have full authority to represent the Service Provider in all matters and at all times during the performance of the Services. The Service Provider shall not replace such representative without the approval of Buy Research.

4.6 Documents and Records. The Service Provider shall: (i) provide Buy Research with such reports, specifications, drawings, models, budgets, and the like, as are appropriate to the nature of the Services to be performed hereunder; (ii) keep accurate records of hours worked; and (iii) make such records available to Buy Research's Authorized Representative for examination upon reasonable notice to Service Provider. The Service Provider shall ensure that all designs prepared by the Service Provider shall comply with all applicable laws, ordinances, permits, regulations of governmental authorities, insurance rules and instructions applicable to the provision of the Services.

4.7 Personnel. In the performance of the Services the Service Provider shall only use employees (i) who are named on the Order related to such Services, or for which the Service Provider has received Buy Research's prior written authorization, and (ii) who are bound by obligations of confidentiality and non-disclosure which are not less stringent than those contained in Section 14. Such personnel shall not be replaced by the Service Provider without the prior written consent of Buy Research, which consent shall not be withheld unreasonably.

4.8 Personnel Identity Card. The Service Provider shall provide for its employees, servants and agents employed in connection with the Agreement a form of identity card for the period they are working on the Site. They shall be required to produce this identity card whenever required by Buy Research.

5 Fees and Payment Terms

5.1 Pricing and Fees. All pricing, fees and other charges to be paid by Buy Research to the Service Provider in connection with Services (hereinafter the 'Service Charge') shall be included in detail in Attachment B. Buy Research shall have no liability, whatsoever, for any charges not included on a properly executed Order.

5.2 Price Adjustments. The prices and discounts set forth in Attachment B shall be guaranteed for [specify agreed period] years following the Effective Date of this Agreement. Thereafter, Service Provider has the right but not the obligation to increase the Service Charge once during any subsequent twelve (12) month period and shall give Buy Research sixty (60) days written notice prior to the effective date of any price changes hereunder. Cumulatively, no price increases during any subsequent twelve (12) month period shall exceed the lower of: (a) three per cent (3%) or (b) the percentage by which the RPI (defined below) increased during the prior twelve (12) month period. 'RPI' means the Retail Price Index as published by the UK Office for National Statistics. Any price decreases for the Services, whether during the Initial Term or any extension thereof, shall be passed on to Buy Research within thirty (30) days of the Service Provider's effective date for any such price decrease.

5.3 Policies. Each Order shall describe in detail all policies and procedures applicable to the Services covered by such Order, including, without limitation, description of any deposits required and any applicable cancellation and refund policies. Each Order shall also clearly describe the acceptable method(s) of payment, and shall set forth in detail the payment terms and/or a payment schedule.

5.4 Payment Terms. Payment terms are thirty (30) days net from date of invoice unless stated otherwise on a related Order.

5.5 Taxes and Applicable Duties. In addition to the Service Charge, Buy Research shall pay to the Service Provider the amount of any applicable sales, use or value-added tax (if applicable) that is imposed as a result of, or measured by, any Services provided hereunder. The value of which is to be shown separately on each invoice.

5.6 Invoicing. The Service Provider shall send to Buy Research either a paper or an electronic invoice for Services provided. Details of invoice frequency agreed and invoice address shall be as specified within the Order.

5.7 Credit Cards. The Service Provider accepts that Buy Research, in sole discretion, may use credit cards including 'procurement cards' to pay any amounts due. The Service Provider will assist Buy Research in arriving at a mutually agreed procedure to suit this application.

5.8 Time and Materials. The Services will be provided on a time and materials basis as further specified in each Order. The Service Provider shall use all commercial reasonable efforts to ensure that, except as a result of a Variation Order as defined in Section 7, the total cost of the Services will not exceed the price estimate as specified in the applicable Order (the 'Budget'). The Parties, however, do acknowledge that in the event that circumstances outside of the Service Provider's control or within the responsibility of Buy Research cause delay to the execution of the Services, this may have an impact on the total costs. If these circumstances occur, the Service Provider will alert Buy Research on the risk and the consequences of these circumstances and will seek upfront written approval from Buy Research for overruns on the Budget before additional costs are made.

5.9 Interest for Late Payment. If any amount payable pursuant to or in connection with this Agreement is not paid when it is due then that amount will bear interest at the rate of two (2) per cent per annum over the base rate of the Bank of England from time to time calculated on a daily basis for the period from the due date to the date of actual payment in full, both before and after any judgment. The Parties agree that this paragraph 5.9 is a substantial remedy for late payment of any sum payable pursuant to or in connection with this Agreement in accordance with section 8(2) of the Late Payment of Commercial Debts (Interest) Act 1998.

6 Acceptance and Non-conformance

6.1 **Progress and Inspection.** The Service Provider shall permit Buy Research employees and representatives to observe and inspect from time to time Service Provider's performance of Services and the results thereof whether on the Site or in the premises of the Service Provider.

6.2 **Rejection.** Buy Research will designate an individual who has the responsibility to review and approve the Services identified in the applicable Order. Buy Research may reject any Services that are not (a) complete, (b) in conformance with this Agreement and the specifications set forth in the applicable Order, and/or (c) delivered in the timeframe set forth in the applicable Order (a 'Deficient Service').

6.3 **Correction.** In the event that Buy Research rejects Services as set forth in Section 6.2, Buy Research shall so notify the Service Provider, and the Service Provider shall correct the deficiencies identified by Buy Research within a reasonable time period, as notified by Buy Research. The Service Provider shall bear the entire cost and expense of any such corrections under this Section 6.3.

6.4 **Defective Service.** If the Service Provider is unable to correct the deficiencies within the designated time period, Buy Research may, at its option, terminate this Agreement and/or a particular Order without any liability whatsoever. Buy Research shall incur no payment obligations for any Services unless and until such Services are accepted by Buy Research, except that Buy Research shall pay the Service Provider any balance due for previously delivered and accepted Services if such accepted Services are not dependent upon delivery and function of Deficient Services.

7 Variation

7.1 Variation Notice. Buy Research may, without invalidating this Agreement, serve notice in writing to the Service Provider to vary the Services ordered under an Order in any respect (hereinafter a 'Variation Notice'). Any such Variation Notice may include a reduction or increase in scope of Services, or a requirement for additions, deletions, substitutions or any other alterations to the Services, or changes to the method, sequence or scheduled dates(s) for completion. In such event, Buy Research shall request the Service Provider to submit in writing within seven (7) calendar days of the receipt of the Variation Notice or such longer period as the Parties may agree, its proposals for a price adjustment or alteration to the sequence or date(s) of the Services, supported with appropriate substantiation in a form acceptable to Buy Research.

7.2 Variation Acceptance. Buy Research shall then, at its sole discretion, either:

(i) proceed with the variation by issuing a variation Order confirming all arrangements made by the Parties in respect of the variation (hereinafter a 'Variation Order'); or

(ii) withdraw the variation.

Any variation to Services shall not be performed until the Service Provider has received a Variation Order from Buy Research. All the provisions, terms and conditions of the Agreement shall remain in full force and effect and apply to each Variation Order issued by Buy Research.

8 Health, Safety and Environmental

8.1 UK Statutory Regulations. The Service Provider shall comply with all health, fire, safety and environmental laws and regulations issued by any duly appointed authority having jurisdiction over the Site and the Services. Without prejudice to the generality of the foregoing obligation, the Services shall be carried out in compliance with the Health and Safety at Work Act 1974 and all applicable regulations made thereunder, or any subsequent re-enactment or amendment thereof for the time being in force.

8.2 Local Regulations. In addition to the requirement to comply with statutory obligations, laws and regulations, the Service Provider shall be responsible for safety related to and during the performance of its own operations and those of any Third-Party Contractor and shall ensure that:

(i) its employees, Third-Party Contractors and anybody working under its control shall be conversant with, and shall at all times comply with the requirements set forth in Attachment C (Buy Research's health, safety and environmental requirements) and any site safety regulations, safe working procedures and health and safety instructions issued to the Service Provider from time to time by Buy Research, Buy Research's Authorized Representative or Buy Research's designated Health and Safety Supervisor;

(ii) a safe working environment is maintained and that no hazardous, unsafe, unhealthy, or environmentally unsound condition or activity over which it has control occurs at the Site;

(iii) all persons in proximity to the Site, whether employed by the Service Provider or any Third-Party Contractor, are properly protected from risk of injury and danger to health arising out of or in connection with the carrying out of the Services; and

(iv) the Site is at all times kept in a clean and tidy condition.

8.4 Environmental Pollution. The Service Provider shall be liable for any environmental pollution arising from its activities at the Site except to the extent that such pollution occurs as the result of the negligence of Buy Research.

9 Disputes

9.1 Dispute Resolution. The Parties shall use their reasonable endeavours to avoid disputes and to negotiate in good faith and settle amicably any disagreement that may arise out of or in relation to this Agreement, or breach thereof, in accordance with the dispute resolution process described in this Section 9. A dispute under this Agreement initially will be referred in writing by the Authorized Representative of one Party to the Authorized Representative of the other Party. If the Authorized Representatives of the Parties are unable to resolve the dispute within ten (10) business days, the dispute shall be referred in writing, by either Party, to the respective nominated Company Director or nominated company principal for resolution (together known as the 'Principals'). The Principals shall meet in order to attempt to resolve the dispute within fifteen (15) business days of the date the dispute is first referred to them.

9.2 Referrals. If the Parties' Principals are unable to resolve a dispute referred to them under Section 9.1 and the period within which to attempt such resolution is not extended by the Parties' Principals in mutual written agreement, the dispute shall, at the election of either Party, be referred for resolution in accordance with Section 18.9.

10 Performance Review Meetings

10.1 Performance Review Meetings. The Parties shall conduct regular performance review meetings ('Review Meetings') at a location to be designated by Buy Research in advance of the meeting. The Service Provider is expected to participate in such Review Meetings, at its cost and expense, and in addition to any agenda items provided by Buy Research and/or the Service Provider, the Service Provider agrees to provide Buy

Research with (i) performance metrics reports as required by Buy Research and as defined within the Agreement or an Order, and (ii) a comprehensive summary of the Services completed in the previous quarter and those that it will be completing, or has agreed to perform, during the next year (the 'Report'). The Report shall include as a minimum a list of all Services performed, along with the costs and expenses associated with such Services, with variations from the budget for such Service where applicable. At the Review Meetings the Service Provider also agrees to address any performance issues between the Parties as concerning this Agreement and also to suggest areas of improvement for the delivery of future Services.

11 Audit

11.1 **Audit rights.** During the Term and for two (2) years after the termination or expiration of this Agreement, the Service Provider shall keep and make available to Buy Research or its public accountants or other representatives for inspection and audit at all reasonable times, all records, documentation, files and inventory relating to this Agreement to ensure pricing consistency and compliance with the terms and provisions of this Agreement and any Order. No more frequent than twice each calendar year, and upon reasonable prior notice, Buy Research shall have the right to examine and copy such records, receipts and supporting data during the Service Provider's normal business hours to verify the accuracy of all fees and reimbursable expenses invoiced under this Agreement. Any such audits or inspections shall be conducted at Buy Research's expense; however, in the event an audit or inspection reveals an overcharge equal to or in excess of five per cent (5%) of the total fees and expenses for the period of the audit, the Service Provider shall bear the cost of the audit together with the amount of each overpayment. Any such audit or inspection shall be subject to the confidentiality obligations contained herein.

12 Insurance

During the Term, the Service Provider agrees that it shall obtain and maintain at all times during the term of this Agreement and for three (3) years thereafter, at its sole cost and expense the following insurance coverage covering its Services provided under this Agreement:

Public Liability

Per Occurrence GBP 1 million.

General Aggregate GBP 10 million.

Products – Completed Operations Aggregate GBP 5 million.

Personal and Advertising – per occurrence GBP 1 million.

Employers Liability

Per Incident GBP 5 million.

Motor Liability

Third-Party Bodily Injury Limit Unlimited.

Third-Party Property Damage Limit – Cars GBP 20 million.

Third-Party Property Damage Limit – Commercial Vehicles GBP 5 million.

To include coverage for owned, hired, rented and leased autos and uninsured and underinsured motorist liability.

Professional Indemnity

Per Claim GBP 1 million.

Annual Aggregate GBP 2 million.

12.1 **Insurer rating.** All insurance obligations of Service Provider under this Agreement shall be met using an insurer that (a) maintains an A.M. Best rating of at least A-(VII) (or Standard & Poor's Rating of BBB), or (b) is otherwise approved by Buy Research.

12.2 Claims-made policies. Any insurance obligations required of the Service Provider in this Agreement may be met using a claims-made coverage form. If a claims-made form is used, then the retroactive date for any policy, any renewal policy thereof, and/or any related extended reporting endorsement(s) to such policies, shall coincide with, or precede, the commencement of the Service Provider Services under this Agreement.

12.3 Certificates of insurance. Before commencing the supply of Services under this Agreement, and thereafter upon Buy Research's request, the Service Provider shall furnish Buy Research a true copy of a certificate of coverage issued by the responsible insurance broker, or carrier, that (a) references this Agreement, (b) designates the insurance coverage required in this Agreement, and (c) specifies the forms or endorsements conferring such status. The Service Provider shall provide Buy Research each year at the inception date of the policies with such a certificate of coverage.

12.4 Notification to Buy Research. The insurance policies required by this Agreement will stipulate that the cancellation, termination or modification of the insurance policies by the insurer for any reason whatsoever, will be promptly notified to Buy Research and will only be enforceable against Buy Research after fifteen (15) calendar days from such notification.

13 Representations and Warranties

13.1 Compliance with Applicable Laws. Service Provider represents and warrants that in the performance of its obligations under this Agreement, it shall comply with all Applicable Laws (meaning all laws, regulations, codes and standards determined by any governmental or regulatory authority and generally applicable industry or self-regulatory standards whether the same are regional, national or international) which apply to such undertaking or to the arrangements under this Agreement.

13.2 Anti-Bribery Representations. Service Provider represents and warrants that it will not offer or give any gratuity to induce any person or entity to enter into, execute or perform the Agreement or any other agreement with Buy Research. Service Provider agrees that it shall not offer, pay, give, or promise to pay or give, directly or indirectly, any payment or gift of any money or thing of value to:

(i) any government official to influence any acts or decisions of such official or to induce such official to use his or her influence with the local government to effect or influence the decision of such government in order to assist the Service Provider in its performance of its obligations under this Agreement or to benefit Buy Research; or

(ii) any political party or candidate for public office for such purpose. In the event of any breach by the Service Provider of this Section this Agreement will automatically be rendered void.

13.3 Standards of Workmanship. The Service Provider warrants that all services performed pursuant to this Agreement, including, without limitation, any Third-Party Contractor, shall be performed in accordance with the highest professional standards of workmanship and that the Service Provider further acknowledges that in performing the Services that Buy Research is reliant on the Service Provider's skill and judgement.

13.4 Authorization. The Service Provider hereby warrants and represents that it is authorized to enter into this Agreement; no provision of this Agreement is in conflict with any other agreement to which the Service Provider is a party; and there is nothing to prevent or restrict in any manner the Service Provider from granting the rights, title and other interests granted by the Service Provider under this Agreement.

13.5 No Conflict. The Service Provider represents that the Service Provider is presently under no obligation to any third party (including any governmental body and others with whom the Service Provider consults) which would prevent the Service

Provider from carrying out the Service Provider's duties and obligations under this Agreement or which is inconsistent with the provisions contained herein.

13.6 Debarment. The Service Provider represents and warrants that it has not been debarred by any relevant governmental or regulatory authority and is not to its knowledge being investigated by any relevant governmental or regulatory authority for breach of Applicable Laws. In the event Buy Research consents to the Service Provider's employment or engagement of any Third-Party Contractor to perform Services under this Agreement, the Service Provider represents that it shall not employ or engage any person or entity that has been debarred by any relevant governmental or regulatory authority.

14 Confidential Information and Non-disclosure

14.1 General. Each Party (including any Authorized Buying Entity) shall maintain as confidential and shall not disclose to a third party, copy, nor use for purposes other than the performance of this Agreement, any information which relates to another Party's or its Affiliates' business affairs, financial data, pricing, customer lists, projects, economic information, systems, plans, procedures, operations, techniques, technology, patent applications, trademarks, trade secrets, know-how, inventions, technical data or specifications, testing methods, research and development activities, clinical studies (including, without limitation, information related to the participants of such studies), marketing strategies, the terms of this Agreement or other confidential or proprietary information (hereinafter 'Confidential Information'), and each agrees to protect that Confidential Information with the same degree of care it exercises to protect its own Confidential Information (but in no event less than a reasonable standard of care) and to prevent the unauthorized, negligent, or inadvertent use, disclosure, or publication thereof.

Each Party may disclose Confidential Information of another Party only to its own employees, consultants or advisors having a need to know for the purposes of this Agreement (which may include, without limitation, temporary and contract employees, attorneys, technical experts and accountants), provided always that such employees, consultants and advisors have signed a non-disclosure agreement with similar and sufficient clauses protecting the disclosure of confidential information as contained herein or are otherwise bound by such a duty of confidentiality.

14.2 **Exceptions.** The obligations set forth in Section 14.1 hereof shall not apply to any Confidential Information which the receiving Party or Authorized Buying Entity (in each instance a 'Receiving Party') can demonstrate:

(i) is or becomes a matter of public knowledge through no fault of the Receiving Party;

(ii) was rightfully in the Receiving Party's possession in a complete and tangible form before it was received from the disclosing Party or Authorized Buying Entity (in each instance, a 'Disclosing Party');

(iii) is furnished to the Receiving Party on a non-confidential basis from a third party, provided that such third party is not bound by an obligation of confidentiality to the Disclosing Party with respect to such Confidential Information;

(iv) is independently developed by the Receiving Party prior to receipt of the Confidential Information; or

(v) is required to be disclosed to comply with applicable laws but only to the extent and for the purposes of such required disclosure and provided that (a) the Disclosing Party is promptly notified by the Receiving Party and (b) the Receiving Party takes all reasonable actions to obtain confidential treatment for such information and, if possible, to minimize the extent of such disclosure.

14.3 Duty to Report. Upon any breach of a Party's obligations under Section 14.1 hereof, such Party shall immediately notify the other, regardless of whether the breaching Party deems such breach to be immaterial.

14.4 Provisional Remedies. It is understood and agreed that any breach of this Section 14 may cause irreparable damage and, therefore, the injured Party or Authorized Buying Entity shall have the right to seek provisional remedies in addition to damages (including reasonable legal fees and expenses) incurred in connection with such breach or by law.

15 Indemnification

15.1 General. Service Provider shall at its sole cost and expense defend, indemnify and hold harmless Buy Research and its Affiliates, including, without limitation, any and all Authorized Buying Entities and their respective officers, directors, agents and employees (each an 'Indemnified Party') from and against claim, loss, liability, damage, cost or expense, including costs of investigation, reasonable legal costs and court costs (collectively 'Damages') made against or incurred by an Indemnified Party arising from:

(i) any inaccuracy in any representation or warranty made by the Service Provider in this Agreement, including, without limitation, any related Attachment or Order;

(ii) any breach of any covenant or obligation of the Service Provider in this Agreement, including, without limitation, any related Attachment or Order;

(iii) any intentional or negligent act, error or omission of the Service Provider, its agents, servants, employees, subcontractors, consultants or other representatives; or

(iv) any allegation of infringement or misappropriation of the patent, trademark, copyright or trade secret rights of the third party, except to the extent that any Damages suffered by an Indemnified Party are directly attributable to instructions given by or on behalf of Buy Research.

15.2 Notice. Each Party shall give the other Party prompt written notice of any fact coming to its attention which may give rise to a claim for indemnification under this Agreement. The Service Provider may, but is not obligated to, assume the defence of any third-party claim to which the indemnification provisions of Section 15 relate or may relate and to such effect may appoint legal counsel responsible for such defence, provided that the Indemnified Party may elect to be represented, at its own expense, in such claim by counsel of its own choosing, and provided further that the Service Provider may not settle any such claim against the Indemnified Party, without consent of the Indemnified Party which consent shall not be unreasonably withheld. Each Indemnified Party and the Service Provider shall cooperate fully in connection with all matters related to the defence of any such claim irrespective of which Party is conducting the defence.

16 Force Majeure

16.1 General. The performance of either Party under this Agreement or an Order may be suspended to the extent and for the period of time that such Party is prevented or delayed from fulfilling its obligations due to causes beyond its reasonable control (including, without limitation, acts of God, acts of civil or military authority including governmental priorities, strikes or other labour disturbances, fires, floods, epidemics, wars, terrorism, or riots), provided that the non-performing Party uses commercially reasonable efforts to avoid or remove such causes of non-performance and continues performance hereunder with reasonable dispatch as soon as such causes are removed. After ten (10) consecutive days of suspension on the part of one Party, the other Party may, at its sole discretion, terminate this Agreement or the relevant Order without further liability.

17 Term and Termination

17.1 **Term.** This Agreement shall commence on the Effective Date and shall continue in force for a period of [   ] [*years/months*] (hereinafter the 'Initial Term'). Unless the Parties agree in writing to extend the Agreement for an additional period (hereinafter each an 'Extended Term'), this Agreement shall automatically end upon expiry of the Initial Term or any Extended Term hereunder without any notice of termination being required.

17.2 **Termination for Convenience.** During the Term, Buy Research may terminate this Agreement or any individual Order upon [*insert reasonable termination period with regard to the specific services*] written notice to the Service Provider, without cause and without liability to Buy Research, other than for charges incurred for Services that are accepted by Buy Research through to the effective date of such termination. Upon termination of the Agreement, the Service Provider shall, if so instructed by Buy Research, continue to provide Services under the terms of this Agreement during said notice period.

17.3 **Termination for Cause.** If one Party materially defaults in the performance of its obligations under this Agreement and such default is not remedied within [ten (10) business days] of its receipt of written notice from the non-defaulting Party (or, in the reasonable opinion of the non-defaulting Party, significant progress is not made towards resolving such default), then the non-defaulting Party shall have the right to terminate this Agreement, effective at the end of such [10-day] cure period, and avail itself of any and all rights and remedies to which it may be entitled by law or in equity.

17.4 **Termination for Insolvency and Bankruptcy.** Either Party may terminate this Agreement effective immediately upon written notice to the other Party if:

    (i) any step, action, application or proceeding is taken by or in respect of the other Party in relation to the whole or any part of its undertaking for a voluntary arrangement or composition or reconstruction of its debts (including any voluntary arrangement as described in the Insolvency Act 1986 or any analogous step, action, application or proceeding taken by or in respect of either Party in a different jurisdiction);

(ii) a receiver (administrative or otherwise), administrator, liquidator or any encumbrancer or security holder takes possession of or is appointed over such other Party or any of its assets (including the appointment of an analogous person or official in a different jurisdiction);

(iii) the other Party has any distress, execution or other process levied or enforced in any jurisdiction (and not discharged within seven days) upon the whole or substantially all of its assets; or

(iv) the other Party ceases or threatens to cease to carry on business or becomes unable to pay its debts or suffers any analogous event in any jurisdiction.

17.5 **Effect of Termination.** Except in the event of termination by the Service Provider pursuant to Section 17.2 hereof, the Service Provider shall honour all Orders that Buy Research has placed prior to the effective date of termination and shall complete any Services covered by such Orders, unless instructed otherwise by Buy Research, and following completion shall return to Buy Research the Free-Issue Materials. Termination shall not affect the rights or obligations of either Party accrued as of such effective date or that may arise subsequently with respect to transactions initiated or completed prior to the effective date of such termination.

17.6 **Miscellaneous.** Termination, expiration or abandonment of this Agreement through any means or for any reason shall be without prejudice to the rights and remedies of either Party with respect to any antecedent breach of any of the provisions of this Agreement.

17.7 **Survival.** All rights and obligations of the Parties set forth herein that expressly or by their nature survive the expiration or termination of this Agreement shall continue in full force and effect subsequent to and notwithstanding the expiration or termination of this Agreement until they are satisfied or by their nature or expire and shall bind the Parties and their legal representatives, successors, and permitted assigns. Without limiting the foregoing, any of the provisions of this Agreement and/or the Attachments dealing with Payment, Limitation of Liability, Warranty, Confidential Information, Indemnification, Compliance with Applicable Laws and Governing Law and Jurisdiction shall survive termination of this Agreement.

18 Miscellaneous

18.1 Assignment. Neither Party shall assign or transfer this Agreement or any Order covered hereunder, in whole or in part, or any interest arising under this Agreement without the prior written consent of the other Party, which consent shall not be unreasonably withheld. Notwithstanding the foregoing, upon written notice to the Service Provider, Buy Research may assign or novate this Agreement (i) to an Affiliate which agrees in writing to assume its obligations hereunder, and (ii) to a successor to its business (whether by merger, a sale of all or substantially all of its assets relating to this Agreement, a sale of a controlling interest of its capital stock, or otherwise) which agrees in writing to assume its obligations hereunder. Any attempted assignment in violation of the preceding sentence shall be of no force or effect. Subject to the provisions of this Section 18.1, this Agreement shall be binding upon the successors and assigns of the Parties.

18.2 Severability. To the extent any clause, term or provision of this Agreement shall be judged to be invalid or unenforceable for any reason whatsoever, such invalidity or unenforceability shall not affect the validity or enforceability of the balance of such clause, term or provision or any other clause, term or provision hereof. The remaining provisions of this Agreement will remain binding and enforceable, and shall be interpreted so as best to reasonably effect the intent of the Parties. The Parties further agree that any such invalid or unenforceable provisions will be deemed replaced with valid and enforceable provisions that achieve, to the extent possible, the business purposes and intent of such invalid and unenforceable provisions.

18.3 Waiver. The failure by a Party at any time to enforce any of the provisions of this Agreement shall not be deemed to be a waiver of such or any other provision hereof. No waiver of any portion of this Agreement will be effective unless in writing signed by the waiving Party. No waiver of any breach of this Agreement will constitute a waiver of any subsequent breach of the same or any other provision of this Agreement.

18.4 Subcontractors. Should performance of the Services require the Service Provider to subcontract all or any portion of the Services to a Third-Party Contractor, the Service Provider agrees, subject to Section 13.6 hereof, that it shall only engage a Third-Party Contractor (i) that is listed on the applicable Order, or (ii) for whom the Service Provider has received Buy Research's prior written authorization. The Service Provider shall incorporate into the terms of any sub-contract with a Third-Party Contractor the like obligations as defined herein as to Confidentiality and Indemnity and shall ensure that the Third-Party Contractor provides the benefit of such obligation to Buy Research. The Service Provider, if so required by Buy Research, shall provide to Buy Research an extract from the sub-contract to establish that it has complied with its obligations under this Section 18.4. The subcontracting of any part of the Services by the Service Provider shall not relieve the Service Provider from any of its obligations under the Agreement and any applicable Order, and the Service Provider shall be fully responsible for the work and services performed by the Third-Party Contractor.

18.5 Relationship of the Parties. The Parties acknowledge and agree that in performing services under this Agreement, the Service Provider shall be acting solely as an independent contractor, and neither the Service Provider nor any of its Affiliates, employees, associated Service Providers or sub-contractors shall be deemed to be employees of Buy Research for any purpose. Neither the Service Provider nor Buy Research shall have the authority to bind, commit or incur any liability on behalf of the other Party or to otherwise act in any way as an agency, representative or partner of the other Party.

18.6 **Publicity**. Both Parties agree to submit to one another all proposed advertising and other promotional materials relating to their relationship in which either Party's name is mentioned or language is used from which the connection with that Party can be inferred. Both Parties agree not to publish or use such advertising or promotional materials without the prior written consent of the other Party. The Service Provider shall not provide Buy Research's name to current or prospective customers as a reference without first receiving prior written approval from Buy Research for each such customer reference. Any information provided by Buy Research to such a customer shall be provided verbally, but not in written form.

18.7 **Notices**. All notices under this Agreement shall be in writing, properly addressed and shall be deemed to have been duly given or received upon the earlier of: (i) actual receipt; (ii) the date of confirmed delivery according to the records of the postal service if sent by registered or certified mail, return receipt requested; (iii) the date of confirmed delivery according to the records of a commercially recognized express courier with tracking capabilities; or (iv) the date of confirmed transmission if sent by e-mail with confirmation of delivery. Any notices not addressed as follows shall be deemed not to have been given or received:

If to the Service Provider:
[Name of Service Provider]
[Address of Service Provider]
Attn: [   ]

If to Buy Research:
[Buy Research Entity]
[Buy Research Address]
Attn: [   ]

18.8 Entire Agreement. This Agreement, together with the Attachments, and any Order (but excluding requests for quotes and quotes issued in respect of an Order) hereunder, contains the entire agreement between the Parties and supersedes all previous written or oral negotiations, commitments, transactions, or understandings. Except as otherwise set forth herein, this Agreement may be modified only in a written instrument, executed by duly authorized officers of both Parties. In the case where any term or condition of this Agreement is in conflict with the terms and conditions set out in an Order, then this Agreement shall govern.

18.9 Governing Law and Jurisdiction. This Agreement shall be governed by and construed in accordance with the laws of England and Wales, including all matters of construction, validity, performance and enforcement, without recourse to its conflict of law principles. Subject to Section 9, the Parties submit to the exclusive jurisdiction of the English courts.

18.10 Third Parties. The terms of this Agreement may be enforced by Authorized Buying Entities subject to and in accordance with the terms of this Agreement and the Contracts (Rights of Third Parties) Act 1999. Notwithstanding that any term of this Agreement may be or become enforceable by a person who is not a party to it, the terms of this Agreement or any of them may be varied, or this Agreement may be suspended, cancelled or terminated by Agreement in writing between the Parties or this Agreement may be rescinded (in each case), without the consent of any such third party.

IN WITNESS WHEREOF, the Parties hereto have caused this Agreement to be executed by their duly authorized representatives as of the Effective Date.

BUY RESEARCH
NAME:
TITLE:
SIGNATURE:

[ENTER SUPPLIER]
NAME:
TITLE:
SIGNATURE:

APPENDIX 18
Miscellaneous terms

Note to readers: the miscellaneous terms set out below are included because they are good standard 'boilerplate', aimed at giving the client organization essential control over the Contractor's performance.

Readers should take suitable advice before adopting them.

1 Obligations of the Contractor

1.1 The Contractor shall:

1.1.1 provide the Services on or before the relevant Completion Date(s) (as set out in Schedule 1);

1.1.2 recruit, employ and provide sufficient numbers of Staff of a suitable grade and calibre, and ensure they hold suitable qualifications to provide the Services and ensure that the Staff are certified in accordance with and meet the requirements necessary for the performance of the Services in accordance with the Service Levels and all Staff shall be suitable, courteous and of neat appearance;

1.1.3 provide BUY RESEARCH LIMITED with copies of its recruitment and employee relations policy documents and all amendments thereto;

1.1.4 when providing the Services, ensure that all Service Levels are met, and preferably exceeded, during the term of the Agreement;

1.1.5 at all times comply fully with the requirements of the Health and Safety Policy Documentation as the same may be amended and notified to the Contractor from time to time and will otherwise itself institute safe systems of work and comply with all Codes which may be deemed by BUY RESEARCH LIMITED to be reasonably relevant to the provision of the Services and immediately notify BUY RESEARCH LIMITED of failure to comply with this clause;

1.1.6 not do or omit to do anything which, in the reasonable opinion of BUY RESEARCH LIMITED, results or may result in damage to the reputation, good name and market perception of any member of the BUY RESEARCH LIMITED Group;

1.1.7 [observe and comply at all times with the Codes (including those relating to fire and security arrangements) and directions, as may be in force or which may from time to time be reasonably given by BUY RESEARCH LIMITED, for the conduct of personnel at each Site and immediately notify BUY RESEARCH LIMITED of failure to comply with this Clause 1.1.7;]

1.1.8 at all times maintain good order and discipline amongst its Staff and ensure that such individuals behave responsibly and in a manner acceptable to BUY RESEARCH LIMITED and, in particular, the Contractor shall ensure that all Staff comply with BUY RESEARCH LIMITED's internal procedures regarding employee behaviour;

1.1.9 [procure on behalf of BUY RESEARCH LIMITED sufficient stocks of uniforms, headgear and safety footwear of a style and pattern acceptable to BUY RESEARCH LIMITED, ensure that all of the Staff and visitors to the Site wear protective uniforms including appropriate headgear and safety footwear whilst on duty. The Contractor hereby fully indemnifies BUY RESEARCH LIMITED for any awards, losses, liabilities, costs, damages and/or expenses incurred by the BUY RESEARCH LIMITED Group as a result of any failure to observe the requirements of this Clause 1.1.9;]

1.1.10 forthwith replace any member of its Staff should BUY RESEARCH LIMITED reasonably require such removal by giving notice to the Contractor in writing;

1.1.11 [forthwith notify BUY RESEARCH LIMITED in the event of any injury or death or near miss occurring on-Site and confirm full details in writing to BUY RESEARCH LIMITED without delay;]

1.1.12 [forthwith notify BUY RESEARCH LIMITED in the event of any breach of the provisions of the Health and Safety Policy Documentation matters whether by the Contractor or any Sub-Contractor or as might affect the Contractor or any Sub-Contractor [and anyone on-Site;]

1.1.13 notify BUY RESEARCH LIMITED as soon as reasonably practicable of any impending or actual disputes with its Staff that do or might reasonably be expected to have an adverse effect on the Services;

1.1.14 inform BUY RESEARCH LIMITED immediately of any material change in the controlling interests or senior management of the Contractor;

1.1.15 ensure that it complies, and that Staff comply, with all internal BUY RESEARCH LIMITED procedures, policy and standards as may be advised from time to time including the Standards of Conduct;

1.1.16 [ensure that all electrical items brought to the Site comply with the Electricity at Work Regulations (1989) and all other applicable regulations relating to electrical appliances and are at all times covered by valid test certificates which will be available at all times for inspection by BUY RESEARCH LIMITED on request;]

1.1.17 [be responsible for the cleanliness, proper use and reasonable care of all facilities and equipment provided by BUY RESEARCH LIMITED and all areas made available to the Contractor and any Sub-Contractor at the Site and shall notify BUY RESEARCH LIMITED if the Site, or facilities and equipment are in need of repair or maintenance during the course of this Agreement;]

1.1.18 [ensure that the Site, and all facilities and equipment are used with due regard to conservation and exercise energy management control in the course of their operation;]

1.1.19 use the facilities provided by BUY RESEARCH LIMITED economically and in line with the operational requirements of the Services provided;

1.1.20 notify BUY RESEARCH LIMITED at the earliest opportunity of any breakdown, failure, malfunction or hazard of [the Site, and] facilities, equipment or services irrespective of whether they have been supplied by BUY RESEARCH LIMITED or the Contractor;

1.1.21 [provide BUY RESEARCH LIMITED with copies of its Health and Safety Policy and the contact details of its Health and Safety Manager and provide BUY RESEARCH LIMITED with Fire Marshalls and qualified First Aiders at each Site and procure their attendance at the BUY RESEARCH LIMITED Health and Safety Committee.]

2 Contract Reporting and Contract Representatives

2.1 For the duration of this Agreement, the Contractor shall provide to BUY RESEARCH LIMITED a Performance Report within [5] [BUY RESEARCH LIMITED to confirm] Working Days after the end of each month, which shall include a summary of the Contractor's performance during the preceding month against the relevant Service Levels.

2.2 The Contractor's Representative and BUY RESEARCH LIMITED's Representative (together the 'Representatives' and each a 'Representative') shall perform the functions set out in Clause 8. Each Party's Representative shall:

2.2.1 serve as the primary point of contact with the other Party;

2.2.2 be responsible for:

(a) co-ordinating and managing the performance of his or her Party's obligations under this Agreement;

(b) monitoring the other Party's performance under this Agreement;

- **2.2.3** have full authority to act for and on behalf of his or her Party concerning all matters relating to this Agreement; and
- **2.2.4** make and communicate decisions on behalf of his or her Party.

2.3 The Representatives shall meet at least every [6 months] [BUY RESEARCH LIMITED to confirm] during the term of the Agreement to discuss the Services, including:

- **2.3.1** the recent Performance Reports produced by the Contractor in accordance with Clause 8.1, including the achievement (or otherwise) of the Service Levels;
- **2.3.2** compliance with the terms of this Agreement;
- **2.3.3** any issue of concern or interest to either Party; and
- **2.3.4** proposed solutions for addressing issues of concern.

3 Tools and Procedures

3.1 Without limiting any of the Contractor's other obligations under this Agreement (including, without limitation, the generation of Performance Reports), as part of its service provision the Contractor shall utilize and implement such tools and procedures as are reasonably necessary to:

- **3.3.1** monitor, manage, measure and report on the performance of the Services in relation to the Service Levels and otherwise in accordance with this Agreement; and
- **3.3.2** detect, prevent, minimize and remedy any problems with, or disruption to, the Services.

4 Service Non-Compliance

4.1 If, at any time, the Contractor's performance of the Services fails to meet the relevant Service Levels or other performance standards set out in this Agreement ('Service Non-Compliance'):

4.1.1 BUY RESEARCH LIMITED may issue a notice to the Contractor requiring the Contractor to end the Service Non-Compliance ('Compliance Notice');

4.1.2 the Contractor shall end the Service Non-Compliance within [5] [BUY RESEARCH LIMITED to confirm] Working Days after receiving the Compliance Notice; and

4.1.3 BUY RESEARCH LIMITED may, if the Contractor fails to comply with its obligation in Clause 10.1.2, terminate this Agreement by further notice to the Contractor.

4.2 The Contractor's obligation to 'end the Service Non-Compliance' as required under Clause 4 shall include:

4.2.1 identifying and investigating the root cause of the Service Non-Compliance;

4.2.2 taking all necessary steps to resolve the Service Non-Compliance and prevent it from re-occurring;

4.2.3 if necessary, re-working relevant deliverables or work (including by correcting errors and rerunning data) each at the Contractor's own cost;

4.2.4 using its best endeavours to minimize any impact on the Services; and

4.2.5 complying with any additional processes as set out in this Agreement.

4.3 BUY RESEARCH LIMITED shall be entitled to Service Credits in relation to Service Non-Compliance in accordance with the methodology for calculating Service Credits set out in Schedule 1. BUY RESEARCH LIMITED shall be entitled to Service Credits from the start of the Service Non-Compliance for the full period of the Service Non-Compliance, regardless of whether such Service Non-Compliance has been remedied by the Contractor in accordance with the timeframes specified in Clause 10.1.2.

4.4 The Contractor shall pay BUY RESEARCH LIMITED the relevant Service Credits promptly after the Service Non-Compliance has been remedied or BUY RESEARCH LIMITED terminates this Agreement under Clause 10.1.3 (as the case may be).

4.5 The purpose of the Service Credits is to give the Contractor an incentive to perform and they are not intended to constitute a penalty for non-performance or to quantify the full extent of BUY RESEARCH LIMITED's losses in relation to Service Non-Compliance.

4.6 If BUY RESEARCH LIMITED recovers any damages for the Service Non-Compliance the amount of any Service Credits also recovered shall be deducted from the damages payable.

4.7 In performing the Services, the Contractor shall disclose to BUY RESEARCH LIMITED any information of which it becomes aware that may have a material impact on the Contractor's ability to carry out the Services effectively and in compliance with any applicable laws and Regulatory Requirements and any requirements of a Regulator.

4.8 The remedies provided in this Clause 10 are without limitation to any other rights and remedies BUY RESEARCH LIMITED has under any other provision of this Agreement or at law in connection with Service Non-Compliance.

5 Dispute Resolution

5.1 Any dispute arising out of or in connection with this Agreement shall, in the first instance, be referred to the Contractor's Representative and the BUY RESEARCH LIMITED Representative for discussion with a view to reaching a mutually agreed resolution.

5.2 If the dispute is not resolved within [10] Working Days of the matter having been referred pursuant to Clause 5.1, the matter will be referred to one or more of the respective managing directors of BUY RESEARCH LIMITED and the Contractor for discussion with a view to reaching a mutually agreed resolution.

5.3 In the event that no settlement is reached within [10] Working Days of the implementation of Clause 5.2, if the Parties agree that it is appropriate to do so, they may attempt to settle the dispute by mediation in accordance with the Centre for Effective

Dispute Resolution ('CEDR') Model Mediation Procedure (the 'Model Procedure').

5.4 To initiate a mediation, a Party by its [managing director] must give notice in writing (the 'ADR notice') to the other Party to the dispute requesting a mediation in accordance with Clause 5.3.

5.5 The procedure in the Model Procedure will be amended to take account of:

5.5.1 any relevant provisions in this Agreement; or

5.5.2 any other agreement which the Parties may enter into in relation to the conduct of the mediation.

5.6 If there is any point on the conduct of the mediation (including as to the appointment of the mediator) upon which the Parties cannot agree within [10] Working Days from the date of the ADR notice, CEDR will, at the request of any Party, decide that point for the Parties, having previously consulted with the Parties.

5.7 The mediation will start not later than [20] Working Days after the date of the ADR notice.

5.8 [In the event that no settlement is reached:

5.8.1 within [10] Days of the implementation of Clause 5.2; or

5.8.2 within [20] Working Days of the implementation of Clause 5.2;

the dispute shall, if the Parties agree that it is appropriate to do so, be referred to and finally resolved by arbitration.]

5.9 [The arbitration shall be conducted in accordance with the JCT 1998 edition of the Construction Industry Model Arbitration Rules (CIMAR) current at the Commencement Date. Provided that if any amendments to the Rules so current have been issued by the JCT after the Commencement Date the Parties may, by a joint notice in writing to the arbitrator, state that they wish the arbitration to be conducted in accordance with the Rules as so amended.]

5.10 The costs of any such referral to mediation [or arbitration, as the case may be], under this Clause 5 shall be apportioned between the Parties as decided by the mediator [or arbitrator] or in the absence of such determination shall be shared equally by the Parties.

5.11 Decisions under this Clause 5 shall be recorded, as the case may require, by way of alteration of or annex to this Agreement, if either Party shall consider the matter sufficiently material to be so recorded or if it is of enduring effect.

5.12 Any amounts found to be payable by one Party to the other following completion of the dispute resolution procedure in this Clause 5 will be immediately payable following resolution.

5.13 Notwithstanding any preceding provision of this Clause 5, however, each Party shall be free to seek injunctive relief without prior reference of any dispute pursuant to the preceding Clauses of this Clause 5.

5.14 This Clause 5 (Dispute Resolution) shall survive termination of this Agreement.

6 Sub-Contracting

6.1 The Contractor may appoint the Sub-Contractors named in Schedule 1 to provide some or all of the Services. The Contractor shall not appoint further or other Sub-Contractors, without the prior consent in writing of BUY RESEARCH LIMITED (such consent not to be unreasonably withheld or delayed). The Contractor shall not, without the prior written consent of BUY RESEARCH LIMITED, terminate or vary the terms of any Sub-Contractor's appointment.

6.2 BUY RESEARCH LIMITED shall not be obliged to pay the Agreement Price or any other payment under this Agreement if the Contractor fails to comply with this Clause 6.[1]

6.3 No sub-contracting by the Contractor under Clause 6.1 or otherwise and no approval or consent by BUY RESEARCH LIMITED in relation thereto shall relieve the Contractor of any liability or obligation under this Agreement. The Contractor shall not be entitled to any additional fees solely by reason of the appointment of any Sub-Contractor.

7 Change Control

7.1 For the purposes of this Agreement a 'Change Request' is:

7.1.1 a request to change (including to cease) any Service or add new services to the Services; or

7.1.2 a request to amend this Agreement or any document attached to it or referred to in this Agreement.

7.2 A Change Request shall become an 'Amendment' when the requirements of the Change Control Procedure have been satisfied and the Change Request is signed by the authorized representatives of both Parties in the form set out in Schedule 11 to signify their approval to the change. For the avoidance of doubt any improvements in performance standards by the Contractor [in compliance with the progressive improvement requirements contained] in this Agreement shall neither result in an increase in the Agreement Price or be deemed to give rise to a Change Request.

7.3 Change Requests may be originated either by BUY RESEARCH LIMITED or by the Contractor and:

7.3.1 where the Contractor originates a Change Request it shall provide, with the Change Request, details of the impact which the proposed change will have upon the Services, any systems or operations of the BUY RESEARCH LIMITED Group which are affected by the Services, the Agreement Price, and the other terms of this Agreement; or

7.3.2 where BUY RESEARCH LIMITED originates a Change Request, the Contractor shall provide BUY RESEARCH LIMITED, within 10 Working Days of receiving the Change Request, details of the impact which the proposed change will have upon the Services; any systems or operations of the BUY RESEARCH LIMITED Group which are affected by the Services; the Agreement Price, and the other terms of this Agreement.

7.4 Unless otherwise stated in this Agreement, neither Party shall be obliged to agree a Change Request originated by the other but such agreement shall not be unreasonably withheld or delayed.

7.5 If either Party is unwilling to accept a Change Request suggested by the other (or any term of any proposed Amendment) then the other Party may require the disagreement to be dealt with in accordance with the Dispute Resolution Procedure.

7.6 The costs of implementing an Amendment shall be borne as set out in the Amendment.

7.7 The identities of the personnel listed in Schedule 3 may be amended by the service of a written notice authorized by either of the BUY RESEARCH LIMITED Representative or the Contractor's Representative, as the case may be, to the other Party as provided in Clause 11.

8 Non-Solicitation

Neither Party shall (except with the prior written consent of the other) during the term of this Agreement, and for a period of [six] months thereafter, solicit the services of any senior staff of the other Party who have been engaged in the provision of the Services or the management of this Agreement or any significant part thereof either as principal, agent, employee, independent contractor or any other form of employment or engagement other than by means of a national advertising campaign open to all-comers and not specifically targeted at such staff of the other Party.

This Clause 8 (Non-Solicitation) shall survive termination of this Agreement.

9 Business Continuity and Disaster Recovery

9.1 Throughout the term of this Agreement, the Contractor shall maintain in accordance with good industry practice, business continuity and disaster recovery plans and the capacity to execute such plans (including the periodic testing of such plans). A copy of the executive summary of the Contractor's business continuity and disaster recovery plans is attached hereto for reference purposes only at Schedule [9].

9.2 Modifications of such business continuity and disaster recovery plans will only be made where they maintain or improve the recovery capability required by BUY RESEARCH LIMITED during the term of this Agreement. On an annual basis and upon request by BUY RESEARCH LIMITED, the Contractor shall provide BUY RESEARCH LIMITED with an executive summary of the Contractor's current business continuity and disaster recovery plans and a detailed description of any plan test results.

9.3 BUY RESEARCH LIMITED shall be entitled, on reasonable notice to the Contractor, to conduct inspections and/or tests of the Contractor's business continuity and disaster recovery plans and the Contractor shall provide BUY RESEARCH LIMITED with all necessary assistance in the conduct of these inspections and/or tests.

9.4 The Contractor shall comply with all business continuity and disaster recovery plans of BUY RESEARCH LIMITED.

10 Assignment

Neither Party shall be entitled to assign the benefit of this Agreement or transfer or delegate any of their duties or obligations without the prior written consent of the other Party, whose consent shall not be unreasonably withheld PROVIDED THAT BUY RESEARCH LIMITED shall always be entitled to assign the benefit or transfer/delegate its duties and obligations to its Holding Company, a Subsidiary of such Holding Company or a Subsidiary of BUY RESEARCH LIMITED, and in the event of the merger or reorganization of BUY RESEARCH LIMITED the consent of the Contractor is deemed to be given.

11 Notices, Instructions, Consents, etc

All notices, instructions, consents and approvals shall be in writing and signed, as the case may be, by the BUY RESEARCH LIMITED Representative or by the Contractor's Representative, and shall be sent to the other Party marked for the attention of their representative at the address set out in this Agreement. Notices may be sent by hand, by first-class mail or by facsimile transmission provided that facsimile transmissions are confirmed within 24 hours by first-class mailed confirmation of a copy. Correctly addressed notices sent by hand shall be deemed to have been delivered at the time of delivery, notice sent by first-class mail shall be deemed to have been delivered 72 hours after posting and correctly directed facsimile transmissions shall be deemed to have been received instantaneously on transmission provided that they are confirmed as set out above.

Endnote

1 This Clause is likely to be unenforceable because the amount you seek to withhold may far exceed the actual damage resulting from the breach of contract by the contractor. Nevertheless, retaining the wording may be an effective deterrent to contractors – but you should be aware that you are unlikely to be able to enforce it, if challenged.

APPENDIX 19
Model form of Statement of Work

Note to readers: this model Statement of Work is considered to be a sound basic template and might be adaptable for specialist professional services-type contract circumstances. Care should be taken where adopting any 'model' template and adaptation to particular circumstances is likely to be required. So proceed with caution!

Model form of Statement of Work

This Statement of Work (SoW) has been executed and delivered pursuant to the Master Services Agreement effective as of [date] between [name] ('the Service Provider') and Buy Research Limited (the 'Agreement') and is a Statement of Work as defined in the Agreement. This Statement of Work shall be incorporated by reference to the Agreement and become a part of and be governed by the Agreement upon execution hereof by both parties. In the event of conflict between these terms and those contained within the Agreement the terms contained within this Statement of Work shall take precedence.

Contract Information

Service provider address (contracting entity)
Project/short description
Supplier contact (contractual)
Buy Research Ltd management negotiator
Buy Research Ltd business representative

Service provider address (contracting entity)	
Effective date	
End date	
Termination period	• At any time/before expiry/none • X days
Value (Excluding VAT)	

1 Services by Service Provider

2 Responsibilities and Deliverables

3 Place of Performance

4 Remuneration and Employees Assigned

The Service Provider will deploy the following employees, and these shall be billed on a time and material basis as defined below.

Name	Function	Grade	Daily rate	Estimated number of days	Currency

A Cost Ceiling of £ [   ] applies.

If day rate does not include all local taxes, state what taxes are payable additionally

OR

the Service Provider will deploy the following employees, whose services shall be provided on a fixed price basis, to be paid on the successful completion of each deliverable specified within Clause 2 of this Statement of Work.

Name: ....   Function: ....   Grade: ....

Deliverable 1 [   ] [   ] total fixed cost
Deliverable 2 [   ] [   ] total fixed cost
Deliverable 3 [   ] [   ] total fixed cost
Deliverable 4 [   ] [   ] total fixed cost

The total fixed cost for the successful completion of ALL Deliverables as defined above, shall not exceed £ [   ].

5 Payment

Payment by Buy Research Limited shall be made monthly in arrears for the work successfully performed, and thirty (30) days following the receipt of a correct and valid invoice.

6 Invoicing

Invoices shall be sent to:

[Name]
[Mail Address]

Invoices shall detail the name of the project, the contract number (if available) and the name of the Buy Research Limited demand/order manager, and any other information that will assist the payment process.

For and on Behalf of

Signed for and on behalf of
[Service Provider]
Name:

Title:

Signature:

Date:

Signed for and on behalf of
Buy Research Limited

Name:

Title:

Signature:

Date:

APPENDIX 20
Letter of comfort

Dear Sirs

Subject Title: ....
** Subject to Contract **

We have pleasure in informing you that it is our intention to award a contract to you for .... generally in accordance with your Tender dated .... as amplified by your letters dated ....

A formal contract will be issued to you if agreement is reached on the following points: ....

Subject to contract, the contract price will be ....

Payment will be made in accordance with ....

The conditions of contract will be as detailed in ....

The programme will be as follows ....

Insurance requirements are ....

Do not start any work until we have signed the formal contract. Nothing in this letter shall be taken to form a binding legal contract. This document remains subject to contract and is not legally binding.

Please acknowledge receipt of this letter.

Yours faithfully

....

APPENDIX 21
Letter of intent (limited liability commence)

Dear Sirs

Subject Title: ....
** Subject to Contract **

We have pleasure in informing you that it is our intention to award a contract to you for .... generally in accordance with your Tender dated .... as amplified by your letters dated ....

A formal contract will be issued to you if agreement is reached on the following points: ....

Subject to contract, the contract price will be £ ....

Payment will be made in accordance with ....

The strict limit of liability under this letter of intent is £ ....

Under the terms of this letter of intent you are authorized to proceed with the following preparatory works/tasks [specify and limit here] in order to progress towards an orderly and timely mobilization under the contract when it is agreed and executed. We confirm that we will meet necessary expenses and disbursements up to but not exceeding the limit of liability sum named above. Any expenses or disbursements incurred by yourselves in excess of this sum shall be at your sole risk and [our firm] shall not be held liable for any such additional costs.

The conditions of contract will be as detailed in ....

The programme is as follows ....

Insurance requirements are ....

Invoices should be sent to ....

Do not start any work beyond that specified above until we have signed the intended formal contract. Nothing in this letter shall be taken to form a binding legal contract except insofar as the limited instruction to proceed. Any work performed as aforesaid within the limited instruction shall be covered by the finally agreed terms of the contract and subsumed into that contract.

Please acknowledge receipt of this letter.

Yours faithfully

....

APPENDIX 22
Inspection arrangements – clause

1. Where [   ] decide that inspection of any of the Articles, whether completed or in the course of production, shall be carried out at the Contractor's factory, or that inspection of employment practices shall be required to satisfy ['s] obligations under the UK Modern Slavery Act 2015, whether during or after performance of the contract in the time limits set out in sub-clause [n] (Availability of Information), the Contractor shall give to the representative of [   ] full and free access to the said premises as and when required for that purpose, and shall at the expense of the Contractor afford to such representative all such reasonable accommodation and facilities as may be required by him therefor and all such appliances, materials, information and labour required for inspection purposes.

2. In cases of doubt about the suitability of any of the material proposed to be used by the Contractor in the execution of the Contract, the Contractor shall communicate with [   ] at as early a stage of the execution of the Contract as possible, drawing attention to any such doubt in order that a preliminary examination or inspection of such material may be made as [   ] may consider necessary, provided that approval of material or such preliminary examination or inspections shall not affect the subsequent right of [   ] of inspection and rejection of the Articles in accordance with the provisions of the Contract for reasons other than unsuitability of such material.

3. All material, parts and components shall be submitted to [   ] for approval at such stages in their manufacture as [   ] may require; failure to comply with these requirements may result in subsequent rejection.

4 All manufacturing and other processes connected with performance of the contract shall be carried out under conditions satisfactory to [   ].

5 The Contractor shall supply [   ] with such unpriced copies of his/her orders on sub-contractors as may reasonably be requested by [   ]. In addition, he/she shall supply priced copies of orders for contingent (casual) labour and otherwise make plain rates of pay and conditions pertaining to pay including any levy made upon such pay.

6 No inspection under this Condition shall relieve the Contractor of any of his obligations under this Contract.

APPENDIX 23
Availability of information – clause

1 The Contractor shall at all times during the course of the contract and for a period of two years after final payment of all sums due under the contract or for a period of three years after final delivery under the contract, whichever period expires sooner, maintain:

a) in accordance with normal procedures, a record of

   i the manufacturing facilities and production plans employed by him for the supply of the Articles; and

   ii the costs incurred by him in the execution of the Contract, including, for example, details of time taken and of wage rates paid;

b) a record of such further particulars of the costs of production of the Articles as [   ] may from time to time reasonably require, as being necessary for the purpose of determining the absence of or non-commission of offences under the UK Modern Slavery Act 2015; and

c) a record of employment arrangements for both permanent employees and contingent (casual) labour, including details of mechanism of recruitment of permanent employees, and a record of the hiring mechanisms and terms associated with employment of contingent (casual) labour,

d) provided that a requirement under sub-clause (a) and (b) shall not apply so as to impose any obligation on the contractor to maintain a record of any such further particulars as aforesaid in respect of any costs of production, including costs of employment, incurred before the date at which this contract became effective.

2 At any time within the period during which sub-clause (1) above applies the Contractor shall, when requested by [   ]

   a) furnish a summary of any of the costs mentioned in said clause (1) in such form and detail as [   ] may reasonably require; and

   b) afford such facilities as [   ] may reasonably require for his representatives to visit the Contractor's premises and examine the records maintained under that clause.

The Contractor shall allow and facilitate without let or hindrance the copying by photocopy or provision of suitably attested and date-stamped electronic files, of all information that may be required by [   ] in order to respond to any investigation to which it is subject under the UK Modern Slavery Act 2015. For the avoidance of doubt this requirement shall not in any circumstances extend to the supply of any information relating to commercial matters that are correctly and reasonably considered to be commercially confidential, it being understood that information relating to employment practices shall not in this regard be considered to be commercially confidential.

3 The Contractor shall ensure that the provisions of this Clause [n] shall be flowed-down into any sub-contracts of relevance to the subject matter of this contract or otherwise directly connected with this contract.

APPENDIX 24
Supply chain transparency – clause

1 Note that [   ] is an obligated company under the UK Modern Slavery Act 2015. Accordingly [   ] requires periodically information regarding without limitation the conditions within which the employees and contingent/casual workers of both Tier 1 suppliers and Tier 2 suppliers and below are working.

2 [   ] requires the right to inspect and for that purpose to enter the workplaces of Tier 1 suppliers. This requirement is to be flowed-down to sub-tier suppliers naming specifically [   ] as a firm that may inspect said sub-supplier under the terms of said sub-contract.

3 Both parties understand that this is a matter beyond their immediate control and that where employment practice deficiencies are exposed, either in comparison with the requirements of the UK Modern Slavery Act 2015 or other relevant official protocols such as the United Nations Guiding Principles on Business and Human Rights 2011, that these deficiencies might take some time and effort to investigate, amend and improve. Both parties undertake to use reasonable endeavours to pursue such investigations and to be party to discussions aimed at said amendment and improvement.

INDEX

Note: **bold** page numbers indicate figures; *italics* indicate tables.

acceptance of goods 200
acceptance/non-conformance in Master Services Agreement 216
adaptive and core styles 107
adjudication 101
administration, contract. *see* contract administration
affiliates in Master Services Agreement 208
alternative dispute resolution (ADR) 101
anti-bribery representations in Master Services Agreement 223
arbitration 100–01
assignment 246
    Master Services Agreement 230
audits
    audit trails 42, 86–87
    Master Services Agreement 220
authorization in Master Services Agreement 223
authorized buying entities in Master Services Agreement 209, 210–11, 213
authorized representatives in Master Services Agreement 209, 212

bankruptcy 204
Basic Contract Materiality Reviews 17–25, 59, 153–57
Boyce, Tim 1–2
business case 130
business interruption 140
business risk of counterparty change in BCMR 22–23
buyers
    contract mobilization 68–69
    monitoring performance 74–79, 75, 78
    rights of 202

cash flow forecasting 111
change
    business 85
    control 244–45
claims against contracts 93–96, **95**, **96**, 98–99
    see also disputes
clarity in contracts 62, **62**
client positioning 27–28, **28**
clients, termination by 182–83
commercial strategy. *see* project strategy
communications
    contract mobilization 80–81
    exit management 180–82
    system for 151–52
condition precedent 194
conditions of contract for purchase
    acceptance of goods 200
    applicable law and jurisdiction 204
    assignment and sub-letting 202
    buyer's rights 202
    consignment stock 205–06
    definitions 198
    delivery date 199
    deterioration 203
    force majeure 201
    free issue materials 203
    incorrect delivery 199
    insolvency and bankruptcy 204
    intellectual property rights 201
    loss or damage in transit 199–200
    notices 204
    passing of property and risk 199
    payment terms 199
    price indexation 206
    progress and inspection 202
    quality 198
    responsibility for information 202
    severance 205
    sub-orders 203
    variations 200–01
    waivers 204–05
    warranties 203–04
conditions of contract in contract management plan (CMP) *146*

Index

confidential information in Master Services Agreement 224–26
consents 247
consequential loss 140
consignment stock 205–06
construction all risks 140
contingency planning 171–72
continuity of business 245–46
contract administration
  benefits of good 7–8
  Contracts Manager 49–50
  defined 3–4, 37–38
  lifecycle of contracts 38–40, **39**, **40**
  money management 50
  tasks 3–4, **40**, 41, 46, **47–49**
  see also contract management; contract management plan (CMP)
contract design
  essential features of contracts 61, **62**
  legal counsel 66
  NEC3 contract system 63–65, **65**, **66**
  precision and clarity 62, **62**
  risk appetite 66–67
contract law 97
contract management
  aspects of 29–30, **30**
  audit trails 86–87
  benefits of good 10–11
  claims against contracts 93–96, **95**, **96**
  competence of teams 70–71
  cost increases 87–88
  cost of 70–71, 75
  counterparty performance management 27–30, **28**, **29**, **30**
  defined 2–3
  disaster recovery 89–90
  force majeure 89–90
  foundations of 32, **33**
  IPR infringement 88–89
  key terms **29**
  market making 33–34, **34**
  need for 84–87
  opportunities 30–31
  performance shortfall 90
  potential problems 10–11, **11**
  pragmatic attitude as alternative 84
  problems, possible 85–86
  remedies for problems 90–93, **91**
  risk areas 87–90
  risks 30, 31–32
  skill sets for 60
  stakeholder management 34–36
  supplier positioning 27–28, **28**
  systems for 111–14
  teams 15–17, **16**
  time delays 88
  see also contract administration; contract management plan (CMP); disputes
contract management plan (CMP)
  clients, plan as most important to 44
  contract administration 38
  within contract management suite 44–45, **45**
  development of 43–44, 45–46
  exit plans as included 115–16
  information for 44–45
  model form 144, *144–49*
  need for 42–43
  responsibility for developing 45–46
  use of 41
contract mobilization
  clients' tasks for 73
  correspondence 80–81
  cost of contract management 70–71
  defined 68
  financial workstream 69
  initiation by both parties 71–72
  monitoring performance 74–79, **75**, **78**
  notices of poor performance 80–82
  objectives for suppliers/clients 73–74
  stakeholder workstream 69–70
  sub-contractors 72–73
  supplier objectives 73
  supplier tasks 72–73
  suppliers/buyers 68–69
  team, assembling 68–69
  variation of contracts 82
  workstreams 68–70, **69**
contract reporting 238–39
contract representatives 238–39
contract strategy 51
  and project strategy **56**

Index

contract value in BCMR 21–22
contractors, obligations of 235–38
contracts
    dimensions of 57–59
    essential features of **62**
    foundations of modern 57
    importance of to business 1–2
    lifecycle of 38–41, **39, 40**
    as sets of promises 12
Contracts Manager
    contract law 97
    core and adaptive styles 107
    escalating actions in disputes 100
    extent of responsibilities 104
    job description 49–50, 107–08, 158–61
    money management 50
    person specification **105**, 105–07
    skill sets for 60
core and adaptive styles 107
corporate strategy 51
correspondence during contract mobilization 80–81
costs
    of contract management 70–71, 75
    increase in 87–88
counterparty performance management 27–30, **28, 29, 30**
credit cards in Master Services Agreement 215

damages at large 92
debarment in Master Services Agreement 224
defective service in Master Services Agreement 216
definitions in Master Services Agreement 208–10
delays 88
deliverables 58
delivery
    acceptance of goods 200
    date 199
    incorrect 199
design of contracts. *see* contract design
detail
    lack of in contracts 62, **62**
    see also documentation and records
deterioration 203
disaster recovery 89–90, 245–46

disclosure of information in Master Services Agreement 224–26
disputes
    adjudication 101
    alternative dispute resolution (ADR) 101
    arbitration 100–01
    claims against contracts 93–96, **95, 96**, 98–99
    contract law 97
    escalating actions 99–101, **100**
    express terms 97
    levers available **97**, 97–99, **98, 99**
    Master Services Agreement 219
    remedies for 85–86, **91**
    resolution of 241–43
    value of the relationship 100
documentation and records
    cash flow forecasting 111
    contract management systems 111–14
    current liabilities, identification of 114, **115**
    enterprise resource planning (ERP) systems 110–11
    management of 108–14, **110, 111, 115**
    Master Services Agreement 213

enterprise resource planning (ERP) systems 110–11
environmental regulations in Master Services Agreement 217–18
examples. *see* model forms
exit management
    accountabilities 177–80
    alternative suppliers 175
    barriers to exit 169–71
    client, termination by 182–83
    communications plan 180–82
    contingency planning 171–72
    exit plans 166, 168–69, 173–82
    in-house capability 176
    incoming/outgoing suppliers, relationship between 185
    issues driving early exit 168, 176, 182–85
    options following exit 168
    performance review during exits 185
    planned exits 179–80, 184

Index

plans, exit 115–16, 166, 168–69
  pre-contract due diligence 168–69
  purpose of exit plans 166
  rationale for planning 166
  repeat of poor contract performance notifications 191–92
  responsibilities 167, 176
  supplier, termination by 183–84
  task list 177–80
  template for plan 173–82
  unplanned exit 171–72, 177–79, 182–84
  unsatisfactory performance, notification of 188–89
expiry of contract in contract management plan (CMP) *149*
express terms 97

family of contract models 63–65, **66**
fees and payments terms in Master Services Agreement 214–16
financial considerations in contract management plan (CMP) **146**
five forces 87–90
force majeure 89–90, 201
  Master Services Agreement 227
formal notices 194
foundations of modern contracts 57
free issue materials 203
  Master Services Agreement 209, 212
frustration of contract 89

health, safety, environmental regulations in Master Services Agreement 217–18

identity cards 214
improved performance, notification of 190
indemnification in Master Services Agreement 226–27
indemnities 58
information
  availability 257–58
  responsibility for 202
insolvency 204
inspection 202, 255–56

Institution of Civil Engineers (ICE) model form 63
instructions 247
insurance
  Master Services Agreement 221–22
  supply risks 139–40
intellectual property rights (IPR) 58, 88–89, 201
interest on late payments in Master Services Agreement 215–16
interviews 77
invoicing in Master Services Agreement 215

job descriptions
  Contracts Manager 49–50, 107–08, 158–61
  Vendor Manager 162–64
  Vendor Relationships and Contracts Manager 158–61

key performance indicators (KPIs) 76
Kraljic Portfolio Purchasing Model 74–75, **75**, 77, 101

legal counsel in contract design 66
legal risk in BCMR 23–24
lessons learnt 197
letter of comfort 252
letter of intent 253–54
liabilities 58
  identification of current 114, **115**
lifecycle of contracts 38–41, **39**, **40**
liquidated damages 92
loss or damage in transit 199–200

management of contracts. *see* contract management
market concentration risk in BCMR 22
market making 33–34, **34**
Master Services Agreement
  acceptance/non-conformance 216
  affiliates 208
  anti-bribery representations 223
  assignment 230
  audits 220
  authorization 223
  authorized buying entities 209, 210–11, 213

Index

authorized representatives 209, 212
Buy Research's
 responsibilities 211–12
confidential information 224–26
credit cards 215
debarment 224
definitions 208–10
disclosure of information 224–26
disputes 219
documentation and records 213
entire agreement 233
fees and payments terms 214–16
force majeure 227
free issue materials 209, 212
governing law 233
health, safety, environmental
 regulations 217–18
identity cards 214
indemnification 226–27
insurance 221–22
interest on late payments 215–16
invoicing 215
no conflict 223–24
notices 232
on-site personnel 209
orders 209, 210
ownership of results 211
parties to the agreement 208
performance reviews 219–20
personnel 213–14
persons 209
policies 214
pricing 214
publicity 232
relationship of the parties 231–32
representation and warranties
 222–24
service charge 209
service provider's authorized
 representative 209
service provider's
 responsibilities 212–14
services 209, 210–11
severability 230–31
site 209–10
standards of workmanship 223
subcontractors 231
taxes 215
termination 228–30
terms 209–10, 228

third party contractors 209–10,
 233
time and materials 215
variation 217
waivers 231
materiality 130
 Basic Contract Materiality
  Reviews 17–25, 59, 153–57
 defined 17–18
 dimensions of risk 18–25, **19**
 monitoring of risks 133–34
 reviews 135–36, 154–57
memo format 150
memo system 151–52
mobilization of contract. *see* contract
 mobilization
model conditions 64
model forms
 contract management plan
  (CMP) *144–49*
 exit plans 173–82
 improved performance, notification
  of 190
 letter of comfort 252
 letter of intent 253–54
 memo format 150
 NEC3 contract system 63–65, **66**
 repeat of poor contract performance
  notifications 191–92
 statement of work 248–51
 unsatisfactory performance,
  notification of 188–89
 variation of contract 186–87
money management 50, 58–59

NEC3 contract system 63–65, **66**
negotiation 141–43
non-compliance 239–41
 see also performance management
non-conformance in Master Services
 Agreement 216
 see also performance management
non-solicitation 245
notices 193–96, 204, 247
 Master Services Agreement 232
 see also performance management
notifications
 improved performance 190
 repeat of poor contract
  performance 191–92

unsatisfactory performance 188–89
see also performance management

on-site personnel in Master Services Agreement 209
orders in Master Services Agreement 209, 210
outputs 58
ownership, passing of title 58
ownership of results
  Buy Research's responsibilities 211–12
  Master Services Agreement 211

parties to the agreement in Master Services Agreement 208
payment management 50
payment terms 199
performance management
  claims against contracts 93–96, **95, 96**
  contract management plan (CMP) *147–48*
  defective service in Master Services Agreement 216
  exit management 185
  monitoring 74–79, **75, 78**
  non-compliance 239–41
  non-conformance in Master Services Agreement 216
  notices of poor performance 80–82, 188–89, 191–92
  repeat of poor contract performance notifications 191–92
  reviews 219–20
  shortfall in performance 90
  unsatisfactory performance, notification of 188–89
  see also disputes
personnel in Master Services Agreement 213–14
persons in Master Services Agreement 209
plans
  communications plan 180–82
  enterprise resource planning (ERP) systems 110–11
  exit 115–16, 166, 168–69, 173–82
  see also contract management plan (CMP)

policies in Master Services Agreement 214
Porter's Five Forces Analysis 101
Portfolio Purchasing Model 74–75, **75**, 77, 101
precision and clarity in contracts 62, **62**
pricing
  indexation 206
  Master Services Agreement 214
  reductions 92–93
privity 57
problems. *see* disputes
professional indemnity 140
Project Memo System 80, 108, 151–52
project strategy
  components of 52–54, **54**
  and contract strategy **56**
  defined 52
  factors feeding into 55
  as first foundation layer 57
  initial questions and thoughts 54–55, **55**
publicity in Master Services Agreement 232

quality 198

recitals 57
record-keeping 108–14, **110, 111, 115**
relationship of the parties
  disputes, and value of the relationship 100
  Master Services Agreement 231–32
repeat of poor contract performance notifications 191–92
representation and warranties
  in Master Services Agreement 222–24
reputation risk in BCMR 24–25
risk in supply/procurement contracts
  analysis of risk 89
  areas of 87–90
  balancing risk 132
  business risk of counterparty change in BCMR 22–23
  contract management 31–32
  contract management plan (CMP) *148–49*
  definitions 129–30

Index

dimensions of risk in BCMR 18–25, **19**
distribution of 14–15, 141–42
evaluation framework 135–39, *137, 139*
evaluation of risk 138–39
identifying and managing risk 131, 132–33, *134*
insurance of supply risks 139–40
legal risk in BCMR 23–24
market concentration risk in BCMR 22
mitigation of risk 133–35
negotiation 141–43
project sourcing phase 132, *133, 134*
reality 128
red-line areas 141, *141*
reputation risk in BCMR 24–25
risk appetite 66–67
risk/reward matrix 138, *139*
special risks 138
summary of recommendations 128–29
third party supplier risks 138–39
typical risks 136, 138
see also materiality
roles and responsibilities
BCMR 19
contract management plan (CMP) *145*
contract management teams 15–17, **16**
exit management 167, 176
information 202
see also Contract Managers

self-assessment reports 77
sellers. *see* suppliers
service charge
Master Services Agreement 209
service level agreements 13
service non-compliance 239–41
service provider's authorized representative
Master Services Agreement 209
service provider's responsibilities
Master Services Agreement 212–14
services in Master Services Agreement 209, 210–11
severability in Master Services Agreement 230–31
severance 205
shortfall in performance 90
site in Master Services Agreement 209–10
size of organization 109, **110, 111**
Sourcing Managers 167
sourcing phase 132, *133,* **134**
specification documents
basic information for 121–22
checklist for equipment 125–26
definition 119
detail and clarity in 120–21
dos and don'ts 125
general principles 120–21
guidelines 124
importance of 119
important areas for 13
problem areas for 13–14
questions prior to signing off 14
R&D/consultancy services 122–24
seller's interest in 120
Supply of Goods and Services Act 1982 120
terms used for 12–13
spend-risk analysis 74–75, **75**
stages of contracts 38–41, **39, 40**
stakeholder management 34–36, 69–70
standard conditions 64
standards of workmanship in Master Services Agreement 223
statements of work 12, 248–51
sub-contractors 72–73
sub-orders 203
subcontractors 202, 231, 243
suppliers
alternative, and exit management 175
contract mobilization 68–69, 72–73
goal setting 33
incoming/outgoing during exit management 185
monitoring performance 74–79, **75, 78**
positioning 27–28, **28**, 85
self-assessment reports 77
Supplier Relationship Managers 167
termination by 183–84
supply chain 259

Index

Supply of Goods and Services Act 1982 120
supply risks 139–40
surveys 77

taxes in Master Services Agreement 215
teams
    competence of 70–71
    contract administration 3–4
    contract management 15–17, **16**
    contract mobilization 68–69
templates. *see* model forms
termination
    Master Services Agreement 228–30
    see also exit management
terms in Master Services Agreement 209–10
terms of reference 12
third party contractors in Master Services Agreement 209–10, 233
third-party liability 140
time 59
    delays 88, **97**, **98**, **99**
    extensions 92
tools and procedures 239

unsatisfactory performance, notification of 188–89
see also performance management

vagueness in contracts 62, **62**
value chains 8–10, **9**, 51
value driver, contract administration as
    benefits of good contract administration 7–8
    commercial context 8–10, **9**
    definition 6–7
    and other value drivers 7, **7**
    potential problems 10–11, **11**
    value chains 8–10, **9**
variation of contracts 200–01
    contract mobilization 82
    costs 88
    Master Services Agreement 217
    model form 186–87
Vendor Managers 130
    exit management 176
    job description 162–64
Vendor Relationships and Contracts Manager job description 158–61

waivers 204–05, 231
warranties 203–04, 222–24